CIVIL AIRCRAFT
1907–PRESENT

THE ESSENTIAL
AIRCRAFT IDENTIFICATION GUIDE

CIVIL AIRCRAFT
1907–PRESENT

PAUL E. EDEN

amber
BOOKS

This edition published in 2012 by
Amber Books Ltd
Bradley's Close
74–77 White Lion Street
London N1 9PF
United Kingdom
www.amberbooks.co.uk
Appstore: itunes.com/apps/amberbooksltd
Facebook: www.facebook.com/amberbooks
Twitter: @amberbooks
Email: enquiries@amberbooks.co.uk

A catalogue record for this book is available from the British Library.

ISBN: 978-1-908696-64-9

Project Editor: Michael Spilling
Design: Brian Rust
Picture Research: Terry Forshaw

Printed in China

Contents

Chapter 1
Pioneers and Perils (1903–19)   6

Chapter 2
Interwar Airlines (1919–39)   18

Chapter 3
Post-War Resurgence (1945–55)   62

Chapter 4
The Modern Era Begins (1949–92)   80

Chapter 5
Widebodies, Regionals and SSTs (1966–2012)   100

Chapter 6
Twenty-first Century Developments (1988–2017)   126

Chapter 7
General Aviation (1924–Present)   134

Chapter 8
Rotary Workhorses (1948–2013)   158

Chapter 9
Special Purpose Aircraft (1935–2012)   172

Index   186

Chapter 1

Pioneers and Perils (1903–19)

Man's fascination with flight is as old as legend, and the Ancient Greeks and Romans created winged gods and icons. For centuries the promise of flight existed as a self-sustaining dream and it was only when men of knowledge came to examine its practicalities that the first steps were made towards manned flight. As a basic understanding of the science of flight emerged, so it took great vision and courage to put this knowledge into practice. Through trial and error these pioneers faced the perils of their obsession head on, often risking – sometimes losing – their lives in search of success.

◀ **Henson's Aerial Steam Carriage**
Englishman William Samuel Henson was perhaps the first person to envisage a complete passenger-carrying machine. His Aerial Steam Carriage, or *Ariel*, of 1842, featured an enclosed fuselage for passengers, crew and steam engine. It was to have been flown by the Aerial Transit Company, but the failure of a steam-powered model proved that the overall concept was flawed.

Early days
1903–07

The origins of civil aviation are the origins of manned flight itself. Almost six centuries passed between the first practical attempts at flight and the Wright brothers' momentous first powered take-off.

THE FIRST RECORDED successful manned flight was in China in 1306, when primitive parachutes were used during coronation celebrations. Marco Polo also noted fourteenth-century Chinese sailors using man-lifting kites. These had little application as a means of transport, but their construction allowed experimentation, especially into the methods for achieving strong, lightweight frameworks.

Lawrence Hargrave, an Australian pioneer, later defined the box kite structure that informed the design of many of the pioneering aircraft to come. As well as his definitive box kite of 1893, Hargrave experimented with aerofoil shapes and concerned himself with how a heavier-than-air machine – not a balloon or airship – might be powered. His invention of the rotary engine in 1889 demonstrated incredible foresight, but the idea was lost, for reinvention early in the twentieth century.

Hargrave built on the fundamental work of Sir George Cayley, an Englishman who began experimenting with model gliders in 1790. Considered the 'father of aerodynamics', Cayley was the first to document the requirements for heavier-than-air flight, deriving the mathematical principles behind it and the features necessary in the construction of an aeroplane. He demonstrated that a curved aerofoil generates lift, as well as building a glider with a monoplane wing and cruciform tail, and a man-carrying glider. Finally, he came to the

▼ **First flight**

Orville Wright was the pilot for the first manned, powered, sustained and controlled heavier-than-air flight, at Kill Devil Hills, Kitty Hawk, North Carolina, on 17 December 1903. The Flyer was launched along a track and flew 36.5m (120ft) in around 12 seconds.

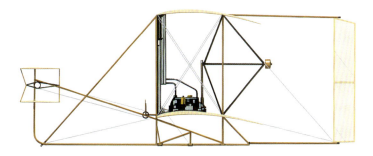

Specifications

Crew: 1	Service ceiling: 3m (10ft)
Powerplant: 9kW (12hp)	Dimensions: Span 12.29m (40f);
Maximum speed: 50km/h (31mph)	length 6.43m (21ft); height 2.81m (9ft)
Range: 36m (120ft)	Weight: 340kg (750lb) loaded

▲ **Wright Flyer**

Kitty Hawk, 17 December 1903

In many ways a culmination of all that had gone before, the *Flyer* was also impractical for meaningful development. The forward-mounted elevator gave the potential for excellent control, but its position close to the wing made handling very sensitive.

▲ **Voisin-Farman 1bis**

Issy-les-Moulineaux, France, 13 January 1908

If aviation was to become a useful means of transport, it needed to demonstrate endurance. Henry Farman completed the first flight in a circuit in this modified Voisin in 1908. He flew to a marker 500m (1640ft) from his take-off point, turned around it and then landed back at his origin.

Specifications

Crew: 1	Service ceiling: Unknown
Powerplant: One 37kW (50hp)	Dimensions: Span 10.2m (33ft 5in);
Maximum speed: 55km/h (34mph)	length 10.5m (34ft 5in); height 3.35m (11ft)
Range: 27km (17 miles)	Weight: 522kg (1150lb) loaded

conclusion that the internal combustion engine was the most promising form of propulsion for a flying machine.

Glider Pioneers

Now the pioneering glider builders worked out the fundamentals of construction and control. Otto Lilienthal, Percy S. Pilcher and Octave Chanute stand out among them. Lilienthal built and flew a series of gliders between 1891 and 1896. Drawing on Cayley's work, he achieved considerable success, but died from injuries received in a crash on 9 August 1896.

In the UK, Pilcher, working on advice from the German Lilienthal and his own experimentation, also built a series of gliders. Unlike the German, who thought that man-powered flight was the way forwards, Pilcher determined to fit an engine to one of his gliders, but he too died after a crash on 2 October 1899.

The American Octave Chanute added to the principles established by Lilienthal and published a history of heavier-than-air flight – *Progress in Flying Machines* – in 1894.

This important book, in conjunction with Chanute's friendship with a pair of brothers who owned a cycle shop in Dayton, Ohio, would eventually lead to the single most important breakthrough in aviation history.

Wilbur and Orville Wright took the best of the available work, from the likes of Lilienthal and Chanute, and applied it in a methodical, logical way to their own gliders. In correspondence with Chanute, and using the expertise gained in their cycle building and repair business, they closed in on a viable, powered aircraft design.

Perhaps their greatest breakthrough was in recognizing the need for three-axis control – yaw, pitch and roll – and perfecting a means to achieve it. Their early work culminated in the *Flyer*, the machine in which Orville Wright conducted the

first powered, sustained, heavier-than-air flight, on 17 December 1903.

The Wrights had entered the history books, but other pioneers were hot on their heels. Europe was soon to become a hotbed of aeronautical creativity and competition, and the Brazilian Alberto Santos-Dumont achieved the continent's first powered, sustained flight on 12 November 1906, in his *14-bis*. Following an alternative line of development, Paul Cornu made the first successful helicopter flight on 13 November 1907; like Santos-Dumont, he lived and worked in France.

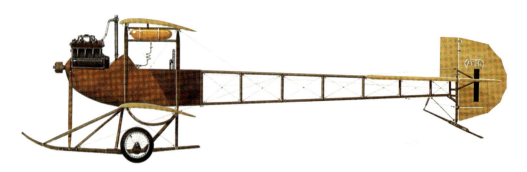

Specifications

Crew: 1	Service ceiling: Unknown
Powerplant: One 26kW (35hp) Green 4-cylinder	Dimensions: Span 9.45m (31ft);
in-line	length 8.53m (28ft); height 2.79m (9ft 2in)
Maximum speed: 78km/h (49mph)	Weight: 227kg (500lb) loaded
Range: Unknown	

▲ **Roe I**

Lea Marshes, Essex, UK, 13 July 1909

Alliot Verdun Roe became the first Briton to fly a British aircraft in July 1909, when he completed a number of 'hops' in his *Roe I* triplane. Later he was able to make longer flights, but only really made progress by developing his primitive machine through a series of improved designs.

Specifications

Crew: 1	Service ceiling: 0.3m (1ft) on first flight
Powerplant: one 18kW (24hp) Antoinette piston	Main rotor diameter: each, 6m (19ft 10in)
engine	Weight: 260kg (573lb)
Maximum speed: not known	

▲ **Cornu twin-rotor**

Lisieux, France, 13 November 1907

Paul Cornu was the first to complete a successful, untethered flight in a rotorcraft, hovering at an altitude of 0.3m (1ft) for 20 seconds in November 1907. Subsequent helicopter development trailed far behind that of fixed-wing aircraft.

Towards a useful concept
1905–19

As pilots became more experienced and their aircraft more capable, the first passengers were taken aloft and longer flights were attempted. Commercial aviation slowly became a reality, through competition and, ultimately, developments driven by World War I.

THE WRIGHTS BECAME INCREASINGLY competent as pilots, but realized that the *Flyer* was far from adequate. They spent 18 months after their first flights perfecting the design, with the resulting *Flyer III* of 1905 far more practical. But maturing the *Flyer* concept had cost them dearly. They had stopped flying to concentrate on design evolution and soon

▶ Louis Blériot
Born in France in 1872, Louis Blériot became wealthy through manufacturing and selling his acetylene car headlamps. He had been interested in flying for some time when he commissioned a Voisin aircraft in 1905. Later, he designed and built his own machines and became a leading light in European aviation.

▼ Blériot XI
Blériot settled on the monoplane configuration for his own aircraft designs. Flown for the first time on 23 January 1909, the Model XI was his first successful design. Blériot famously flew an XI across the Channel, but the type's achievements were legion and included the UK's first official airmail flight, in 1911.

▲ Blériot XI

Within two days of the Channel flight, more than 100 orders had been placed for the *Blériot XI*. Louis Blériot had designed the aircraft with Raymond Saulnier and now he was forced to establish himself as a manufacturer, making extensive use of subcontractors. The *XI* was subsequently developed into new variants, including two- and three-seaters.

Specifications

Crew: 1

Powerplant: one 16–19kW (22–25hp) Anzani 3-cylinder fan-type engine

Maximum speed: 75.6km/h (41 knots, 47mph)

Dimensions: span 7.79m (25ft 7in); length 7.62m (25ft 0in); height 2.69m (8ft 10in)

Weight: 230kg (507lb) empty

AVIATION FIRSTS

Date	Event	Aircraft type	Personality
1843	First modern fixed-wing aircraft design patented	Aerial Steam Carriage	William Samuel Henson, designer
17 December 1903	First heavier-than-air sustained powered manned flight	*Wright Flyer*	Orville Wright, pilot and designer
9 November 1904	First flight exceeding five minutes	*Wright Flyer II*	Wilbur Wright, pilot and designer
12 November 1906	First accredited sustained flight in Europe	14-bis	Alberto Santos-Dumont, pilot and designer
1907	First powered flight in UK	Multiplane	Horatio Phillips, pilot and designer
13 January 1908	First circuit flight in Europe	Voisin biplane	Henry Farman, pilot
14 May 1908	First passenger	Wright biplane	Charles W. Furnas, passenger, Wilbur Wright, pilot and designer
29 May 1908	First passenger in Europe	Voisin biplane	Ernest Archdeacon, passenger, Henry Farman, pilot
8 July 1908	First female passenger	Voisin biplane	Thérèse Peltier, passenger, Léon Delagrange, pilot
25 July 1909	First crossing of the English Channel	*Blériot XI*	Louis Blériot, pilot and designer
7 September 1909	First pilot fatality in a crash	Wright Type A	Eugène Lefebvre
28 March 1910	First take-off from water	Hydravion	Henri Fabre, pilot and designer
12 July 1910	First British pilot fatality in a crash	Wright biplane	Honourable Charles Stewart Rolls
7 November 1910	First airfreight	Wright Model B	Philip O. Parmalee, pilot
12 April 1911	First non-stop London-Paris flight	Blériot monoplane	Pierre Prier, pilot
23 September 1911	First US official airmail flight	Queen monoplane	Earl L. Ovington, pilot

they would trail the Europeans in piloting skills and technology.

If the aeroplane were to become truly useful, however, it would need to carry more than one person, and although some early airframes had second – and even third – seats, the limiting factor was engine power. Contemporary engines were heavy and inefficient. Any increase in their modest power output came with a large increase in weight, not only from the engine itself, but also from the systems required to cool and fuel it.

The Wrights were nevertheless first with a passenger flight. They returned to flying on 6 May 1908, after a three-year suspension of their piloting activities, and Wilbur took the first ever passenger aloft on 14 May. It was a sign of just how well the Europeans were progressing that the world's second aeroplane passenger, Ernest Archdeacon, had flown in France before the end of the month; and during July the first woman was taken aloft, again by a European and in Europe.

Promoting Innovation

Archdeacon provided a series of large cash prizes for aviators who successfully rose to his challenges. Such competition promoted a spirit of innovation in Europe, where pilots and designers often competed for prize money, which was then invested in further development. Britain's *Daily Mail* newspaper was among the more notable benefactors, providing prizes for forward-thinking challenges into the 1930s. Having first offered a prize for a model aeroplane exhibition and competition in 1907 – won by Alliot Verdun Roe, who used the £75 to fund his *Roe I*

13 May 1913	First four-engined aircraft to fly	*Le Grand*	Igor Sikorsky, pilot and designer
27 August 1913	First loop	Nieuport Type IV	Lieutenant Nesterov, pilot, Russian Army
21 September 1913	First sustained inverted flight	Blériot monoplane	Adolphe Pégoud, pilot
1 January 1914	First scheduled airline – St Petersburg–Tampa Airboat Line – begins operations	Benoist flying boat	Anthony Jannus, pilot
5 October 1916	First British airline – Aircraft Transport & Travel Limited – registered		George Holt Thomas, founder
28 July 1918	First UK–Egypt flight, arrived 8 August	Handley Page O/400	Major A.S. McLaren and Brigadier-General A.E. Borton
29 November 1918	First Egypt–India flight, arrived 12 December	Handley Page O/400	Captain Ross M. Smith, captain
10 January 1919	First London–Paris passenger and mail services, No. 2 (Communications) Squadron, RAF	Airco DH.4A	
5 February 1919	First sustained daily passenger service, Deutsche Luft-Reederi	AEG and DFW biplanes	
8 May 1919	First transatlantic crossing, arrived 31 May	Curtiss NC-4	Commander John H. Towers, captain, US Navy
14 June 1919	First non-stop transatlantic crossing, arrived 15 June	Vickers Vimy	Captain John Alcock and Lieutenant Arthur Whitten Brown
25 June 1919	First purpose-designed, all-metal commercial transport flown	Junkers F.13	Hugo Junkers, designer
25 August 1919	First scheduled international airline flight, flown by AT&T, London-Paris	de Havilland DH.16	Cyril Patteson, pilot
12 November 1919	First UK–Australia flight, arrived 10 December	Vickers Vimy	Captain Ross and Lieutenant Keith Smith, pilots
27 December 1919	First Boeing commercial aircraft flown	Boeing B-1	William Boeing, designer

Specifications

Crew: 2

Powerplant: One 125hp (93kW (125hp)
Straight-6 piston engine

Maximum speed: 121 km/h (75mph)

Range: 518km (320 miles)

Service ceiling: Unknown

Dimensions: Span 15.86m (52ft);
length 8.38m (27ft 6in)

Weight: 1272kg (2800lb) loaded

▲ Sopwith Tabloid

Monaco, France, Schneider Trophy, 20 April 1914

The Schneider Trophy contest began in April 1913 as a competition to encourage seaplane development. Initially won by a Deperdussin, the trophy went to a British Sopwith Tabloid in 1914. The event did much to promote seaplane design, but later developed into a primarily military competition.

▼ Boeing Model 1

An unimposing design of enormous significance, the Model 1 was first in the Boeing dynasty of commercial and military aircraft. Just two Model 1 floatplanes were built and both were sold in New Zealand. Seattle's Museum of Flight has a replica machine.

triplane – the *Daily Mail* offered £1000 to the first pilot successfully crossing the English Channel.

The Wrights, meanwhile, faced a storm of criticism from their home press, much of which refused to believe their flying claims. By 1906, this derisive attitude was also rife in Europe, and in summer 1908 the brothers decided to fight back. Orville remained in the United States, while Wilbur travelled to Europe. He made his first flight in foreign skies near Le Mans, France, on 8 August.

The demonstration was brief – less than two minutes – but the level of control that he exhibited stunned Europe's aviators, including Louis Blériot. On 21 September, Wright made the longest flight to date, covering 66.5km (41.33 miles) and laying down a challenge to his rivals.

Unfortunately, the Europeans took up the challenge and, spurred on by the *Daily Mail* cross-Channel prize money, they were soon establishing their superiority.

Crossing the Channel

On 12 June 1909, Louis Blériot flew for the first time with two passengers, even as he was working towards a Channel attempt. Blériot's cross-Channel flight is recognized as a key achievement, but it fell to him only through an engine failure. The Englishman

Hubert Latham attempted to fly his *Antoinette IV* monoplane over the Channel on 19 July 1909, only to be defeated by an engine problem. He was forced to put down in the sea and returned to land courtesy of the French navy.

Latham was unable to replace his aircraft before Blériot took off for his own attempt at the prize on 25 July. The Frenchman was more fortunate, coming down in England, near Dover Castle, to claim the £1000 prize, although the undercarriage and propeller of his *Blériot XI* monoplane were damaged.

Blériot's instant celebrity added to a rising public interest in flying, an interest fuelled by spectacular meetings, such as the first international air meeting, at Reims, France, which lasted from 22 to 29 August; followed by the first British meeting, at Doncaster, between 15 and 23 October.

The *Daily Mail* kept up its good work, offering £1000 for the first British pilot to fly a one-mile circular route – JTC Moore-Brabazon claimed the prize on 30 October, flying a Short No. 2 biplane. One of a series of six Short biplanes – copies of the Wright biplane – his machine had been built under an agreement between Eustace Short and Wilbur Wright. These Shorts were the first ever aircraft built in series, making Short Brothers the first aircraft manufacturing company.

▼ **Vickers Vimy Commercial**

S. Instone & Co Ltd/Croydon, UK, 9 May 1920

A derivative of the wartime Vimy bomber, the Vimy Commercial first flew on 13 April 1919. G-EASI was one of three used by Instone from 1920 on routes to the Continent. Forty more Commercials pioneered airmail routes in China.

Specifications

Crew: 2 + 10 passengers	Service ceiling: 3200m (10,500ft)
Powerplant: Two 268.5kW (360hp) Rolls-Royce	Dimensions: Span 20.47m (67ft 3in);
Eagle VIII engines	length 13m (42ft 8in); height 4.76m
Cruising speed: 135km/h (84mph)	(15ft 7in)
Range: 720km (450 miles)	Weight: 5670kg (12,500lb) loaded

Further and Further

Now the potential of the aeroplane as a commercial tool began to emerge. On 2 June 1910, the Honourable Charles S. Rolls used his French-built Wright for a non-stop flight from Dover to Sangatte, France, and back to Dover. He dropped a letter for the aeroclub at Sangatte and returned to land at his take-off point, with no damage to his aircraft.

A Blériot machine again crossed the Channel successfully on 17 August 1910. This time it was a two-seater, in which pilot John B. Moisant flew a passenger from Calais to Dover cross Channel for the first time.

Aside from passengers, two other commodities would soon become vital to commercial flying – freight and mail. The first aerial freight, two parcels of silk, was flown between Dayton and Columbus, Ohio, on 7 November 1910.

A Wright Company biplane flew the goods to promote a sale being held by The Home Dry Goods Store, which was delighted by the service, the publicity and the handsome profit. Elsewhere, experiments with mail were made, but the first official airmail flight was not until 18 February 1911, when Henri Pequet flew 6500 letters from Allahabad, 8km (5 miles) across the Jumna River to Naini Junction in India.

Route Proving

It was now possible to produce reasonably reliable aircraft, with good endurance and predictable behaviour. So the pioneers turned their attention to the earliest route proving flights. Pierre Prier debuted the route from London to Paris, in a Blériot, on 12 April 1911 and in the United States, Callbraith P. Rodgers completed the first coast-to-coast crossing of the country. A series of short flights in his Burgess-Wright biplane began on 17 September and he reached his destination on 5 November, some 19 days outside the 30-day limit that he needed to satisfy to claim a US$50,000 prize.

Earl L. Ovington was more successful on 23 September when he flew the first official US airmail service, covering 9.6km (6 miles) across New York. Progress in aircraft construction and flying techniques now accelerated: the Russians flew the world's first four-engined aeroplane, designed by Igor Sikorsky and named *Le Grand*, on 13 May 1913; the Russian pilot Nesterov and the Frenchman Pégoud established the basics of aerobatics; and the first scheduled airline began operations between St Petersburg and Tampa, Florida, on 1 January 1914. But war was looming and although the UK's first airline was registered as Aircraft

▲ **Handley Page 0/400**

War surplus bombers were obvious subjects for conversion into multi-engine airliners. Handley Page Transport was the first airline to use a converted 0/400, flying a service from Cricklewood to Manchester on 1 May 1919.

Transport & Travel Ltd in October 1916, civil aviation all but ceased until the Armistice of 1918.

Nevertheless, the expediencies of war had driven tremendous development in airframe and engine technology. As early as July 1918, an ambitious flight departed the UK for Egypt, using one of the new O/400 bombers, while sustained commercial operations began in Europe when Deutsche Luft-Reederi flew the first of its services between Berlin and Weimar, Germany, on 5 February 1919.

▲ **Handley Page O/10**

Handley Page Transport Ltd, London, 1920

This machine was one of nine O/10 airliners converted from surplus O/400 airframes. Equipped for 12 passengers, the aircraft were used by the manufacturer's own airline. G-EATN was also used in trials of the Aveline Stabilizer.

Specifications

Crew: 2 + 12–16 passengers	Service ceiling: 2590m (8500ft)
Powerplant: Two 268.5kW (360hp) Rolls-Royce	Dimensions: Span 30.48m (100ft);
Eagle VIII V-12 engines	length 19.16m (62ft 10in); height 6.7m (22ft)
Cruising speed: 117km/h (110mph)	Weight: 6350kg (14,000lb) loaded
Range: 724km (450 miles)	

Specifications

Crew: 2 + 12 passengers	Range: 400km (249 miles)
Powerplant: Two 194kW (260hp) Salmson CM-9	Service ceiling: 4000m (13,125ft)
9-cylinder radials	Dimensions: Span 26.5m (86ft 11in);
Cruising speed: 120km/h (75mph) at 2000m	length 14.33m (47ft); height 4.91m (16ft 1in)
(6500ft)	Weight: 4770kg (10,516l) loaded

▲ **Farman F60 Goliath**

Air Union, France

The Goliath helped pioneer French operations in Europe. The first Paris–London commercial flight was made on 8 February 1919, by a Goliath belonging to the Farman brothers.

Chapter 2

Interwar Airlines (1919–39)

The interwar years were a time of austerity, of trailblazing, of experimentation and, ultimately, of expansion. In Europe there was an immediate need for air transport between the British Isles and the European continent in support of Armistice treaty arrangements. Meanwhile, aircraft manufacturers saw demand for their military products dry up almost overnight and soon began converting surplus aircraft for civil use, even as they explored new concepts in commercial and private aviation. And in the United States, the real possibilities for airmail services emerged and began to drive airliner development towards ever faster, safer operations. By the mid-1930s, the world's first truly modern commercial aircraft were entering service just as the clouds of war descended once again.

◀ **Boeing 247**

More than any other design, the Boeing 247 established the formula for the modern airliner. This machine was delivered to United in July 1933 and upgraded to Model 247D standard in 1937, although it apparently retained the forward-raked windscreen of the earlier model. After several changes of ownership, including serving time as a crop sprayer, it was restored in the 1960s. In 2012 it was with the Seattle Museum of Flight Restoration Center and potentially airworthy.

European expansion
1919–29

World War I saw aircraft and associated technologies develop rapidly. With the end of hostilities in 1918, aircraft manufacturers turned their attention to the needs of the nascent airline business.

EUROPE'S AVIATION INDUSTRY emerged from World War I having taken great technological strides forwards. In particular, several of the British and French manufacturers had grown into industrial giants of the time. Even Anthony Fokker, latterly planemaker to the Kaiser, was thriving. His wartime achievements had led Allied pilots to fear his machines above all others – his game-changing E-series monoplanes were responsible for the bloody Fokker scourge of 1915–16, his Dr.I triplane became synonymous with the 'Red Baron' and his D.VII was the only aircraft type identified for immediate handover to the victorious powers under the terms of the Armistice.

A great deal of the technology, and many of the flying techniques developed in the constant struggle for air supremacy in the 1914–18 war, were directly applicable to civil aviation. At the beginning of hostilities, aircraft were unarmed observers, but soon they were mounting weapons. Weapons brought with

▲ **Alcock and Brown**

Lieutenant Arthur Whitten Brown (left) and Captain John Alcock crossed the Atlantic non-stop on 14–15 June 1919. The pair overcame navigational difficulties and poor weather, narrowly averting disaster, before making landfall over Ireland.

▲ **Junkers F13**

Luft Hansa, 1926

Deutsche Luft Hansa took over a number of F13s from Junkers Luftverkehr in 1926. A rugged, dependable type, the F13 served the state airline until 1938, an impressive record for a design first flown in 1919.

Specifications

Crew: 2	Service ceiling: 5000m (16,400ft)
Passengers: 4	Dimensions: Span 14.8m (48ft 6.3in);
Powerplant: One 118kW (160hp) Mercedes	length 9.59m (31ft 5.3in); height 3.50m
D.IIIa engine	(11ft 5.7in)
Maximum speed: 173km/h (107mph)	Weight: 1640kg (3620lb) loaded
Range: 1400km (870 miles)	

them additional weight and these early warplanes had barely sufficient power to lift themselves and a pilot. Aeroengine technology was therefore driven at pace and by the end of the war, fast, agile fighters, armed with twin machine-guns and powerful enough for sustained aerial combat, were being built. Delivering enough power for a fast-paced fighter, those same engines also delivered enough power for a heavier, rather more modestly performing airliner.

Aircraft structures had also become rather better understood, as had the techniques for successful navigation, while the need to bomb an enemy's territory had led to the construction of large bombers, capable of covering hundreds of miles while carrying heavy loads. It was clear to see that such a machine might be modified to carry passengers and baggage, rather than bombs, over a similar distance.

It was also clear that machines such as the Handley Page O/400 bomber would be eminently suitable for pioneering long-distance flights. With thoughts already of Empire and making the farther-flung corners of Britain's territories more easily accessible, British and Commonwealth pilots began exploring the possibilities for air travel.

The big Handley Page had been selected for UK–Egypt and Egypt–India explorations in 1918,

▲ **Vickers Vimy**
The Vickers Vimy achieved fame as a bomber in World War I and for making the first non-stop crossing of the Atlantic Ocean, by Alcock and Brown, in June 1919.

INTERWAR FOKKER CIVIL AIRCRAFT

Model	First flown	Powerplant	Description
F.II	October 1919	One 185hp (138kW) BMW IIIA inline piston engine	Single-pilot, open-cockpit airliner; four passengers in cabin, one in open-cockpit
F.III	April 1921	One 240hp (179kW) Armstrong Siddeley Puma inline piston engine	Single-pilot, open-cockpit airliner; five passengers in cabin
F.VII	1924	One 360hp (268kW) Rolls-Royce Eagle inline piston engine	Two-crew, enclosed-cockpit airliner; eight passengers
F.VIIa	1925	One 480hp (358kW) Bristol Jupiter radial piston engine	Two-crew airliner; eight passengers
F.VIIa-3m	September 1925	Three 200hp (149kW) Wright Whirlwind J-4 radial piston engines	Two-crew airliner; 10 passengers
F.VIIb-3m	1928	Three 300hp (224kW) Wright Whirlwind J-6 radial piston engines	Two-crew airliner; 10 passengers
F.VIII	12 March 1927	Two 480hp (358kW) Gnome-Rhône (Bristol) Jupiter VI radial piston engines	Two-crew airliner; 15 passengers
F.IX	26 August 1929	Three 500hp (373kW) Gnome-Rhône (Bristol) Jupiter VI radial piston engines	Two/three-crew airliner; 18 passengers
F.XII	1930	Three 425hp (317kW) Pratt & Whitney Wasp C radial piston engines	Two-crew airliner; 16 passengers
F.XVIII	1932	Three 420hp (313kW) Pratt & Whitney Wasp C radial piston engines	Two/four-crew airliner; 13 passengers
F.XX	1933	Three 640hp (477kW) Wright R-1820-F Cyclone radial piston engines	Three-crew airliner; 12 passengers
F.XXII or F.22	June 1934	Four 500hp (373kW) Pratt & Whitney R-1340-T1D1 radial piston engines	Four-crew airliner; 22 passengers

with the possibility that these two routes might one day be connected to form a through service. However, it was the Vickers Vimy, a bomber just too late to see wartime service, that caught the public attention in the most dramatic style.

As important as the Empire was, Britain also looked towards North America, while the Americans, for their part, had an enduring fascination with Europe. Only the North Atlantic stood between the continents and the promise of a relatively brief crossing by air, compared to four days by liner, was attractive. The US Navy had crossed the Atlantic in stages in May 1919, but on 14 June, Captain John Alcock and his navigator, Lieutenant Arthur Whitten Brown, left Newfoundland in their Vimy, bound for the British Isles. They came down next day in County Galway, Ireland, making an ignominious crash landing, but claiming a £10,000 *Daily Mail* prize. The Atlantic had been conquered, but it would be another three decades before regular transatlantic crossings by passenger aircraft became a reality.

British Progress

Ironically, the possibilities for civil aviation were actually quite slow in realization. The victorious combatants were left with fleets of redundant aircraft. Some surplus machines were quickly adapted for civil operations, although the market for such conversions, as well as for new-build civil types, was limited. Civil aviation had progressed very little since the beginning of the war and there was not yet any real demand for air travel.

In the UK, Handley Page O/400 bombers were modified into O/10 airliners for Handley Page Transport Ltd, the manufacturer joining Airco in establishing its own airline subsidiary. As an airliner, the O/10 was less than ideal, however. The internal fuselage bracing of the O/400 limited its utility and Handley Page set about improving the type. It designed an outwardly similar fuselage based on a different structure and equipped with cabin windows. To this it added the wings of its late-war V/1500 bomber, albeit in reduced form. A series of evolved W.8 variants was then built in small numbers for Handley Page Transport and Belgium's SABENA. Some of the aircraft were produced under licence in Belgium and some variants featured three engines, while the final W.9 and W.10 models were built for Imperial Airways and Handley Page transport, respectively. The last W.10 served Imperial until 1933.

Airco had established AT&T as long ago as 1916. The airline tentatively began carrying passengers from London to Paris in the summer of 1919, employing single-engined ex-RAF DH.4A aircraft of Airco design. It also served routes to Amsterdam, before taking the purpose-designed DH.16 on strength in August. The Aircraft Manufacturing Co Ltd (Airco) had been responsible for some of the most important British combat aircraft, including the DH.4 and DH.9. In the immediate post-war period its chief designer, Geoffrey de Havilland, set in motion the design of a four-seat airliner based on the DH.9A. This DH.16 added a new, wider fuselage to DH.9A wings and seated all four of its passengers in an enclosed cabin.

▲ **Handley Page W.8b**

Handley Page Transport, 1922

The W.8 was a more refined airliner development of the O/400. First flying on 2 December 1919, it led to the W.8b production variant (seven were built), which entered service with Handley Page Transport on 4 May 1922.

Specifications

Crew: 2	Range: 805km (500 miles)
Passengers: 12–14	Service ceiling: 3280m (10,700ft)
Powerplant: Two 261kW (350hp) Rolls-Royce	Dimensions: Span 22.86m (75ft);
Eagle VIII 12-cylinder liquid-cooled V-type	length 18.31m (60ft 1in); height 5.18m (17ft)
engines	Weight:5443kg (12,000lb) loaded
Maximum speed: 145km/h (90mph)	

▲ **Bristol Type 62 10-Seater**

Bristol Aeroplane Company, 1921

The Type 62 was first flown on 21 June 1921 and remained on manufacturer's trials until being moved to Croydon in August. During the trials the forward undercarriage units were removed, the machine then flying services from Croydon before undergoing official testing.

Specifications

Crew: 1	Range: 965km (600 miles)
Passengers: 9	Service ceiling: 2590m (8500ft)
Powerplant: One 336kW (450hp) Napier Lion	Dimensions: Span 17.07m (56ft);
radial engine	length 12.34m (40.6ft); height 3.35m (11ft)
Maximum speed: 177km/h (110mph)	Weight: 3064kg (6755lb) loaded

INTERWAR DE HAVILLAND CIVIL AIRCRAFT

Model	First flown	Powerplant	Description
DH.16	March 1919	one 320hp (239kW) Rolls-Royce Eagle inline piston engine	Single-pilot, open-cockpit airliner; four passengers in cabin
DH.18	February 1920	one 450hp (336kW) Napier Lion W-type piston engine	Single-pilot, open-cockpit airliner; eight passengers
DH.34	26 March 1922	one 450hp (336kW) Napier Lion W-type piston engine	Three-crew, open-cockpit airliner; eight passengers
DH.50	3 August 1923	one 230hp (112kW) Siddeley Puma inline piston engine	Single-pilot, open-cockpit airliner; four passengers
DH.61 Giant Moth	December 1927	one 500hp (373kW) Bristol Jupiter XI radial piston engine	Single-pilot, open-cockpit airliner; 10 passengers
DH.66 Hercules	30 September 1926	three 420hp (313kW) Bristol Jupiter VI radial piston engine	Two-crew, enclosed-cockpit airliner; 14 passengers
DH.83 Fox Moth	29 January 1932	one 130hp (97kW) de Havilland Gipsy Major inverted inline piston engine	Single-pilot, open-cockpit airliner; three passengers
DH.84 Dragon	12 November 1932	two 130hp (97kW) de Havilland Gipsy Major I inverted inline piston engines	Single-pilot, enclosed-cockpit airliner; eight passengers
DH.86	14 January 1934	four 200hp (149kW) de Havilland Gipsy Six inverted inline piston engines	Two-crew airliner; 10 passengers
DH.88 Comet 1934	8 September	two 230hp (170kW) de Havilland Gipsy Six R inverted inline piston engines	Two-seat racer and mailplane
DH.89 Dragon Rapide	17 April 1934	two 200hp (149kW) de Havilland Gipsy Six inverted inline piston engines	Single/two-crew airliner; eight passengers
DH.90 Dragonfly	12 August 1935	two 130hp (97kW) de Havilland Gipsy Major II inverted inline piston engines	Single-pilot airliner; four passengers
DH.91 Albatross	20 May 1937	four 525hp (391kW) de Havilland Gipsy Twelve I inverted-Vee piston engines	Four-crew airliner; 22 passengers
DH.95 Flamingo	28 December 1938	two 930hp (694kW) Bristol Perseus XVI radial piston engines	Three-crew airliner; 20 passengers

Airco had boldly invested in a civil design, but the general downturn in aircraft manufacturing soon saw it closed down. In another bold move, de Havilland took selected key members of the Airco staff and established himself as an aircraft manufacturer. He took responsibility for the DH.16 with him and stated his aim of concentrating his design efforts on civil aircraft. A European aircraft manufacturing legend was in the making.

Given the limited market for civil aircraft, de Havilland might have been expected to fail almost immediately. Instead the company set about designing the DH.18, a much larger airliner than the DH.16. AT&T began using the first example on the lucrative Croydon–Paris service in spring 1920, with examples also going to Daimler Hire and Instone Air Line. Nevertheless, the market was limited and RAF contracts for the overhaul of DH.9As were critical for de Havilland's survival.

The company's next design, the DH.34, was a very reliable aircraft for its time, establishing a fine reputation for de Havilland, even though six of the 11 aircraft built were lost in accidents. At the insistence of Instone and Daimler Hire, the aircraft was completed with the same Napier Lion engine already used in the DH.18. Given the limited market that de Havilland had to address, it made sense to bow to its major and, most likely, only customers, but it established a precedent that was to stifle British airliner manufacturing in years to come. Indeed, Instone and Daimler were the primary customers, with Dobrolet of the Soviet Union taking a single machine.

Another of Britain's great aircraft manufacturers, Bristol, won great acclaim for its F.2 Fighter during

World War I. The Fighter formed the basis for the post-war Tourer, a three-seater enclosing its passengers in a mid-fuselage cabin. Built in small numbers, but exported widely, the Tourer found only limited favour with the airlines, although six were used on mail routes in Australia and another was flown by QANTAS, before going on the Flying Doctor Service. Meanwhile, Bristol made an attempt on the airliner market with its Type 62 Ten-Seater. An ungainly creation, it sold just two commercial examples. The first was used by Instone before passing to Handley Page Transport, while the second, revised aircraft, designated Type 75, was also flown by Instone.

Fokker Production

As soon as hostilities ceased, Anthony Fokker turned his attention to civil aircraft, working on his abortive F.I and the rather more successful F.II at Schwerin. When Allied restrictions threatened to curtail F.II production, he moved his work to his Netherlands homeland, establishing a line of airliners that would come to dominate the world's airways into the mid-1930s. He had the F.II prototype flown out of Germany illegally on 20 March 1920, a tactic that allowed him to develop the production aircraft unhindered. In the event, 30 F.IIs were built, the majority of them, ironically, in Germany. Karl Grulich was technical manager at Deutsche Aero

▲ **de Havilland DH.34**

Bristol Aeroplane Company, 1921

Daimler Hire operated the DH.34 briefly, before becoming Daimler Airways. Instone was also a DH.34 operator and of the 11 built, Instone took four, Daimler six and the USSR's Dobrolet the eleventh.

Specifications

Crew: 1	Range: 587km (365 miles)
Passengers: 9	Service ceiling: 4420m (14,500ft)
Powerplant: One 336kW (450hp) Napier Lion engine	Dimensions: Span 15.65m (51ft 4in); length 11.89m (39ft); height 3.66m (12ft)
Cruising speed: 177km/h (110mph)	Weight: 3266kg (7200lb) loaded

▲ **de Havilland DH.50J**

Sir Charles Wakefield Flight to Australia, 1926

De Havilland's DH.50 saw service in small numbers with airlines around the world. It was especially popular in Australia, most likely as a result of Sir Alan Cobham's England–Australia return flight in the DH.50J. Sir Charles Wakefield, whose company developed the Castrol brand of lubricants, sponsored the flight.

Specifications

Crew: 1	Range: 612km (380 miles)
Passengers: 4	Service ceiling: 4450m (14,600ft)
Powerplant: One 287kW (385hp) Armstrong Siddeley Jaguar radial engine	Dimensions: Span 13.03m (42ft 9in); length 9.07m (29ft 9in)
Cruising speed: 180km/h (112mph)	Weight: 3.35m (11ft) loaded

▲ **Airco DH.9C**

Northern Air Lines, 1925

The DH.9C was perhaps the ultimate DH.9 conversion for airline use. Northern Air Lines took *G-EBIG* on charge in 1925, for use on its Stranraer–Belfast service. Later, it operated two of the type for joyriding from Manchester's brand new Barton Airport, which Northern also managed.

Specifications

Crew: 1	Service ceiling: 5105m (16,750ft)
Passengers: 3	Dimensions: Span 14.01m (45ft 11in)
Powerplant: One 313kW (420hp) Packard	length 9.22m (30ft 3in); height 3.45m
Liberty 12 V-12 piston engine	(11ft 4in)
Cruising speed: 176km/h (109mph)	Weight: 2107kg (4645lb) loaded
Range: 933km (580 miles)	

Lloyd and under his influence a Fokker-Grulich F.II was created for the German airline. F.IIs also served KLM and SABENA, and some passed to Deutsche Luft-Reederi and, ultimately, Luft Hansa.

Buoyed by the success of his F.II, Fokker developed the F.III, which also sold well and was also built in Germany. More importantly, however, it bridged the gap to the unsuccessful F.V, which itself led the way to the F.VII. A single-engined, long-range airliner aimed primarily at KLM's routes to the Dutch East Indies, the F.VII sold in considerable numbers. But when it was redesigned with three engines for increased power and enhanced safety as the F.VII-3m, it became the most successful transport aircraft of the 1920s. Hundreds of F.VII-series aircraft were built, many of them under licence in other European countries and the type also became a favourite of explorers and adventurers. More importantly for Fokker perhaps, the type was also built in the United States, where Atlantic Aircraft was founded as a Fokker subsidiary.

Atlantic's products became the benchmark against which US manufacturers were measured, and it was some years before the Americans managed to build an indigenous airliner of comparable quality.

German Resurgence

After World War I, the Allied Control Commission placed restrictions on aircraft production in Germany. Like Anthony Fokker, who quickly evacuated his work to the Netherlands, Germany's nascent indigenous civil aircraft manufacturers also established themselves abroad during the early 1920s. From these foreign locations they were able to supply Germany's burgeoning airline industry, with Dornier and Junkers taking leading roles.

Of the two, Dornier was perhaps the most prolific in terms of design output, while Junkers made the most technologically significant advances. Its wartime output had included small numbers of all-metal monoplanes in several variants. Extremely advanced for the time, they featured metal frameworks and skinning,

INTERWAR ARMSTRONG WHITWORTH CIVIL AIRCRAFT

Model	First flown	Powerplant	Description
Argosy	March 1926	Three 420hp (313kW) Armstrong Siddeley Jaguar IVA geared radial piston engines	Two/three-crew, open-cockpit airliner; 20 passengers in cabin
A.W.XV Atalanta	6 June 1932	Four 340hp (254kW) Armstrong Siddeley Serval III radial piston engines	Three-crew, enclosed-cockpit airliner; 17 passengers in cabin, plus freight
A.W.27 Ensign	24 January 1938	Four 850hp (634kW) Armstrong Siddeley Tiger IXC radial piston engines	Five-crew airliner; 40 passengers

▲ Armstrong Whitworth Argosy

Imperial Airways, 1926

The 20-seat Argosy first flew in March 1926, before entering service on Imperial Airways' Croydon–Paris route on 16 July. *G-EBLF* was the first Argosy in service. Imperial had been formed through an amalgamation of the UK's major airlines in 1924.

Specifications

Crew: 2	Range: 652km (405 miles)
Passengers: 20	Service ceiling: 4000m (13,120ft)
Powerplant: Three 287kW (385hp) Armstrong	Dimensions: Span 27.64m (90ft 8in); length
Siddeley Jaguar IIA 14-cylinder radial engines	20.07m (65ft 10in); height 6.05m (19ft 10in)
Maximum speed: 145km/h (90mph)	Weight: 8165kg (18,000lb) loaded

▲ de Havilland DH.66 Hercules

Imperial Airways, 1926

Designed specifically for services in Africa and Asia, where what would today be called 'hot-and-high' conditions adversely affected aircraft performance, the DH.66 entered Imperial Airways service in December 1927.

Specifications

Crew: 3	Service ceiling: 3960m (13,000ft)
Passengers: 8	Dimensions: Span 24.23m (79ft 6in);
Powerplant: Three 313kW (420hp) Bristol	length 16.92m (55ft 6in); height 5.56m
Jupiter VI radial engines	(18ft 3in)
Cruising speed: 177km/h (110mph)	Weight: 7067kg (15,600lb) loaded
Range: 845km (525 miles)	

▲ Fokker F.III

KLM, 1921

A linear development of the F.II with a longer, wider fuselage, the F.III entered KLM service on 14 April 1921, just days after its first flight. As well as buying direct from Fokker, the airline also built its own F.III airframes.

Specifications

Crew: 1	Service ceiling: 3960m (13,000ft)
Passengers: 5	Dimensions: Span 17.68m (36ft 4in);
Powerplant: One Armstrong Siddeley Puma,	length 11.0 m (36ft 4in); height 3.20m
170kW (230hp)	(10ft 6in)
Cruising speed: 135km/h (84mph)	Weight: 1905kg (4200lb) loaded
Range: 1000km (621 miles)	

INTERWAR JUNKERS CIVIL AIRCRAFT

Model	First flown	Powerplant	Description
F13	25 June 1919	One 185hp (138kW) BMW IIIA inline piston engine	Two-crew, open-cockpit airliner; four passengers in cabin
K16	3 March 1921	One 65hp (49kW) Siemens-Halske Sh4 piston engine	One-crew, open-cockpit airliner; two passengers in cabin
A20L	1923	One 160hp (118kW) Mercedes D.IIIA in line piston engine	Two-crew, open-cockpit mailplane
A35	1926	One 310hp (231kW) Junkers L-5 inline piston engine	Two-crew, open-cockpit mailplane
G24	19 September 1924	Three 310hp (231kW) Junkers L-5 inline piston engines	Three-crew, open-cockpit airliner; nine passengers in cabin
G31 (G31fo) 1926	7 September	Three 525hp (386kW) BMW-built Pratt & Whitney Hornet radial piston engines	Four-crew, open-cockpit airliner; 15 passengers in cabin
A48	15 September 1929	One 590hp (440kW) BMW-built Pratt & Whitney Hornet radial piston engine	Two-crew, open-cockpit sporting aircraft
G38	6 November 1929	Four 750hp (560kW) Junkers Jumo 204 inline piston engines	Six-crew, enclosed-cockpit airliner; 34 passengers in cabin
Ju 46	March 1932	One 590hp (440kW) BMW 132 (Pratt & Whitney Hornet) radial piston engine	Two-crew, enclosed-cockpit freighter/mailplane
Ju 52	3 September 1930	One 680hp (507kW) BMW VIIaU radial piston engine	Two-crew airliner; 17 passengers
Ju 52/3m	7 March 1932	Three 550hp (410kW) BMW Hornet A radial piston engines	Two-crew airliner; 17 passengers
Ju 60	8 November 1932	One 590hp (440kW) BMW Hornet A2 radial piston engine	Two-crew airliner; six passengers
Ju 86	4 November 1934	Two 590hp (440kW) Junkers Jumo 205 inline piston engines	Three-crew airliner; 10 passengers
Ju 160	30 January 1934	One 660hp (490kW) BMW 132A radial piston engine	Two-crew airliner; six passengers
W33	17 June 1926	One 310hp (231kW) Junkers L-5 inline piston engine	Two-crew freighter/mailplane/airliner; six passengers
W34 (W34h)	7 July 1926	One 660hp (490kW) BMW 132 radial piston engine	Two-crew airliner; six passengers

the later examples employing corrugated duralumin skin panels, which were both strong and light.

Junkers applied this construction method to its F13 of 1919. The world's first all-metal airliner, it went on to sell over 320 examples across Europe, Asia and into the Americas. Its basic structure and layout informed the later W33 and W34. Of course, by the time that Junkers was working on these later designs it had been forced out of Germany, establishing facilities in Spain, Sweden and the Soviet Union.

Now unhindered by the Allies, Junkers was able to extrapolate the F13/W33 line through the Ju 46 to the Ju 52. The latter was a single-engined freighter of little consequence, except that when modified for the three-engine powerplant then in vogue, it became the Ju 52/3m, an airliner of crucial importance during the 1930s and the basis of a warplane and military transport of considerable capability.

For its part, Dornier kept Europe's airlines – primarily those of Germany – supplied with modern, capable aircraft, including the Merkur and Komet. Again, the aircraft were built in large numbers for the period and exported widely. The company's ungainly Delphin flying boats were less successful, but its Wal series revolutionized seaplane operations. The Wal was first flown in 1922, by which time Dornier had been forced out of Germany. While landplane production was transferred to Switzerland,

▲ **Fokker F.VIIb-3m**

LOT, 1930

It was typical of the F.VIIb-3m that 19 of the type were built under licence in
Poland by E. Plage and T. Laskiewicz, for the national carrier LOT. Given the
country's severe winter weather, LOT's Fokkers adopted skies for operations
off snowbound airfields.

Specifications

Crew: 2	Range: 1200km (746 miles) with extra fuel
Passengers: 8–10	Service ceiling: 4400m (14,435ft)
Powerplant: Three 224kW (300hp) Wright J6	Dimensions: Span 21.71m (71ft 3in); length
Whirlwind 9-cylinder radial engines	14.57m (47ft 7in); height 3.9m (12ft 10in)
Cruising speed: 178km/h (111mph)	Weight: 5300kg (11,684lb) loaded

Costruzioni Meccaniche Aeronautiche SA (CAMSA)
was established in Italy for flying boat work.

The Wal allowed air services to reach previously
inaccessible communities, established a number of
records and formed the basis for a series of
extraordinarily successful civil and military flying boats.
Dornier's experience with the Wal also informed the
splendid Do X of 1929. At the time of its first flight, the
12-engined Do X was the world's largest aircraft.
Designed and built in Switzerland, it was not a
commercial success, but when British manufacturers
were still producing open-cockpit biplane flying boats,
it should have come as a warning of just how capable
Germany's estranged designers had become.

French Manufacturing

Like Britain, France emerged from World War I with
a powerful, large-scale aircraft manufacturing base.
And in common with their British counterparts, the
French aircraft companies turned to civil aviation as
the market for their military products all but dried
up. More than 5000 Breguet 14s had been built
during the war and in the immediate post-war
period the type proved attractive in modified form as
the Bre.14T2 Salon. Comparable to the DH.4 and
Bristol Tourers, the salon was considerably more
successful than either, with more than 130 examples
entering service. Compagnie de Messageries
Aériennes pioneered Salon service on its
Paris–London route from 1919 and the type was
subsequently developed into a number of variants for
several operators. Breguet subsequently found

sufficient work on military contracts, returning to
civil aircraft only in 1928, with its Bre.280T. An
attractive biplane airliner for six passengers, it met
with only moderate success.

Louis Blériot had continued in the aircraft
manufacturing business through Blériot Aéronautique,
purchasing the SPAD company in 1914. Post-war,
Blériot-SPAD produced the S.33 airliner, first flown in
December 1920. The aircraft offered accommodation
for five passengers, one of them sitting alongside the
pilot in an open cockpit behind the engine. The S.33
was built in several variants and in considerable
numbers. It was of particular importance to the
Compagnie Internationale de Navigation Aérienne,
serving on its routes throughout Europe.

Farman had also been a pre-war manufacturer and
was working on its F.F.60 bomber at war's end.
With little prospect of the design entering military
service, the two prototypes became airliners and one
of the most important transports of the early 1920s
was created. An F.60 flew the first ever airline
passengers on the Paris–London route on 8 February
1919, and of the 60 or so aircraft built, many formed
the backbone of French commercial aviation through
the 1920s.

Finally, with the aim of equipping its own airline,
Latécoère developed a series of parasol-wing airliners,
beginning with the Latécoère 17 of 1925. Carrying
five passengers in its cabin, but providing open
accommodation for its pilot, the type was followed by
the rather more successful Latécoère 25 airliner and
26 mailplane.

Trail blazing
1919–29

The 1920s was a time of civil aviation trail blazing in every sense of the expression. While manufacturers developed aircraft and technologies, pilots took flying to its long-range extremes.

IN TERMS OF AIRCRAFT technology and airline operations, the 1920s was a decade of gradual improvement and growth. A level of competency in navigation had been reached, but navigational techniques would develop little until the widespread application of radio equipment to aircraft in the 1930s. In the meantime, map, compass, clock and dead reckoning were the tools of the pilot's trade, with all help from railway lines and roads gratefully received. Nevertheless, tentative steps were being taken and the Frenchman Georges Aveline developed his Stabilizer, a primitive autopilot that was tested in an 0/10. His work added to similar systems developed and tested as early as 1912 by Sperry but, again, it would be some years before autopilots became a feature of regular operations.

As commercial aviation expanded, albeit slowly, it was only a matter of time before accidents involving passengers occurred. The first accident on a scheduled airline flight in Britain happened on 14 December 1920. A little after take-off from a foggy London airfield, a Handley Page Transport O/400 crashed, killing its pilot and flight engineer, and two passengers. Four other passengers survived the accident, but the occupants of a Daimler Airways DH.18 that crashed on 7 April 1922 were less fortunate. Their aircraft hit an F.60 travelling towards them, as the pilots of both aircraft used a road below for navigation. All seven people involved in the accident were killed as the aircraft came down near Beauvais, France.

New Decade, New Types

Several significant new aircraft types appeared in the 1920s. In some instances, the machine itself was important in signalling the arrival of a future force in aviation; in other cases, the aircraft heralded a revolution in itself. The *ANT-1* of 1923 was an unremarkable, one-off single-seater, built to demonstrate the metal manufacturing techniques of its designer, Andrei Nikolayevich Tupolev. Tupolev's design bureau was in full swing by 1925, building the first in a series of military and commercial aircraft

▲ **Douglas DWC**

US Army Air Service, April 1924

Four Douglas World Cruiser (DWC) aircraft took off from Seattle, Washington, for an around-the-world attempt on 6 April 1924. The success of the staged flight provided a powerful indicator of aviation's reach, although only two aircraft – *CHICAGO* and *NEW ORLEANS* – completed the journey. *SEATTLE* crashed early on, while *BOSTON* – shown here – sank in the Atlantic.

Specifications

Crew: 2

Powerplant: One 89.5kW (120hp) Liberty 12A 12-cylinder liquid-cooled V-type engine

Cruising speed: 161km/h (100mph)

Range: 2655km (1650 miles)

Service ceiling: 2135m (7000ft)

Dimensions: Span 15.24m (50ft); length 10.82m (35ft 6in); height 4.14m (13ft 7in)

Weight: 3173kg (6995lb) loaded

that continues today. Also of tremendous significance, at least for general and sporting aviation, de Havilland's latest creation, the DH.60M Moth, flew for the first time in 1925. Of more importance for the airlines, the superlative Fokker F.VIIa-3m flew later that same year, with America's first airliner of quality, the Ford Tri-Motor, joining them in in 1926.

Airline Developments

Queensland And Northern Territory Aerial Service (QANTAS), the Australian national carrier, was formed in 1920, while the Soviet Union's first state airline, Dobrolet, was established in 1923.

Daimler Airways expanded its scheduled services to Berlin in 1923, before disappearing into Imperial Airways a year later, as Britain's disparate and struggling airlines were brought together as one company. By 1929, Imperial had expanded sufficiently to begin the first commercial service from London to India, building on the pioneering O/400 flights of 1918.

In the United States, experimental airmail flights bore fruit as the first commercial mail routes were opened in 1926, serviced by Varney Air Service. Now long since forgotten by all but airline historians, Varney Air Service became United Air Lines in 1933,

▲ Breguet Bre.19 Super Bidon
Point d'interrogation, September 1929

Dieudonne and Bellonte flew Super Bidon (Super Petrol Can) *Point d'interrogation* (Question mark) from Paris to Qiqihar, Manchuria, between 17 and 19 September 1929. In so doing, they set a world straight-line distance record. In September 1930, they flew the same aircraft from Paris to New York, reversing Lindbergh's route.

Specifications

Crew: 2	Service ceiling: 6700m (22,000ft)
Powerplant: One 485kW (650hp) Hispano-Suiza	Dimensions: Span 18.3m (60ft);
12Nb 12-cylinder liquid-cooled V-type engine	length 10.41m (34ft 1in); height 4.06m
Cruising speed: 245km/h (152mph)	(13ft 3in)
Range: 9000km (5592 miles)	Weight: 6150kg (13,558lb) loaded

▲ Bernard 191GR
Oiseau Canari, 13 June 1929

Bernard built a handful of transport aircraft in its 180 and 190 series during the late 1920s. Of these, three 191GR machines were built for long-range flights. *Oiseau Canari* (Canary Bird) completed the first French crossing of the North Atlantic. Its three crew discovered that they had a stowaway soon after take-off, a stowaway who thus became the first transatlantic air passenger.

Specifications

Crew: 2	Service ceiling: 3700m (12,140ft)
Passengers: 8	Dimensions: Span 17.30m (56ft 9in);
Powerplant: One 447kW (600hp) Hispano-Suiza	length 12.58m (41ft 3in); height 3.59 m
12Lb piston engine	(11ft 9 in)
Maximum speed: 216 km/h (134 mph)	Weight: 3400kg (7496lb) loaded
Range: 1000 km (620 miles)	

NOTABLE 1920s' EVENTS AND PIONEERING FLIGHTS

Date	Event	Aircraft type	Personality
1920	First automatic pilot installed – Aveline Stabilizer	Handley Page O/10	
4 February 1920	First UK–South Africa flight, arrived 20 March	Vickers Vimy & Airco DH.9	Lt Col Piere van Ryneveld and Sqn Ldr Christopher Quintin Brand
16 November 1920	First Australian airline – QANTAS – formed		Sir Fergus McMaster, chairman
14 December 1920	First fatal UK commercial accident	Handley Page O/400	R. Bager, pilot, flight engineer and two passengers
13 March 1922	First South Atlantic crossing, completed	Fairey IIIC & IIID	Capts Gago 16 June Coutinho and Sacadura Cabral
March 1923	First Soviet state airline – Dobrolet – formed		
10 April 1923	First scheduled London–Berlin air service, Daimler Airways		
2 May 1923	First non-stop crossing of United States, completed 3 May	Fokker T-2	Lts O.G. Kelly and J.A. Macready
21 October 1923	First Tupolev aircraft flown	ANT-1	Andrei N. Tupolev, designer
1 April 1924	First UK national airline – Imperial Airways – formed	de Havilland DH.34, Supermarine Sea Eagle, Handley Page W.8b & Vickers Vimy	
6 April 1924	First around-the-world flight, completed 28 September	Douglas DWC	Lts Lowell H. Smith and Leslie P. Arnold & Lts Erik Nelson and John Harding, Jr, successful crews
22 February 1925	First flight of DH.60M	de Havilland DH.60M	
4 September 1925	First flight of F.VIIa-3m	Fokker F.VIIa-3m	
16 November 1925	First London–Cape Town flight, arrived 17 February 1926, returned London 13 March	de Havilland DH.50	Alan Cobham (pilot), A.B. Elliot (engineer), B.W.G. Emmott (cameraman)

a mega-carrier that survives today. Another of North America's most historically important airlines, Pan American Airways, flew its first service in 1927, operating to South America.

Pioneers and Explorers

The 1920s was also a time of great piloting endeavour, especially in terms of distance flying, both by individuals and crews. Aircraft had already been flown over huge distances, but now pilots were looking to cover long ranges non-stop. Prize money, fame and personality were often at the heart of these attempts, although many were also sponsored by the military. Whatever the motivation, they served the airlines well, publicly demonstrating what air travel

could do. The first of the great long-distance flights was that of Lieutenants Kelly and Macready, who flew their Fokker T-2 non-stop across the United States in 1923. Another Fokker found fame in 1926, when Lieutenant Commander Byrd and Floyd Bennet flew 2575km (1600 miles) over the North Pole. Fokkers, a C-2 and an F.VIIb-3m, respectively, completed further non-stop feats: in 1927, flying from the continental United States to Hawaii; and in 1928, the first crossing of the Tasman Sea.

The most famous long-range flight of the period, and perhaps the most famous ever, however, was that of Charles Lindbergh. He crossed the North Atlantic solo, in his single-engined *Ryan* NYP on 20–21 May 1927. Just eight years had elapsed since Alcock and

Date	Event	Aircraft type	Personality
6 April 1926	First US commercial airmail flights, Varney Air Service Speed Lines	Laird Swallow	Walter T. Varney, founder; Leon Cuddeback, pilot
9 May 1926	First flight over the North Pole	Fokker F.VIIa-3m	Lt Cdr Richard E. Byrd and Floyd Bennet
11 June 1926	First successful US airliner flown	Ford 4-AT Tri-Motor	
30 June 1926	First UK–Australia return flight, returned 1 October 1926	de Havilland DH.50	Alan Cobham (pilot) and A. B. Elliot (engineer)
20 May 1927	First non-stop transatlantic crossing, completed 21 May	Ryan NYP	Capt. Charles Lindbergh
28 June 1927	First non-stop US mainland–Hawaii crossing, completed 29 June	Fokker C-2	Lts Albert F. Hegenberger and Lester J. Maitland
14 October 1927	First non-stop South Atlantic crossing, arrived 15 October	Breguet Bre.19GR	Capt. Dieudonne Cross and Lt Cdr Le Brix
19 October 1927	First Pan American Airways service	Fairchild FC-2	Juan Terry Trippe, founder
12 April 1928	First non-stop east–west transatlantic crossing, completed 13 April	Junkers W33	Hermann Köhl, Capt. J. Fitzmaurice and Baron von Hunefeld
15 May 1928	Australian Flying Doctor Service established	de Havilland DH.50	Rev. J. Flynn, OBE, founder; Dr K. H. Vincent, first pilot
31 May 1928	First transpacific flight, completed 9 June	Fokker F.VIIb-3m	Capt. Charles Kingsford Smith and C.T.P. Ulm (pilots)
10 September 1928	First crossing of Tasman Sea, completed 11 September	Fokker F.VIIb-3m	Capt. Charles Kingsford Smith and C.T.P. Ulm (pilots)
30 March 1929	First commercial London–India route inaugurated, Imperial Airways	Armstrong Whitworth Argosy, Short Calcutta, de Havilland DH.66	
24 April 1929	First non-stop UK–India flight, completed 26 April	Fairey Long Range Monoplane	Sqn Ldr A.G. Jones Williams, pilot; Flt Lt N.H. Jenkins, navigator
28 November 1929	First flight over the South Pole	Ford 4-AT Tri-Motor	Cdr Richard E. Byrd and Bernt Balchen (pilots)

Brown had struggled across to crash land in Ireland, but now Lindbergh made it to Paris, landing to global celebrity. But it is typical of history that second place is often forgotten: the Frenchmen Costes and Le Brix flew the first non-stop crossing of the South Atlantic in their Breguet Bre.19GR biplane on 14–15 October, while a German-led crew completed the much more difficult east–west crossing of the North Atlantic (against prevailing winds) less than a year after Lindbergh's famous flight, in April 1928.

▶ **Charles Lindbergh and Ryan NYP**
Ryan built the NYP (New York–Paris) specifically for Lindbergh's transatlantic attempt. Here, Lindbergh (the tall man under the aircraft's wing) poses in France for publicity photographs with a sponsor's banner.

▲ **Fokker F.VIIb-3m**

Southern Cross, 1928

Pilots Charles Kingsford Smith and Charles Ulm, along with their radio operator and navigator, used *Southern Cross* for a successful transpacific flight in 1928. Later that year, they used the same machine for the first ever crossing of the Tasman Sea.

Specifications

Crew: 4

Powerplant: Three 179kW (240hp) Wright Whirlwind radial engines

Cruising speed: 170km/h (106mph)

Range: 2600km (1616 miles) with extra fuel

Service ceiling: 4700m (15,420ft)

Dimensions: Span 19.31m (63ft 4in); length 14.57m (47ft 10in); height 3.9m (12ft 10in)

Weight: 3986kg (8788lb) loaded

North American developments
1918–26

In North America, commercial aviation took a very different path to that followed in Europe. For the United States, airmail was the crucial commodity, while in Canada, previously isolated settlements could be linked to the nearest railhead.

AMERICA'S PIONEERING PILOTS and aircraft builders were quick to see the potential of the aeroplane in speeding the delivery of mail between the country's scattered settlements. The first experiments with airmail were flown as early as 1911 and although the Post Office Department was enthusiastic, no government funding could be secured until 1916. Interested parties were then invited to tender for mail routes, but with no suitable aircraft available, no bids were submitted.

Once again, World War I provided the developmental impetus necessary to push commercial aviation forwards. A start on providing the United States with a national airmail service was made on 15 May 1918, when US Army Air Service pilots inaugurated a route between Washington, Philadelphia, and New York, using Curtiss JN-4 Jenny biplanes. The Post Office stepped in on 12 August, taking over the service and introducing new equipment in the form of Standard JR-1B aircraft built as mailplanes.

A more significant development came when the Post Office bought 100 war-surplus examples of the DH-4B, a US-built version of the Airco DH.4. The DH-4B allowed coast-to-coast services, albeit as a series of sectors joining major cities. The final sectors were opened on 8 September 1920 and an attempt was made to fly mail in both directions from 22 February 1921.

In order to make the service as fast as possible, it was decided that some of the flying should be at night and this, combined with the challenges of long-range, single-engined flying, led to problems, including a fatal accident eastbound. The westbound route was abandoned due to bad weather. Ultimately, the surviving eastbound mail reached New York after 33 hours 20 minutes, proving the practicality of airmail services.

In an effort to improve safety and ease navigation, the beginnings of a lighting system for the full 3860km (2400-mile) route were laid in 1922. Completed late in 1925, the system placed flashing beacons at 4.8km (3-mile) intervals along the route, with powerful beacons at designated stops and less powerful lights at emergency airfields.

Nevertheless, in 1926–27, the Post Office ceased its airmail operations, opening the route segments to tender by private companies. In doing so, it laid the foundations for the United States' future airline industry, with many of the successful bidders going on to form into passenger-carrying airlines.

Canadian Operations

In Canada, the demographic was even more difficult than in the United States. Canada's vast tracts of forested, often mountainous wilderness were sparsely populated across hundreds of remote, inaccessible settlements. Aircraft represented potentially useful tools for reaching and supplying these settlements,

but the emphasis was not on mail or passenger routes; the aim was often to connect populations with their nearest railhead.

Canada is blessed with a great many water features, and in 1920 a survey of air routes for seaplanes and landplanes was conducted. In 1921, the first flight into the Northwest Territories was made, and in 1923, the first airmail was flown between Newfoundland and Labrador.

Due to its terrain, the aircraft used in Canada had to be rugged and easily maintained. A choice of wheeled or float landing gear was useful depending on location, while the option of skies for the winter months was a bonus.

◀ **Curtiss Model 40 Carrier Pigeon**
National Air Transport, 1926
Designed against a US Post Office requirement, the Carrier Pigeon entered service with NAT just as the Post Office was divesting itself of the airmail routes. Carrying mail in holds fore and aft of the cockpit, 10 production aircraft and the prototype entered service.

Specifications

Crew: 1	Service ceiling: 5100m (16,700ft)
Powerplant: One 300kW (400hp) Liberty L-12	Dimensions: Span 12.78m (41ft 11in);
water-cooled V12 engine	length 8.776m (28ft 9.5in); height 3.68m
Maximum speed: 201km/h (125mph)	(12ft 1in)
Range: unknown	Weight: 2223kg (4900lb) loaded

Specifications

Crew: 2	Range: 1000km (620 miles)
Passengers: 6	Service ceiling: 4300m (14,100ft)
Powerplant: One 447kW (600hp) BMW Hornet C	Dimensions: Span 17.75m (58ft 3in); length
6-cylinder radial engine	10.27m (33ft 8in); height 3.53m (11ft 7in)
Cruising speed: 150km/h (93mph)	Weight: 2500kg (5511lb) loaded

▲ **Junkers W34f**
Canada, 1931–59
Rugged and dependable, the W34 could be flown with wheels, floats or skis, making it entirely suitable for Canadian operations. The radial engines used in the W34 were more powerful than the inlines of the W33 and more easily maintained. Delivered in March 1931, *CF-AQB* served until 1959.

Imperial Airways
1924–39

Imperial Airways brought the UK's airlines together as one organization, improving safety and facilitating the expansion of Britain's air routes across the Empire. The company was disbanded in 1939, on the eve of war.

As COMMERCIAL AVIATION spread its reach across Europe, so the hazards inherent in flying became apparent. Accidents through mechanical failure and navigational error were frequent, and it became apparent that government backing might be necessary to help the continent's nascent airlines fund safer aircraft and develop new operational techniques.

British airlines already received subsidies on their cross-Channel routes and on 2 January 1923 the government began an examination of these subsidies, as well as an assessment of airline services. The conclusion was that a '…heavier than air transport company to be called The Imperial Air transport Co. Ltd' should be formed. The heavily subsidized company would absorb the country's major airlines.

On 31 March 1924, Imperial Airways was formed. At the same time, British Marine Air Navigation, Daimler Airways, Handley Page Air Transport and Instone Air Line all ceased to exist, being amalgamated into the new entity. Three of these carriers were well established, the exception being British Marine Air Navigation, which had been plying its Southampton–Guernsey route with Supermarine Sea Eagle flying boats only since 25 September 1923. Alongside 18 ex-military aircraft, Imperial inherited three Handley Page W.8bs, seven DH.34s, two Sea Eagles and a Vimy Commercial. A month elapsed – while pilots agreed on salaries and administrative issues were straightened out – before services began.

Imperial's first outing was a Croydon–Paris run, flown on 26 April 1924. With government backing, the airline was quick to prosper on routes from the UK to Amsterdam, Basle, Berlin, Brussels, Cologne and Zurich, as well as Paris. As its success became evident, it was able to dictate its requirements to the aircraft industry, commissioning aircraft that were not only more efficient and safer, but which were also suited to its ambition to serve the furthest corners of the Empire.

New Routes, New Aircraft

By 1930, Imperial's routes stretched as far as Budapest and the airline was preparing to place one of a new breed of aircraft, built to its requirements, into service. Handley Page flew its H.P.42 for the

▲ **Avro 618 Ten**

Imperial Airways, 1930

A licence-built Fokker F.VIIb-3m, the Avro Ten was named after its seating capacity, for two crew and eight passengers. The type was primarily used on Imperial's charter business across Europe.

Specifications

Crew: 2	Range: 644km (400 miles)
Passengers: 8	Service ceiling: 7270m (16,000ft)
Powerplant: Three 179kW (240hp) Armstrong	Dimensions: Span 21.72m (71ft 3in); length
Siddeley Lynx IVB or IVC radial engines	14.48m (47ft 6in); height 3.89m (12ft 9in)
Maximum speed: 185km/h (115mph)	Weight: 4818kg (10,600lb) loaded

INTERWAR SHORT CIVIL AIRCRAFT

Model	First flown	Powerplant	Description
S.8 Calcutta	14 February 1928	Three 540hp (403kW) Bristol Jupiter XI radial piston engines	Three-crew, open-cockpit flying-boat airliner; 15 passengers in cabin
S.16 Scion	18 August 1933	Two 75hp (56kW) Pobjoy R radial piston engines	One-crew, enclosed-cockpit airliner; six passengers
S.17 Kent	24 February 1931	Three 555hp (414kW) Bristol Jupiter XFBM radial piston engines	Four-crew flying-boat airliner; 15 passengers plus airmail
L.17 Scylla	March 1934	Four 595hp (444kW) Bristol Jupiter XFBM radial piston engines	Four-crew airliner; 39 passengers
S.20 Mercury	5 September 1937	Four 340hp (254kW) Napier Rapier H inline piston engines	Two-crew mailplane floatplane (upper component of Mayo Composite)
S.21 Maia	27 July 1937	Four 920hp (686kW) Bristol Pegasus XC radial piston engines	Three-crew mothership flying-boat (lower component of Mayo Composite)
S.22 Scion Senior	1935	Four 90hp (67kW) Pobjoy Niagara III radial piston engines	Two-crew floatplane airliner; 10 passengers
S.23 Empire/'C'-class	3 July 1936	Four 920hp (686kW) Bristol Pegasus XC radial piston engines	Five-crew flying-boat airliner; 17 passengers plus airmail
S.30 Empire/'C'-class		Four 890hp (664kW) Bristol Perseus XIIC radial piston engines	Long-range flying-boat mailplane
S.33 Empire/'C'-class		Four 920hp (686kW) Bristol Pegasus XC radial piston engines	Long-range flying-boat airliner and mailplane
S.26 'G'-class	21 July 1939	Four 1380hp (1029kW) Bristol Hercules IV radial piston engines	Seven-crew flying-boat airliner; 38 passengers

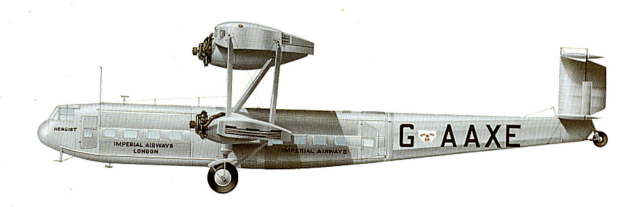

▲ Handley Page H.P.42W

HENGIST, Imperial Airways, 1930

The H.P.42Ws carried 38 passengers, while the more arduous operating conditions faced by the 'E' restricted its load to 24. Passengers enjoyed a walkway between the fore and aft saloons, the facilities of a central bar and the welcome relief of onboard toilets.

Specifications

Crew: 4

Passengers: 38

Powerplant: Four 365kW (490hp) Bristol Jupiter
XIF 9-cylinder radial engines

Cruising speed: 160km/h (100mph)

Range: 805km (500 miles)

Service ceiling: 4420m (14,500ft)

Dimensions: Span 39.62m (130ft);
length 28.09m (92ft 2in); height 8.23m (27ft)

Weight: 12,701kg (28,000lb) loaded

first time in November, with the aircraft entering service in June 1931. The H.P.42 was designed in two variants, the standard H.P.42W (Western) for services from routes in Western Europe and the H.P.42E (Eastern), with supercharged engines, for services in Africa and on to India.

The H.P.42 heralded a new era in more comfortable travel, under what Imperial called its Silver Wings Service.

Middle East Services

Another airliner built specifically for Imperial, the DH.66 Hercules, had entered service on the Croydon–India route on 27 December 1926. The type allowed services to be extended not only to India, but also down to South Africa, but neither route was flown entirely by the DH.66. Both routes began at Croydon on the Armstrong Whitworth Argosy, with passengers eventually leaving Europe by Short Calcutta flying boat, crossing the Mediterranean to Africa. From 1931, the Short Kent was also in service on the Mediterranean legs, and Imperial turned to Short to develop an even more luxurious supplement to the H.P.42 on its Western services.

Imperial asked Short for a landplane version of its Kent and two aircraft were built, each featuring dual passenger cabins, toilets and a buffet. Like the

H.P.42s, the Short landplanes, named *Scylla* and *Syrinx*, served until early in World War II.

Out to Australia

On 4 April 1931, the first of two joint RAF, Imperial Airways and QANTAS attempts at flying mail from London to Australia was launched. Imperial was to fly the mail as far as Darwin, where it would be transferred to a QANTAS aircraft for carriage to Sydney and Melbourne.

A DH.66 was chosen for the flight and the intrepid biplane made it as far as Timor, where its load had to be collected by a QANTAS machine, flown by Charles Kingsford Smith, on 25 April. The second attempt began that same day, the mail reaching its final destination on 14 May.

In 1933, it became clear that if a regular service were to be established, permanent co-operation between Imperial and QANTAS would be needed. A new attempt was made under this arrangement, one of the new Atalanta monoplanes leaving London on 29 May. The trip was successful, although not without its difficulties, and it was not until 8 December 1934 that scheduled flights began. On 13 April 1935, the route also became available to passengers.

Beginning in the UK on DH.86 biplanes, the route included the Kent flying boat, H.P.42 and

---

IMPERIAL TO THE CAPE

Imperial Airways' 11-day route to Cape Town began at Croydon, London's international airport of the time. The weekly departure for Cape Town began with passengers boarding an Armstrong Whitworth Argosy bound for Paris. The same aircraft then took them on to Basle, where passengers and mail were transferred onto a luxury train service for the journey to Rome.

Now multiple legs were flown to Alexandria, Egypt, by Short S.17 Kent flying boat. Alighting in coastal waters, the Kent left Rome to stop off at Naples, then across Italy to Brindisi, over to Corfu, then Crete, then out of Europe for the first time, to land at Tobruk, Libya. One more flight brought passengers and mail to Alexandria, where they again boarded a train, this time for Cairo.

At Cairo it was back onto an Argosy, and a multi-stage journey along the Nile, via Assiut and Assuan in Egypt, and Wadi Halfa and Atbara, Sudan, to Khartoum.

Khartoum saw a second flying boat type involved, with the Short S.8 Calcutta continuing the route via rivers and lakes at Kosti, Malakal and Juba in Sudan, then across to Kisumu, on Lake Victoria, Kenya.

Originally the journey to Cape Town was completed overland from Lake Victoria, but in 1932 the air route was extended all the way to the South African city by de Havilland DH.66 Hercules. The Hercules flew from Kisumu to Nairobi, then into Tanzania at Moshi. Dodoma was the next stop, then Mbeya, before flying into Rhodesia (now Zambia) and landing at Mpika. Still in Rhodesia, the Hercules flew on to Broken Hill, Salisbury (now Harare, capital of Zimbabwe) and then Bulawayo.

South Africa was reached at last when the DH.66 reached Pietersburg (now Polokwane). From there it was on to Johannesburg, Kimberley, Victoria West, Beaufort West and, finally, Cape Town.

Atalanta. At Singapore, a QANTAS Empire Airways (an Imperial/QANTAS joint venture) DH.86 took over for the final stages of the journey.

When the British Government announced that all mail to destinations served by Imperial would be delivered as airmail, the airline recognizcd that its antiquated equipment was not up to the task and neither could it rival the DC-2s that KLM was using on its Far East routes. An order for 28 Short 'C'-class flying boats was placed and the type flew its first Empire Air Mail Programme service on 23 February 1938. The time to Australia was cut to nine days, but the glorious days of the 'C'-class were short-lived, as Imperial was amalgamated with British Airways to form British Overseas Airways Corporation on 4 August 1939.

▲ de Havilland DH.86

DAEDALUS, Imperial Airways, 1935

The four-engined DH.86 served the London–Brindisi section of the route to Australia. Ironically, QANTAS Empire Airways had commissioned the type for the Singapore–Brisbane legs, on which it was also used.

Specifications

Crew: 2	Range: Not known
Passengers: 10	Service ceiling: 5305m (17,400ft)
Powerplant: Two 149kW (200hp) de Havilland	Dimensions: Span 19.66m (64ft 6in);
Gipsy 6 in-line engines	length 14.05m (46ft 1in); height 3.96m (13ft)
Cruising speed: 233km/h (145mph)	Weight: 4649kg (10,250lb) loaded

▲ Boulton & Paul P.64 Mail Carrier

Boulton & Paul, 1933

Imperial's policy of aircraft commissioning did not always bear fruit. Designed to a company requirement for a mailplane with a 453.6kg (1000lb) payload and 1609km (1000-mile) range, the P.64 was an abject failure, crashing just seven months after its first flight and never entering service.

Specifications

Crew: 2	Range: 966km (600 miles)
Passengers: 13	Service ceiling: 4575m (15,000ft)
Powerplant: two 365kW (490hp) Armstrong	Dimensions: span 16.46m (54ft); length
Siddeley Jaguar VIA radial engines	13.46m (44ft 2in); height 4.62m (15ft 2in)
Cruising speed: 314km/h (195mph)	Weight: 4309kg (9500lb) loaded

Lufthansa
1926–35

If Imperial Airways was intent on spanning the British Empire, then Lufthansa set out to span the globe. It reached across the Atlantic and eastwards to China; it also became a proving ground for new aviation technologies.

Regular daily passenger schedules began in Germany in February 1919, Deutsche Luft-Reederi (DLR) employing ex-military aircraft on its primitive services. DLR continued trading until 1923, when it was absorbed by Deutscher Aero Lloyd to become a rival to the newly formed Junkers Luftverkehr.

As had been the British experience, however, it proved impossible to develop a safe, efficient air transport network without government backing. In 1926 Luft Hansa was therefore created, absorbing Germany's two primary airline players and creating a global mega carrier that continues in operation today.

Mail, Freight and Passengers

In reality, there was little immediate call for passenger services in Germany, but a great deal of interest in the rapid movement of mail and freight. Luft Hansa therefore mainly focused its effort on creating high-speed, reliable services and the aircraft to operate them. Passengers were an important part of the Luft Hansa vision, however, and its passengers travelled in relative luxury; its aircraft featured enclosed, heated cabins and the seats on the F13 even boasted safety belts.

Always pushing the boundaries, Luft Hansa began the world's first scheduled passenger night flight on 1 May 1926, using a Junkers G24. By 1929–30, all of the airline's pilots were receiving blind flying training and it began training crews from around the world. It also began experimenting with radio communication and radio direction finding, work that helped to expand its network and lay the foundations for the systems that would later lead the *Luftwaffe's* bombers over Europe.

Extended Reach

Luft Hansa began flying over the Alps, from Munich to Milan, in May 1927. Using three-engined Rohrbach Roland monoplanes, the flights were little more than experiments, although regular mail and freight services began the following year. In May 1932, scheduled services began over the mountains to Rome, thanks to the legendary Ju 52/3m.

Meanwhile, in 1926, Luft Hansa had sent a pair of G24s on an exploratory flight to Peking, the aircraft arriving after a troubled 37-day trip. Efforts to reach the Far East were continued into the 1930s, but lack of infrastructure and other difficulties combined to prevent any real success.

▲ **Dornier Merkur**

Luft Hansa, 1925

Developed from the early Komet, the Merkur flew for the first time in 1925 and at the peak of its operations as many as 30 were in Luft Hansa service. It was especially useful on overnight services and at least 22 were engaged on the nocturnal Berlin–Moscow route, which was run in co-operation with Deruluft.

Specifications

Crew: 2	Range: 1050km (650 miles)
Passengers: 10	Service ceiling: 5200m (17,060ft)
Powerplant: One 447kW (600hp) BMW VI	Dimensions: Span 19.60m (64ft 4in);
12-cylinder V-type engine	length 12.50m (41ft); height 3.45m (11ft 4in)
Cruising speed: 180km/h (112mph)	Weight: 3600kg (7936lb) loaded

Specifications

Crew: 3

Passengers: 19

Powerplant: Four 362kW (485hp) Napier
Lion VIII W-12 in-line engines

Cruising speed: 210km/h (130mph)

Range: 2000km (1243 miles)

Dimensions: Span 28.60m (93ft 10in);
length 24.60m (80ft 8in); height 6.0m
(19ft 8in)

Weight: 14,000kg (30,864lb) loaded

▲ Dornier Do R2 Super Wal

Luft Hansa, 1926

Dornier built several Wal variants, all developments of the original Do J Wal of 1922. While the 8-tonne (7.8-ton) and 10-tonne (9.8-ton) Wals were the mainstay of Luft Hansa's South Atlantic routes, the Super Wal was the ultimate 'boat in the series, with accommodation for 19 passengers.

▲ Junkers Ju 52/3m

Luft Hansa, 1933

Perhaps the single most important development for Luft Hansa's commercial success, the Ju 52/3m first reached the airline in 1932. Seating 17 passengers, it offered new levels of performance and reliability.

Specifications

Crew: 1

Passengers: 17

Powerplant: three 447kW (600hp) Pratt
& Whitney Wasp radial engines

Cruising speed: 245km/h (152mph)

Range: 915km (568 miles)

Service ceiling: 5200m (17,000ft)

Dimensions: Span 29.25m (95ft 11in);
length 18.90m (62ft); height 6.1m (20ft)

Weight: 9200kg (20,282lb) loaded

Elsewhere, the airline's expansion was proceeding at pace. Luft Hansa had now reached beyond Europe to the south, as far as Cairo. It was also becoming a master at transatlantic work, using seaplanes and tenders to make regular staged crossings of both the North and South Atlantic.

Indeed, South America had become a very important market for Luft Hansa and by the end of March 1935 the carrier was offering a three-day journey from Germany to Rio de Janeiro, Brazil, at the same time introducing its latest Ju 52/3m equipment to the region. The seaplane part of the operation had been initiated with 8-tonne (7.8-ton) Wal flying boats on 6 June 1933. The early services carried only mail, with the aircraft alighting alongside a seaplane tender before being winched aboard for refuelling. When it was ready for departure, the aircraft was catapulted off and flew to the next tender. Eventually, the 10-tonne (9.8-ton) Wal took over on the South Atlantic route, and was ultimately replaced by the excellent Do 18.

Interestingly, the majority of South America's indigenous airlines were also established by German enterprise, bringing the latest airliner equipment to the continent, as well as German operating procedures. Later, as war clouds began to gather over Europe and the rest of the world, this German interest also caused problems – the United States became uncomfortable with 'Nazi' assets so close to its back door.

Air mail and flying boats
1925–35

A major change in the US Government's transport policy brought about upheaval among the nation's emerging airlines. By 1931, four major carriers had been produced through a process of consolidation.

IN FEBRUARY 1935, the Contract Air Mail Act, or Kelly Act, was passed into US law. The Act marked the beginning of the end for US Post Office airmail flying, as the routes were handed over to commercial enterprise. It was followed in May 1926 by the Air Commerce Act, under which designated routes for mail and passengers were created, navigational procedures established, and pilots and aircraft licensed.

Ryan Airlines had pre-empted the government by starting a regular, sustained passenger service under its Los Angeles–San Diego Air Line brand, on 1 March 1925, but the exponential growth of air transport in the United States really began on 7 October 1925, when an initial five airmail routes were awarded to private operators.

First among the successful bidders, the Ford Motor Company had already been flying an express parcel service with Ford 2-AT monoplanes. It now added airmail routes to its operation. Other contracted companies, as more routes were issued, included Varney Air Lines (Curtiss Swallow), Robertson Aircraft Corporation, Western Air Express (WAE,

Douglas M-2), Colonial Air Transport (Fokker), Philadelphia Rapid Transit Service (PRT, Fokker F.VIIa-3m), and National Air Transport (NAT, Curtiss Carrier Pigeon). PRT bucked the trend by prioritizing passengers over mail, the latter being the major commodity for most operators, with passengers 'squeezed in' as capacity allowed.

Carriers and routes continued to be established, Boeing building Model 40A biplanes to service its own contracts, while Florida Airways, Pacific Air Transport (PAT), Pitcairn Aviation, Standard Airlines and Transcontinental Air Transport (TAT) also entered the fray.

New Aircraft

The United States' first truly successful airliner appeared in June 1926, when the Ford Tri-Motor flew for the first time. It represented the realization that safety, performance and, eventually, passengers were all becoming vital for successful operations. Other new aircraft entering service in the late 1920s and into the 1930s included the Boeing Model 80 and Curtiss Condor. However, these larger-capacity

▲ **Northrop Alpha**

Transcontinental and Western Air, 1930

The Alpha entered service with TWA in 1931 and was typical of the high-speed mailplane/passenger transport. The ability to carry mail was paramount, with passenger comfort a secondary consideration.

Specifications

Crew: 1	Range: 2650km (1650 miles)
Passengers: 6	Service ceiling: 5885m (19,300ft)
Powerplant: one 313kW (420hp) Pratt &	Dimensions: span 12.8m (41ft 10in);
Whitney Wasp R-1340-SC1 engine	length 8.7m (28ft 5in); height 2.7m (9ft 0in)
Maximum speed: 285km/h (177mph))	Weight: 2045kg (4500lb) loaded

machines were often flown with small passenger loads, and in a mistaken belief that smaller, fast airliners might be the way ahead, both Lockheed and Northrop produced impressive high-speed mail/ passenger carriers.

Meanwhile, the Post Office forced the merger of TAT and WAE to form Transcontinental and Western Air (TWA), before awarding the new company the prime central transcontinental route. Consolidation continued as American Airways was

formed out of several existing operators in the south of the country, while United Air Lines represented the merger of Boeing Air Transport, NAT, PAT and Varney.

Pitcairn and Florida Airways had already merged as Eastern Air Transport, and so, by 1931, the four major carriers had been established as TWA, American, United and Eastern, while an entirely separate operation, Pan American Airways (PAA), had begun operations into South America.

Specifications

Crew: 1	Service ceiling: 6705m (22,000ft)
Passengers: 6	Dimensions: Span 13.04m (42ft 9.25in);
Powerplant: One 410kW (550hp) Pratt &	length 8.64m (28ft 4in); height 2.95m
Whitney Wasp S1D1 engine	(9ft 8in)
Maximum speed: 354km/h (220mph)	Weight: 2359kg (5200lb) loaded
Range: 1159km (750 miles)	

▲ **Lockheed Orion**

Varney Speed Lanes, 1931

Lockheed's Orion was also built to the concept of the high-speed, small-capacity airliner. It saw widespread service with US airlines, carrying passengers and mail, but such aircraft could not compete in the longer term, as flying became more popular. Varney's Speed Lanes operation became Continental Airlines in 1937.

Specifications

Crew: 3	Range: 1610km (1000 miles)
Passengers: 20–32	Service ceiling: 3050m (10,000ft)
Powerplant: Two 429kW (575hp) Pratt &	Dimensions: Span 30.48m (100ft); length
Whitney Hornet B 9-cylinder radial engines	18.79m (61ft 8in); height 5.82m (19ft 1in)
Cruising speed: 174km/h (108mph)	Weight: 11,460kg (25,265lb) loaded

▲ **Consolidated Commodore**

Pan American Airways, 1930

Although US airline developments were mostly focused on internal routes, some carriers were looking towards South America. The New York, Rio & Buenos Aires Line began its services with Commodores in December 1929. On 15 September 1930, the airline was taken over by PAA, which subsequently operated all 14 Commodores built.

▲ Northrop Gamma 2D

Transcontinental and Western Air, 1934

A development of the Alpha, the Gamma perpetuated the high-speed mail/passenger concept. TWA's 2Ds were built to order, with the majority of Gammas being built either for military customers, record-breaking flights or expedition work.

Specifications

Crew: 1
Powerplant: One 530kW (710hp) Wright R-1820
   Cylone 9-cylinder Radial engine
Maximum speed: 359km/h (223mph)
Range: 3170km (1970 miles)

Service ceiling: 7130m (23,400ft)
Dimensions: Span 14.57m (47ft 9½in);
   length 9.5m (31ft 2in); height 2.74m (9ft 0in)
Weight: 3334kg (7350lb) loaded

Specifications

Crew: 2
Passengers: 12
Powerplant: Two Wright Cyclone 9-cylinder
   radial engines
Cruising speed: 268km/h (167mph)

Range: 1152km (716 miles)
Service ceiling: 7010m (23,000ft)
Dimensions: Span 24.99m (82ft); length
   14.81m (48ft 7in); height 4.98m (16ft 4in)
Weight: 7938kg (17,500lb) loaded

▲ Curtiss AT-32-B Condor II

American Airways, 1934

A peculiar combination of traditional biplane design and future airliner technology, the Condor II allowed airlines to advance from their 1920s equipment relatively cheaply, without having to commit to the more modern monoplanes then entering service. This machine crashed into a mountain in June 1934.

▲ Lockheed Model 10 Electra

Northwest Airlines, 1934

By comparison with the Curtiss Condor, the Electra was very much of the modern era. The 10-passenger airliner established Lockheed as a major producer of transport aircraft and first entered service with Northwest in 1934. The airline had been established as a mail carrier in 1926.

Specifications

Crew: 2
Passengers: 10
Powerplant: two 336kW (450hp) Pratt &
   Whitney Wasp Junior SB radial piston engines
Maximum speed: 325km/h (202mph)

Range: 1305km (809 miles)
Service ceiling: 5915m (19,400ft)
Dimensions: Span 16.76m (55ft);
   length 11.76m (38ft); height 3.07m (10ft 1in)
Weight: 4672kg (10,278lb) loaded

Specifications

Crew: 5

Passengers: 32

Powerplant: Four 52kW (70hp) Pratt & Whitney
  Hornet S51DG 9-cylinder radial engines

Cruising speed: 267km/h (166mph)

Range: 1250km (775 miles)

Service ceiling: 5790m (19,000ft)

Dimensions: Span 34.79m (114ft 2in);
  length 21.08m (69ft 2in); height 5.28m
  (17ft 4in)

Weight: 19,051kg (42,000lb) loaded

▲ Sikorsky S-42

Pan American Airways System, 1935

In its quest to conquer the Pacific, PAA employed several flying boat designs.
The S-42 flew route proving trials in support of the later Martin M-130, as well
as ultimately carrying PAA's service all the way down to New Zealand.

Specifications

Crew: 6–9

Powerplant: Four 708kW (830hp) Pratt
  & Whitney R-1830-S2A5G Twin Wasp
  14-cylinder radial engines with hydromatic
  propellers

Maximum speed: 290km/h (180mph)

Range: 5150km (3200 miles)

Service ceiling: 3048m (10,000ft)

Dimensions: Span 39.7m (130ft);
  length 27.7m (90ft 10½in); height 7.5m
  (24ft 7in)

Weight: 23,701kg (52,252lb) loaded

▲ Martin M-130

CHINA CLIPPER, Pan American Airways, 1935

Martin's M-130 took off for its first PAA airmail service on 22 November 1935. The
aircraft reached its destination, Manila, on the 29th. Just three M-130s were built,
all for PAA. They began passenger flights in October 1937.

▲ Ford 5-AT Tri-Motor

Scenic Airways, 1980

Having flown for the first time in 1929, this remarkable Tri-Motor was still making
regular sightseeing flights with Scenic Airways in 1980. The aircraft remained
airworthy in early 2012, testament to the sturdy build of Ford's masterpiece.

Specifications

Crew: 3

Passengers: 10

Powerplant: Three 313kW (420hp) Pratt
  & Whitney Wasp C 9-cylinder radial engines

Maximum speed: 241km/h (150mph)

Range: 885km (550 miles)

Service ceiling: 5640m (18,500ft)

Dimensions: Span 23.72m (77ft 10in);
  length 15.32m (50ft 3in); height 3.86m
  (12ft 8in)

Weight: 6120kg (13,500lb) loaded

Aviation adventures
1930–39

The 1930s were a time of record-breaking long-range flights that saw the emergence of several outstanding female pilots. It was also a decade of improvement in aircraft design that produced the first truly modern airliner.

SEVERAL AVIATORS COMPLETED meritorious flights during the 1930s, usually in single-engined lightplanes over enormous distances, but above all else the decade saw the rise of the aviatrix. First among these pioneering women was Britain's Amy Johnson. She departed Croydon for Australia on 5 May 1930, flying her Gipsy Moth *Jason* and with just 75 hours' flying time and a longest flight of 237km (147 miles) to her credit.

Johnson survived a crash landing en route to complete the journey on 24 May. A little over a year later she was off again, this time in a Puss Moth named *Jason II*, bound for Japan. She reached Tokyo on 6 August. In 1932, she married fellow aviator Jim Mollison and they competed unsuccessfully in the 1934 MacRobertson race. Amy Johnson took the London–Cape Town record in 1936, before withdrawing from the European aviation scene.

Amelia Earhart became globally famous through her aviation exploits of the 1930s. A society darling, Earhart was married to the renowned publisher and promoter George P. Putnam. She became the first woman to cross the North Atlantic solo on 20–21 May 1932, flying from Newfoundland to Northern Ireland. In August of the same year she flew non-stop from Los Angeles to New Jersey to become the Unites States' first female non-stop transcontinental pilot. She remained faithful to the Lockheed Vega of her previous records when she flew from Honolulu, Hawaii to Oakland, California on 11–12 January 1935; again, she was the first woman to achieve the feat.

Several other women pilots achieved great things during the decade, but perhaps just one more must be mentioned here. New Zealand's Jean Batten flew a DH.60M Moth from England to Darwin, Australia, from 8 to 23 May 1934, taking more than four days off Johnson's record for the journey. Later, Batten completed the first solo flight across the South Atlantic by a woman, flying a Percival Gull from the UK to Senegal and then across the ocean to Natal, Brazil, during 11–13 November 1935.

▲ **de Havilland DH.60G Gipsy Moth**

Jason, Amy Johnson, 1930

Amy Johnson flew *Jason* solo to Darwin, Australia, from Croydon, England, in 1930. On completing the journey she won a £10,000 *Daily Mail* prize and entered into a world of publicity that caused her to have several emotional breakdowns. She was lost during a wartime flight in 1941.

Specifications

Crew: 1	Service ceiling: 3965m (13,000ft)
Passengers: 1	Dimensions: Span 8.84m (29ft);
Powerplant: One 45kW (60hp) ADC Cirrus I	length 7.16m (23ft 6in); height 2.68m
engine	(8ft 7in)
Cruising speed: 137km/h (85mph)	Weight: 611kg (1350lb) loaded
Range: 515km (320 miles)	

And Airmen, Too

Of course, men were also excelling in the air, none more so than Wiley Post and his navigator Harold Gatty, who circled the globe in their Vega *WINNIE MAE* between 23 June and 1 July 1931. Post repeated the effort – solo – from 15 to 22 July 1933, in the same aircraft, but was killed in an accident in 1935.

Hugh Herndon Jr and Clyde E. Pangborn became the first to fly non-stop from Japan to the US on 4–5 October 1931, while Sir Charles Kingsford Smith and Captain P.G. Taylor completed a staged crossing of the Pacific from Australia to America in their Lockheed Altair *Lady Southern Cross,* between 22 October and 4 November 1934.

Newly married to Amy Johnson, Jim Mollison set out from Ireland to attempt the first solo east–west crossing of the North Atlantic on 18 August 1932. His DH.80A Puss Moth *The Heart's Content* landed safely in New Brunswick 31 hours later. In spring 1933, he used the same aircraft to fly solo from the UK to Natal, Brazil, to complete not only the first

▲ **Lockheed Vega**

WINNIE MAE, Wiley Post, 1933

Wiley Post made a second circumnavigation of the world in 1933. On successful completion of the 25099km (15,596-mile) trip, *WINNIE MAE* was painted with the names of all the aircraft's stops made during the seven-day, 18-hour, 49-minute adventure.

Specifications

Crew: 1 + 7

Powerplant: one 335kW (450hp) Pratt & Whitney Wasp 9-cylinder radial engine

Maximum speed: 265km/h (165mph) at 3050m (10,000ft)

Range: 885km (550 miles)

Service ceiling: 5500m (18,000ft)

Dimensions: span 12.5m (41ft); length 8.4m (27ft 7in); height 2.6m (8ft 6in)

Weight: 2155kg (4750lb) loaded

▲ **Curtiss BT-32 Condor II**

Second Byrd Antarctic Expedition, 1933-1935

Richard E. Byrd led five Antarctic expeditions. He was among the growing number of explorers and adventurers to appreciate the relevance of the aircraft as an expedition tool. His first expedition employed three aircraft, while his second used the Condor above. In 1930, Curtiss had officially become Curtiss-Wright, but the new name was seldom used.

Specifications

Crew: 2

Passengers: 12

Powerplant: Two 529kW (710 hp) Wright Cyclone 9-cylinder radial engines

Cruising speed: 268km/h (167mph)

Range: 1152km (716 miles)

Service ceiling: 7010m (23,000ft)

Dimensions: Span 24.99m (82ft); length 14.81m (48ft 7in); height 4.98m (16ft 4in)

Weight: 7938kg (17,500lb) loaded

solo flight from England to South America, but also the first solo east–west crossing of the South Atlantic. At the same time he became the only pilot to have flown both the North and South Atlantics solo.

Mollison contested the MacRobertson Air Race with his wife, flying as a team in a de Havilland DH.88 Comet on the route from England to Australia. Unfortunately, their entry was scuppered by engine problems, but the race was won by another Comet, while one of the new DC-2 airliners came in second.

New Equipment

The 1930s was also a great time for new aircraft developments. Boeing flew its first civil monoplane, the Model 200 Monomail, in 1930. A highly advanced machine, it provided a taste of great things to come. In 1933, the company flew the first Model 247, an aircraft so technologically superior that it is considered to be the first of the truly modern airliners. Remarkably, Boeing was able to follow the ground-breaking 247 with the Model 307 Stratoliner, the world's first pressurized airliner, which entered service on 31 December 1938.

Boeing's products were initially available only to the United group airlines, however, spurring TWA to request a competitor to the 247 from Douglas. The result was the DC-1 of 1933, which led to the production DC-2 and ultimately to the legendary DC-3, which first flew on 17 December 1935.

In the UK, Imperial Airways introduced its 'C'-class flying boat to service on 30 October 1936, before beginning inflight-refuelling trials with the type in January 1938. Perhaps applicable to mail flights, but not those carrying passengers, the trials were generally successful.

NOTABLE 1930s' EVENTS AND PIONEERING FLIGHTS

Date	Event	Aircraft type	Personality
6 May 1930	First Boeing commercial monoplane flown	Boeing Model 200 Monomail	
15 May 1930	First flight by airline stewardess; Boeing Air Transport		Ellen Church
25 October 1930	First coast–coast US passenger service inaugurated; TWA	Armstrong Whitworth Argosy & Short S.8 Calcutta	
28 February 1931	First London–Central Africa service inaugurated; Imperial Airways		
4 October 1931	First non-stop Japan–US flight, completed 5 October	Bellanca Skyrocket	Hugh Herndon Jr and Clyde E. Pangborn
8 February 1933	First flight of Boeing 247	Boeing Model 247	
3 April 1933	First flight over Mount Everest	Westland PV-3 & Westland Wallace	Marquess of Clydesdale (PV-3) and Flt Lt D.F. McIntyre (Wallace)
1 July 1933	First flight of DC-1	Douglas DC-1	Carl A. Cover, pilot
8 August 1933	First non-stop Canada–UK flight, completed 9 August	de Havilland Dragon	L.G. Reid and J.R. Ayling
20 October 1934	UK–Australia MacRobertson Race begun, completed 23 October	de Havilland DH.88 Comet, Douglas DC-2, Bellanca Model 28, Boeing 247D	Charles W.A. Scott and Tom Campbell Black, winners (DH.88)
22 October 1934	First Australia–US flight, completed 4 November	Lockheed Altair	Sir Charles Kingsford Smith and Capt. P.G. Taylor
17 December 1935	First flight of DC-3	Douglas DC-3	Carl A. Cover, pilot
3 July 1936	First flight of S.23 Empire	Short S.23 Empire	John Lankester Parker, pilot
15 August 1937	Transatlantic trials with depot ships begun; Deutsche Lufthansa	Blohm und Voss Ha 139	
31 December 1938	First flight of Stratoliner	Boeing Model 307 Stratoliner	
20 May 1939	First regular airmail service over North Atlantic inaugurated; Pan Am	Boeing Model 314	

Europe's airlines
1919–39

During the early 1920s, airlines were formed across Europe. They linked the continent's major cities and in many cases provided hitherto unavailable access to foreign lands.

GIVEN THE TREMENDOUS achievements of Imperial Airways and Luft Hansa in particular, it is all too easy to forget that airlines were forming all over Europe. Generally, these served domestic markets and what would today be called regional routes, but some also took on longer, international sectors.

In France, a bewildering array of airlines was quickly established after World War I, often in association with a particular aircraft manufacturer.

The prime route was over the Channel to London, but very soon services were being flown to Corsica and North Africa, and the major challenge was to establish links to South America and the Far East.

By April 1920, Lignes Aériennes Latécoère had reached Casablanca and by 1925 – under the company name Compagnie Générale d'Enterprises Aéronautiques – its West African route had been extended to Dakar, as the first stage in reaching South

▲ **Blériot-SPAD S.33**

Compagnie Internationale de Navigation Aérienne, 1933

Seating up to five passengers internally and flown by a single pilot in an open cockpit, the S.33 remained an important type throughout the 1920s and into the 1930s. CIDNA relied on the type for its European schedules.

Specifications

Crew: 1	Service ceiling: 3800m (12,470ft)
Powerplant: One 194kW (260hp) Salmson CM.9 radial engine	Dimensions: Span 11.66m (38ft 3in); length 9.08m (29ft 10in); height 3.2m (10ft 6in)
Maximum speed: 180km/h (112mph)	
Range: 1060km (670 miles)	Weight: 2062kg (4546lb) loaded

▲ **Fokker F.VIIa**

KLM, 1925

KLM's single-engined Fokker F.VIIa airliners were used in Europe and on its routes to the Far East. Among the type's innovations was the standard provision of toilet facilities and radio communications for the crew.

Specifications

Crew: 2	Service ceiling: 4700m (15,420ft)
Passengers: 8	Dimensions: Span 19.31m (63ft 4in); length 14.57m (47ft 7in); height 3.9m (12ft 10in)
Powerplant: Three 179kW (240hp) Wright Whirlwind radial engines	
Cruising speed: 170km/h (106mph)	Weight: 3986kg (8788lb) loaded
Range: 2600km (1616 miles) with extra fuel	

EUROPE'S PRE-WAR AIRLINES

Airline	Country of origin	Founded	Ceased operations	Notes
AB Aerotransport (ABA)	Sweden	2 June 1924	1946	
Ad Astra Aero	Switzerland	15 December 1919	1931	
Aer Lingus Teoranta	Ireland	22 May 1936	Operational in 2012	
Aero Lloyd Warschau	Poland	1922	1925	
Aero O/Y	Finland	1 November 1923	1968	
Aero TZ	Poland	1922	1929	
Aeroflot	USSR	1932	1992	Absorbed Dobrolyot USSR
Aerolot	Poland	1925	1929	
Aéropostale	France	1930	1933	
Air Bleu	France	1933	1940	Domestic Air France affiliate
Air France	France	1933	Operational in 2012	Merger of CGTA, CIDNA, Air-Orient and Air Union. Absorbed Compagnie General Aéropostale
Air Union	France	1923	1933	Absorbed Compagnie des Grands Express Aériens and Compagnie des Messageries Aériennes
Aircraft Transport & Travel Company	UK	5 October 1916	17 December 1920	Merged with Daimler Air Hire Ltd
Air-Orient	France	1930	1933	
Ala Littoria	Italy	1934	1945	
Avio Linee Italiane	Italy	1926	1939	Re-established in 1947
Balair	Switzerland	1925	1931	
British Airways	UK	1935	1940	
British Marine Air Navigation Company	UK	1923	1924	
British Overseas Airways Corporation (BOAC)	UK	24 November 1939	1974	Merger of British Airways and Imperial Airways
Ceskoslovenské Letecká Spolecnost (CLS)	Czeckoslovakia	1927	1939	
Ceskoslovenské Statni Aerolinie (CSA)	Czeckoslovakia	28 July 1923	1939	
Compagnie des Grands Express Aériens	France	20 March 1919	1 January 1923	
Compagnie des Messageries Aériennes	France	1919	1923	
Compagnie Franco-Roumaine de Navigation Aérienne, later Compagnie Internationale de Navigation Aérienne (CIDNA)	France	1920	1933	
Compañía Aérea Transportes (CAT), or Iberia	Spain	1927	1929	
Compañía Española de Tráfico Aéreo (CETA)	Spain	1921	1929	
Concessionaria Lineas Aéreas Subvenciondas SA (CLASSA)	Spain	13 March 1929	8 April 1932	Absorbed CAT, CETA and UAE
Crilly Airways	UK	1935	1936	
Daimler Hire Ltd	UK	7 June 1919	1921	
Daimler Airways	UK	1921	1 April 1924	Merger of Aircraft Transport & Travel Company and Daimler Air Hire Ltd
DET Danske Luftfart-selskap (DDL)	Denmark	7 August 1920	1946	
de Havilland Aeroplane Hire Service	UK	1921	1925	
Det Norske Luftfartselskap (DNL)	Norway	April 1928	1948	

Airline	Country of origin	Founded	Ceased operations	Notes
Deutsche Luft Hansa (Deutsche Lufthansa)	Germany	6 January 1926	Operational in 2012	Government take-over of Deutscher Aero Lloyd and Junkers Luftverkehr
Deutsche Luft-Reederi	Germany	1919	1923	
Deutscher Aero Lloyd	Germany	1923	1926	Absorbed Deutsche Luft-Reederi
Deutsch-Russische Luftverkehrs (Deruluft)	USSR/Germany	11 November 1921	1937	
Dobrolyot (Dobrolet)	USSR	March 1923	1929	
Dobrolyot (Dobrolet)	USSR	1929 1930	29 October Zakavia and Deruluft	Merger of Ukrvozdukhput, USSR
Handley Page Transport Ltd	UK	1919	1924	
Imperial Airways	UK	31 March 1924	1940	Merger of British Marine Air Navigation Company, Daimler Airways, Handley Page Transport and Instone Air Line
Instone Air Line	UK	1920	1924	
Junkers Luftverkehr	Germany	1923	1926	
Koninklijke Luchtvaart Maatschappij (KLM)	Netherlands	7 October 1919	Operational in 2012	
Lignes Aériennes Farman (Compagnie Générale de Transport Aérien – CGTA)	France	1919	1926	
Lignes Aériennes Latécoère (LAT, later Compagnie Générale d'Enterprises Aéronautiques, then Compagnie Generale Aéropostale)	France	1918	1946	
Líneas Aéreas Postales Españolas (LAPE)	Spain	1932	1936	Superceded CLASSA
Lineas Aereas de Espana (Iberia)	Spain	1927	Operational in 2012	
Linile Aeriene Romane Exploate cu Statul (LARES)	Romania	1932	1939	
Malert	Hungary	1928	1939	
Österreichische Luftverkehrs (OLAG)	Austria	1923	1938	
Northern Air Lines	UK	1925	1933	
Polskie Linje Lotnicze (LOT)	Poland	1 January 1929	Operational in 2012	Government take-over of Aerolot and Aero TZ
Società Anonima di Navigazione Aerea	Italy	1925	1934	Absorbed by Ala Littoria
Société Anonyme Belge d'Exploitation de la Navigation Aérienne (SABENA)	Belgium	23 May 1923	2001	
Société Générale de Transports Aériens (SGTA, later Lignes Farman)	France	1919	1933	
Swissair	Switzerland	March 1931	2001	Merger of Ad Astra Aero and Balair
Syndicat National d'Etude du Transport Aérienne (SNETA)	Belgium	31 March 1919	1923	
Transadriatica	Italy	1925	1931	
Turkiye Devlet Hava Yollari (THY)	Turkey	20 May 1933	Operational in 2012	
Ukrainski Vosdukhni Put (Ukrvozdukhput)	Ukraine	1 June 1923	1929	
USS	Spain	1925	1929	
Zakavia	Georgia	1923	April 1925	

▲ **Junkers Ju 46hi**

Luft Hansa, 1932

Luft Hansa employed the He 46 primarily as a mailplane, flying off the ocean liners *Bremen* and *Europa*, this aircraft being marked for the latter. The German carrier invested heavily in technologies for launching transatlantic floatplane services.

Specifications

Crew: 2	Service ceiling: 4240m (13,900ft)
Powerplant: One 485kW (650hp) BMW 132E	Dimensions: Span 17.8m (58ft 5in);
9-cylinder single-row radial engine	length 11.06 m (36 ft 3.5in); height 3.9m
Cruising speed: 200km/h (125mph)	(12 ft 9.5in)
Range: 2000km (1242 miles)	Weight: 3200kg (7054lb) loaded

▼ **Breguet Bre.393T**

Air France, 1934

F-ANEJ served on Air France's Toulouse–Casablanca route in 1934. A three-engined machine, the Bre.393T accommodated 10 passengers in some comfort, each of them sitting adjacent to a large cabin window.

Specifications

Crew: 2	Range: 975km (606 miles)
Passengers: 10	Service ceiling: 5850m (19,190ft)
Powerplant: Three 261kW (350hp) Gnome-	Dimensions: Span 20.71m (67ft 11in);
Rhone 7Kd Titan Major radial engines	length 14.76m (48ft 5in); height not known
Cruising speed: 249km/h (155mph)	Weight: 6000kg (13,228lb) loaded

America. Simultaneously, Compagnie Franco-Roumaine de Navigation Aérienne had begun operations into eastern Europe as a first step to reaching Asia. By 1923 the airline had penetrated as far as Belgrade.

Elsewhere in Europe, Belgium's Syndicat National d'Etude du Transport Aérienne (SNETA) paved the way for the formation of Société Anonyme Belge d'Exploitation de la Navigation Aérienne (SABENA) in 1923, while Koninklijke Luchtvaart Maatschappij (KLM) was established in the Netherlands in 1919.

Overseas Territories

Belgium, France and the Netherlands all had extensive overseas territories and saw the potential for serving them with airmail routes. SNETA was first off the mark, joining Kinshasa with N'Gombé in the Congo, from 1 July 1920. By early 1921, the route extended

the length of the Congo River, SNETA's three-seat Lévy-Lepen flying boats reaching as far as Kisangani.

On 1 January 1925, France's Franco-Roumaine became Compagnie Internationale de Navigation Aérienne (CIDNA) and under this title it worked to extend its eastern routes to Baghdad. Ultimately, however, it was Air Union, in partnership with Air Asie to form a new concern, known as Air Orient, which took French airmail to Baghdad. By 1938, the route stretched to Saigon, as the responsibility of Air France, the latter taking it to Hong Kong in 1939, using Dewoitine D.338 airliners.

KLM came relatively late to long-range international routes, inaugurating its Amsterdam–

◤ Fokker F.XXXVI
AREND, KLM, 1934

Fokker stuck doggedly to the construction techniques and technologies that had served it so well on the F.VII line. Unfortunately, by the time the F.XXXVI appeared – it was a contemporary of the DC-2 – Fokker's design philosophy was clearly obsolete.

Specifications

Crew: 2–3	Service ceiling: 6930m (22,750ft)
Passengers: 14	Dimensions: Span 25.9m (85ft 0in);
Powerplant: Two 540kW (730hp) Wright GR-	length 19.1m (62ft 6in); height 4.8m
1820-F-53 Cyclone 9-cylinder radial engines	(15ft 10in)
Maximum speed: 338km/h (210mph)	Weight: 8420kg (18,560lb) loaded
Range: 1750km (1085 miles)	

Specifications

Crew: 4	Service ceiling: Unknown
Passengers: 32	Dimensions: Span 33.0m (108ft 2in);
Powerplant: Four 560kW (750hp) Wright	length 24.0m (78ft 8in); height 8.3m
Cyclone SGR-1820-F2 radial piston engines	(27ft 3in)
Cruising speed: 280km/h (165mph)	Weight: 16,500kg (36,366lb) loaded
Range: 600km (960 miles)	

▼ Douglas DC-2
KLM, 1934

Ironically, Fokker also began building the DC-2 under licence in 1934. *PH-AJU* was the first of its DC-2s. It went on to gain fame by taking second place in the 1934 MacRobertson Air Race.

Batavia (Jakarta) service on 1 October 1931 with Fokker F.XII monoplanes, but subsequently introducing a revolution to European air travel. The Dutch airline was the first of the European carriers to introduce one of the advanced American airliners, entering a DC-2 into the 1934 MacRobertson Air Race and running the type on its services to Indonesia from June 1935. The new equipment shaved four days off the 10-day schedule, even though the F.XII had been replaced by the F.XVIII on the route in 1932.

By comparison with KLM's latest equipment, Imperial Airways' aircraft were beginning to show their obsolescence, but it was not until Imperial gained a direct competitor that this lack of modernity began to tell. British Airways was formed in 1937, on a European route network served by Lockheed Electras and, subsequently, Lockheed 14s. Imperial had nothing with which to offer a comparable service and the two airlines were merged in 1939 to form the British Overseas Airways Corporation (BOAC).

While Imperial was struggling with modern developments, Luft Hansa had become Lufthansa and was matching everything its European rivals could offer, with a series of advanced indigenous aircraft. By now seen as a powerful, global expression of National Socialism, Lufthansa introduced the high-speed Heinkel He 70 on special European Express services, as well as the 10-seat He 111, while it expanded its transatlantic capability by introducing a fleet of new depot ships in 1937.

Airlines Across Europe

Airlines were now popping up all over Europe. Austria had Österreichische Luftverkehrs, while Poland's Polskie Linje Lotnicze (LOT) was more ambitious in flying not only European routes, but also to Palestine. Like British Airways, LOT later employed Lockheed airliners, while its Czechoslovak contemporaries, Ceskoslovenské Letecká Spolecnost and Ceskoslovenské Statni Aerolinie, adopted the DC-2 and Savoia-Marchetti S.73, respectively.

Spain had begun airmail services in October 1921, Compañía Española de Tráfico Aéreo using DH.9s between Seville and Morocco. Several small airline concerns were then established, including the original Iberia, before the industry was consolidated as Líneas Aéreas Postales Españolas (LAPE) in 1932. LAPE survived as the national airline until civil war broke out in 1936, latterly flying DC-2s.

Switzerland's Astra Aero and Balair combined to form Swissair, the flag carrier introducing DC-2 and DC-3 equipment, as well as the Lockheed Orion, which spurred Lufthansa to compete with the He 70.

First among Scandinavia's airlines, Det Danske Luftfartselskab (DDL) began a seaplane service from Copenhagen to Warnemünde on 7 August 1920, but was soon using landplanes. Finland's Aero O/Y, Norway's Det Norske Luftfartselskap (DNL) and Sweden's AB Aerotransport (ABA) all began their operations on seaplanes Aero O/Y and ABA initially relying on F13s, while DNL was established somewhat later, on the Ju 52/3m.

▲ Junkers G38ce

Lufthansa, 1932

Junkers' extraordinary G38 had seats for 22 passengers in two fuselage cabins; it also seated three passengers in each inner wing. The two G38s flew widely, *D-APIS* surviving into 1941 in Luftwaffe service, although *D-AZUR* crashed in 1936.

Specifications

Crew: 7/8	Range: 2000km (1200 miles)
Passengers: 32–34	Service ceiling: 5800m (19,000ft)
Powerplant: Four 559kW (750hp) Junkers Jumo	Dimensions: Span 44m (144ft 4in);
204 12-cylinder diesel engines	length 23.2m (76ft); height 7m (23ft)
Maximum speed: 210km/h (130mph)	Weight: 25,488kg (56,074lb) loaded

▲ Dornier Do X

Luft Hansa, 1931

With as many as 12 engines, a navigation and control room, an engineering room, a bar, washrooms and rugs on the floor of its dining room, the Do X was another extraordinary German airliner. The type undertook a transatlantic odyssey from November 1930 to May 1932, but never entered revenue service with Luft Hansa. Two Do Xs were built for Società Anonima di Navigazione Aerea, but saw little use.

Specifications

Crew: 4–5	Service ceiling: 5900m (19,352ft)
Passengers: Variable	Dimensions: Span 27m (88ft 7in);
Powerplant: Three 746kW (1000hp)	length 22m (72ft 2in); height 5.75m
BMW-Bramo Fafnir radial engines	(18ft 10in)
Cruising speed: 295km/h (183mph)	Weight: 17,800kg (39,249lb) loaded
Range: 2900km (1801 miles)	

▲ Caudron C.640 Typhon

LOUIS BLÉRIOT, 1935

Named *LOUIS BLÉRIOT*, *F-AOOR* was the fifth Typhon. Only seven of the high-speed mailplanes were built, early aerodynamic problems having never been properly overcome, and keeping the type out of airline service.

Specifications

Crew: 2

Powerplant: Two 164kW (220hp) Renault 6Q inline piston engines

Cruising speed: 400km/h (249mph)

Range: 3725km (2315 miles)

Service ceiling: 7000m (22,965ft)

Dimensions: Span 11.5m (47ft 6.75in); length 10.95m (35ft 11in); height 3m (9ft 10in)

Weight: 3400kg (7496lb) loaded

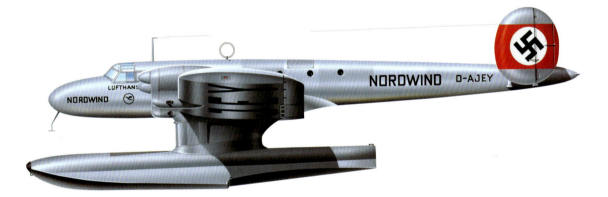

Specifications

Crew: 4–5

Powerplant: Four 440kW (592hp) Junkers Jumo 205 diesel engines

Maximum speed: 307km/h (191mph)

Range: 4990km (3100 miles)

Service ceiling: 3690m (12,100ft)

Dimensions: Span 27m (88ft 7in); length 19.5m (64ft); height 4.4m (14ft 7in)

Weight: 17,460kg (38,500lb) loaded

▲ Blohm und Voss Ha 139

NORDWIND, Lufthansa, 1937

When Lufthansa issued a challenging specification for a seaplane to be launched from its new depot ships, Blohm und Voss responded with an advanced floatplane. The four-engined Ha 139 began trials in August 1937 and the type entered service over the South Atlantic just prior to World War II.

▲ Dewoitine D.338

Air France, 1936

Air France took 30 D.338 trimotors and the type provided excellent service. The carrier operated its route to Saigon and beyond with the Dewoitine and also re-established services post-war on the type.

Specifications

Crew: 1

Powerplant: Three 485kW (650hp) Hispano-Suiza V16/17 radial engines

Maximum speed: 301km/h (187mph)

Range: 1950km (1212 miles)

Service ceiling: 4900m (16,075ft)

Dimensions: span 29m (95ft 1.75in); length 22.13m (72ft 7.25in); height 5.57m (18ft 3in)

Weight: 11,150kg (24,582lb) loaded

▲ **Savoia-Marchetti SM.83**

SABENA, 1938

SABENA ordered the Italian SM.83 to supplement the S.73 on its Belgian Congo
route. Three of the four SM.83s ordered had been delivered before the outbreak
of war, while several S.73s were evacuated to the UK.

Specifications

Crew: 3–4	Range: 1500km (932 miles)
Passengers: 10	Service ceiling: 8400m (27,559ft)
Powerplant: Three 560kW (750hp) Alfa Romeo	Dimensions: Span 21.2m (69ft 7in);
126 9-cyl air-cooled radial piston engines	length 16.2m (53ft 2in); height 4.1m
Maximum speed: 444km/h (276mph) at 4000m	(13ft 5in)
(13,123ft)	Weight: 10,300kg (22,708lb) loaded

The modern airliner evolves
1934–45

**In the United States, rivalry between United and TWA led to the superlative DC-3, while Europe's
aircraft manufacturers struggled to keep up. Ultimately, World War II brought an end to several
advanced European airliner designs.**

UNITED AIR LINES ordered 60 Model 247s from
Boeing, the type representing a sea change in
capability. It had twin engines, retractable
undercarriage, was made entirely of metal and seated
10 passengers. In terms of safety, not only could it
maintain height with one engine stopped, but it
could still climb, and it cruised at 250km/h
(155mph). All of the United States' airliners were
rendered obsolete on the day that the 247 entered
service, but Douglas was working on a rival, the
DC-2. Similar in concept to the Boeing, the Douglas
proved to have the greater development potential and
longevity, but TWA's plans for it were thrown into
disarray on the eve of its service entry.

On 9 February 1934, President Roosevelt
cancelled the primary airmail contracts. He believed
that some airlines had been unfairly favoured when
contracts were awarded and called for a shake-up of
the system. Incensed, TWA's Jack Frye joined with
World War I ace Eddie Rickenbacker to fly the
DC-1 prototype across the country in just 13 hour
4 minutes, demonstrating how far civil aviation had

advanced. But the president remained steadfast and
the Army Air Corps took on the airmail, using a
selection of generally unsuitable aircraft, flown by
pilots who lacked the training necessary for long
cross-country flights that were often at night and in
bad weather.

The Army continued its efforts until 1 June, by
which time the deaths of 10 pilots had convinced the
president that he was wrong. The airmail contracts
were reinstated and America's airlines reorganized as
American Airlines, Eastern Air Lines, TWA and
United Air Lines. The operators were no longer
permitted to have associations with particular
manufacturers, but generally their work continued as
before, with new contracts being fulfilled and routes
re-established.

Developed Equipment

Boeing's Model 247 was well established in service by
the time that the airmail contracts were passed back
into commercial hands, while the DC-2 began
servicing TWA's transcontinental route on 1 August

Specifications

Crew: 3

Passengers: 10

Powerplant: Two 410kW (550hp) Pratt & Whitney S1H1-G Wasp radial engines

Maximum speed: 320km/h (200mph)

Range: 1200km (745 miles)

Service ceiling: 7620m (25,400ft)

Dimensions: Span 22.6m (74ft 1in); length 15.7m (51ft 5in); height 3.8m (12ft 5in)

Weight: 7621kg (16,770lb) loaded

▼ Boeing 247D

United Air Lines, 1935

United took new-build Model 247Ds, and had some of its original aircraft, including NC13326, upgraded. Compared to the Model 247, the 247D had revised elevators and powerplant, an aft-raked windscreen and more fuel.

▲ Short Mayo Composite

S.20 Maia and S.21 Mercury, Imperial Airways, 1938

Major Robert Mayo, Imperial Airway's technical manager, came up with the concept for a composite aircraft capable of launching a transatlantic mailplane. Laden with fuel and mail, the S.21 upper component of the resulting Mayo Composite could be launched at weights much higher than that at which it could leave the ground under its own power.

Specifications

Crew: 5

Passengers: 20

Powerplant: Four 679kW (910hp) Bristol Pegasus XC radial engines

Cruising speed: 265km/h (165mph) at 1524m (5000ft)

Range: 1360km (850 miles)

Service ceiling: 6100m (20,000ft)

Dimensions: Span 34.7m (114ft); length 25.9m (84ft 11in); height 9.95m (32ft 7in)

Weight: 17,237kg (38,000lb) loaded

1934. Ironically, it was the introduction of an airliner anachronism that saw the 247 surpassed and one of the greatest transport aircraft of all time created. American Airlines had begun a transcontinental sleeper service on 5 May 1934 using the Curtiss Condor II. The Curtiss biplanes were unable to compete with the DC-2 in terms of speed, but American was keen to maintain its edge in sleeper services. It therefore asked Douglas for an enlarged DC-2, a machine that emerged in December 1935 as the Douglas Sleeper Transport (DST). American subsequently revised its order for 10 DSTs to eight of the Sleepers and 12 standard transports. The latter were designated DC-3.

Meanwhile, Lockheed had also been working on advanced airliner designs and its 10-seat Electra entered service with Northwest on 11 August 1934. It followed the type with the 12-seat Model 14, but its next airliner, the superlative Constellation, went the way of a similar machine from Douglas, the DC-4, which was destined to enter service with the US Army Air Force during World War II. The United States' 'big four' airlines had joined with PAA in 1936 to fund development of a large Douglas airliner. The four-engined DC-4E was tested in 1939, but proved deficient. Subsequently, it was revised for military service as the C-54 and by far the majority of 'DC-4s' in airline service post-war were ex-military C-54s.

But the last inter-war laugh was undoubtedly Boeing's. Only 10 of its Model 307 Stratoliners were built, but the type pushed airliner travel to yet another level. A four-engined machine, the Stratoliner featured cabin pressurization. As such, it paved the way for higher-altitude, faster flights when it entered service with TWA in July 1940. PAA used its Stratoliners on routes to South America, but in 1941 it was forced to add its fleet to those of TWA, flying wartime transatlantic services.

European Rivals

While US aircraft manufacturers were taking great technological leaps forwards, Europe's industry was taking a rather more conservative approach to airliner evolution. France, Germany, Great Britain, Italy and

▲ **Focke-Wulf Fw 200 Condor**

WESTFALEN, Lufthansa, 1938

WESTFALEN was the second Fw 200 prototype. Flown for the first time in 1937, it was taken on strength by Lufthansa for ongoing trials in early 1938. Four Fw 200B production aircraft were ordered for Lufthansa, while two Fw 200A airliners entered service with DDL.

Specifications

Crew: 5	Range: 3560km (2212 miles)
Passengers: 30	Service ceiling: 6000m (19,700ft)
Powerplant: Four 895kW (1200hp) BMW/Bramo	Dimensions: Span 32.85m (107ft 9in);
nine-cylinder air-cooled radial engines	length 23.45m (76ft 11in); height 6.30m
Maximum speed: 360km/h (224mph) at 4800m	(20ft 8in)
(15,750ft)	Weight: 24,520kg (50,057lb) loaded

Specifications

Crew: 2	Service ceiling: 7070m (23,200ft)
Passengers: 21	Dimensions: Span 28.96m (95ft);
Powerplant: Two 746kW (1000hp) Wright	length 19.65m (64ft 5in); height 4.97m
Cyclone SGR-1820 9-cylinder radial engines	(16ft 3in)
Cruising speed: 298km/h (185mph)	Weight: 10,886kg (24,000lb) loaded
Range: 2414km (1500 miles)	

▲ **Douglas DC-3**

'Flagship Detroit', American Airlines, 1936

Many of American's DST/DC-3 aircraft were given *Flagship* names, including *Flagship Rochester*. The first commercial DST/DC-3 service was flown by *Flagship Illinois*, non-stop from Chicago to New York on 25 June 1936. Passengers paid $47.95 for a one-way ticket.

the Netherlands all possessed thriving aircraft companies capable of developing modern airliners to rival those of the United States.

In France, a series of new types allowed Air France to offer safer, faster, more reliable services. Typical of these machines, the Bloch 220 was an all-metal equivalent to the DC-3, while the Dewoitine D.338 was a long-range tri-motor, also of all-metal construction. Both types entered Air France service, and offered impressive performance, but World War II cut their use, and sales potential, short.

Britain's manufacturers were firmly locked into satisfying the needs of Imperial Airways, an airline that was failing to compete with the modern aircraft being introduced by its European rivals. There were moments of inspiration, however, and in response to a government requirement for a high-speed, long-range mailplane, de Havilland flew its DH.91 Albatross for the first time on 20 May 1937. The company had built a solid reputation through its touring and training aircraft, as well as its conservative biplane airliners, but now it produced a four-engined machine of remarkable performance. Unfortunately, technical difficulties kept the Albatross from service and World War II brought an end to its airliner potential, with just two machines flying BOAC services into 1943.

Specifications

Crew: 10	Range: 6760km (4200 miles)
Passengers: 40–74	Service ceiling: 4085m (13,400ft)
Powerplant: Four 1193kW (1600hp) Wright	Dimensions: Span 46.32m (152ft);
GR-2600 Double Cyclone 14-cylinder radial	length 32.3m (106ft); height 8.4m (27ft 7in)
engines	Weight: 38,100kg (84,000lb) loaded
Cruising speed: 294km/h (183mph)	

▲ Boeing 314A Clipper

CALIFORNIA CLIPPER, Pan American Airways, 1939

While Boeing and Douglas were trading punches over landplane supremacy, the flying boat was far from forgotten. Representing the pinnacle of inter-war flying boat airliner design, the Clipper entered PAA service on 20 May 1939 and could seat as many as 70 passengers.

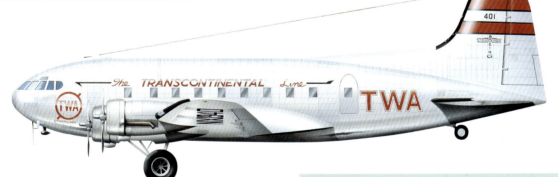

▲ Boeing 307 Stratoliner

TWA, 1940

TWA operated the largest Stratoliner fleet – five aircraft – introducing the type to service in July 1940 between Los Angeles and New York. The aircraft were impressed into military service, but returned to airline flying in 1944.

Specifications

Crew: 5	Service ceiling: 7985m (26,200ft)
Passengers: 33	Dimensions: Span 32.7m (107ft 3in);
Powerplant: Four 671kW (900hp) Wright	length 22.7m (74ft 4in); height 6.3m
GR-1820 Cyclone radial engines	(20ft 9in)
Cruising speed: 355km/h (220mph)	Weight: 19,050kg (42,000lb) loaded
Range: 3846km (2390 miles)	

GERMAN 'AIRLINER' DEVELOPMENTS

During the 1930s, Germany's aircraft industry created a number of very advanced aircraft. Many of these were produced as erstwhile civil aircraft, but with future *Luftwaffe* service in mind. However, others were genuinely among the most advanced civil aircraft designs of their time, subsequently swept up in the tide of war before they had a chance to become widely known in commercial service.

Type	First flown	Powerplant	Description
Blohm und Voss BV 142	11 October 1938	Four 880hp (656kW) BMW 132H-1 radial piston engines	Designed as long-range mailplane; served as maritime and strategic reconnaissance aircraft
Blohm und Voss BV 222	7 September 1940	Six 1,200hp (895kW) Bramo Fafnir 323R-2 radial piston engines	Designed as transatlantic airliner flying boat; served as maritime patrol and reconnaissance aircraft
Dornier Do P	31 March 1930	Four 500hp (373kW) Bristol Jupiter radial piston engines	Designed as a bomber; publicly revealed as a freighter, as with related Do Y
Dornier Do 17	1934	Two 660hp (492kW) BMW VI inline piston engines	Designed as a high-speed mailplane/airliner; served as bomber, reconnaissance and night-fighter aircraft
Focke-Wulf Fw 200 Condor	27 July 1937	Four 720hp (537kW) BMW 132G radial piston engines	Designed as a transatlantic airliner; served as an airliner, military transport and maritime reconnaissance-bomber
Heinkel He 111	24 February 1935	Two 660hp (492kW) BMW VI inline piston engines	Designed as a bomber or high-speed airliner; served as a bomber
Junkers Ju 52/3m	7 March 1932	Three 550hp (410kW) Pratt & Whitney Hornet radial piston engines	Designed as an airliner; served as an airliner, bomber and military transport
Junkers Ju 86	4 November 1934	Two 590hp (440kW) Junkers Jumo 205 inline piston engines	Designed as a bomber or high-speed airliner; served as an airliner, bomber, military transport and strategic reconnaissance aircraft
Siebel Si 204	1940	Two 592hp (441kW) Argus As 411 inline piston engines	Designed as a light airliner; served as a military communications, training and transport aircraft

Undoubtedly the most important of Britain's advanced airliners, the Short S.23 flying boat entered Imperial service in November 1936. It flew the routes to Australia and South Africa, and its performance was magnificent, but again, war curtailed operations. In 1938, however, Imperial used a variation on the S.23, the S.20, to prove a unique concept in civil aviation. On 6 February, S.20 Maia released S.21 Mercury, a four-engined mailplane. The concept behind the so-called Mayo composite was that Maia gave Mercury a boost in range and payload, before releasing it over the Atlantic for a non-stop run to the United States. The idea might well have worked, but was abandoned as war loomed.

In Italy, Savoia-Marchetti produced the 16-seat, fixed-undercarriage S.73 tri-motor and the larger, more advanced SM.83. The latter had retractable undercarriage and better performance, but the S.73 was cheaper and remained popular even as production switched to wartime needs. In the Netherlands, the proud Fokker tradition was fading as the company failed to embrace the new construction techniques and technologies of its rivals, especially those in the United States. The story was very different in Germany, however, where the aircraft industry seemed without restraint.

In answering Lufthansa's calls for aircraft to rival the best in service, the German aircraft companies produced a succession of advanced designs, many of them eminently suitable for conversion to military use, others produced with military roles in mind, but under the cover of civilian specifications. A fascinating mix of civil and pseudo-civil aircraft resulted, from Dornier, Focke-Wulf, Heinkel and Junkers, placing Germany firmly at the top of the commercial aircraft tree, but also establishing names in the minds of Europe's population that would come to cause terror in the not too distant future.

Specifications

Crew: 4

Passengers: 62

Powerplant: Two 1500kW (2000hp) Pratt
& Whitney R-2800-51 two-row 18-cylinder
radial engines

Maximum speed: 433km/h (269 mph)

Range: 4750km (2950 miles)

Service ceiling: 8410m (27,600ft)

Dimensions: Span 32.9m (108ft 1in);
length 23.27m (76ft 4in); height 6.63m
(21ft 9in)

Weight: 22,000kg (48,000lb) loaded

▼ Curtiss C-55

BOAC, 1941

Curtiss began work on a DC-3 rival in 1936, flying a prototype of its CW-20 in 1940. By then the DC-3 was well established and the CW-20 failed to become an airline hit. Huge numbers were built for the US military, however, while the CW-20 prototype, redesignated as the sole military C-55, served BOAC's wartime routes between 1941 and 1943.

Specifications

Crew: 2

Passengers: 18

Powerplant: Two 653kW (875hp) Pratt
& Whitney Hornet S1E2-G engines

Maximum speed: 428km/h (266mph)

Range: 4025km (2500 miles)

Service ceiling: 7740 (25,400ft)

Dimensions: Span 19.96m (65ft 6in);
length 15.19m (49ft 10in); height 3.6m
(11ft 10in)

Weight: 7938kg (17,500lb) loaded

▼ Lockheed Lodestar

BOAC, 1941

BOAC maintained regular schedules throughout World War II, often in support of the military. It used the Lodestar on its African routes as well as on the 'ball-bearing' run between Sweden and Scotland. Essential ball bearings, as well as documents and personnel, were regularly flown between the two countries at great risk to their crews.

Specifications

Crew: 2

Powerplant: Two 1103kW (1480hp) Rolls-Royce
liquid-cooled V12 engines

Maximum speed: 610km/h (366 mph)

Range: 1500km (900 miles)

Service ceiling: 8839m (29,000ft)

Dimensions: Span 16.52m (54ft 2in);
length 13.57m (41ft 2in); height 5.3m
(17ft 5in)

Weight: 8028kg (17,700lb) loaded

▼ De Havilland Mosquito FB.Mk IV

BOAC, 1943

BOAC flew *G-AGGE* on the 'ball-bearing' run until 1945. These daring flights were often flown at ultra low level and always at high speed. Sometimes an unfortunate, but generally very important, passenger was carried in the aircraft's modified bomb bay.

Chapter 3

Post-War Resurgence (1945–55)

World War II severely curtailed airline operations in Europe. Very basic services were maintained between principal destinations in Allied countries, or between those of combatants and neutral states, but generally the continent's once-proud airline system was in disarray. In terms of equipment, some aircraft manufacturers had looked forwards to the end of the conflict and had begun laying grand plans for new airliner designers, while the British Government had had the foresight to assess future air travel needs, but much remained to be done. In the United States, airline travel had been less curtailed, while some of the big airline players had also been involved in military contract work. US industry had also developed the C-54 and Constellation for the military and found itself ideally placed to build a new generation of airliner.

◀ DC-3

Douglas had built the DC-3 in considerable numbers before the war, but the type had been built in its thousands for the wartime military, in several different versions. With the end of hostilities, ex-military C-47s were readily available for airliner or freight conversion. The type appeared just about everywhere, offering an unbeatable combination of availability, rugged design, reliability and low ownership costs.

Wartime survivors
1945–50

Although World War II had driven aerospace technology to new heights, in the immediate aftermath of conflict surplus military aircraft supplied the majority of the world's air transport.

JUST AS WORLD WAR I had generated the technologies necessary to make commercial aviation a reality, so World War II paved the way for new aircraft and new services in the post-war years. Wartime operations had introduced and honed technologies that included radar and the jet engine. They had also demanded larger aircraft capable of covering great ranges, producing the components necessary for the globe-shrinking jetliners that were to come.

Aftermath of War

But in the immediate months and years after the end of the war in Europe in May 1945, and in the Pacific in August, the world's airlines – those that survived – had to make do with whatever equipment and infrastructure they could find. For most airlines, that meant using ex-military C-47s hastily modified for civil passenger operations, but in some cases airliner projects that had stagnated during the war finally bore fruit. Aircraft like the Savoia-Marchetti SM.95 had been conceived just before the war and were finally able to enter service as 'new' equipment for new airlines.

In the UK, a great deal of ingenuity was applied to converting existing bombers and transports, producing the Halton airliner from the Handley Page Halifax and the Avro Lancastrian from the Lancaster. With plenty of cheap transport aircraft and experienced pilots looking for post-war employment, small airlines and cargo carriers began springing up, especially in the UK, the United States and parts of Asia.

For the new British outfits, a major fillip came from an unexpected direction. In June 1948, Soviet authorities enforced a blockade on Berlin, aimed at forcing a political confrontation with the West. When the West refused to negotiate, the Soviets effectively cut West Berlin off from the supplies of food, fuel and other necessities that had been keeping its 2.3 million residents alive. The Western response was to mount an airlift of gargantuan proportions, and while the majority of traffic was military, several British companies took up contracts to supply more difficult goods. Fuel, especially liquid fuel, became a major commodity for these operators, as they did much to establish standards of operation for British and European commercial operators.

Specifications

Crew: 2	Service ceiling: 7070m (23,200ft)
Passengers: 21	Dimensions: Span 28.96m (95ft);
Powerplant: Two 746kW (1000hp) Ash-621R	length 19.65m (64ft 5in); height 4.97m
radial engines	(16ft 3in)
Maximum speed: 298km/hr (185mph)	Weight: 11,280kg (24,872lb) loaded
Range: 2414km (1500 miles)	

▼ **Douglas C-47**

Ethiopian Airlines, 1946

Ethiopian Airlines was typical of many post-war airlines, in operating C-47s and being set up with the aid of an established airline. Ethiopian began trading on 8 April 1946 with an all C-47/DC-3 fleet and assistance from TWA.

Specifications

Crew: 7

Passengers: 10

Powerplant: Four 1205kW (1615hp) Bristol
  Hercules XVI radial engines

Maximum speed: 454km/hr (282mph)

Range: 3000km (1860 miles)

Service ceiling: 7315m (24,000ft)

Dimensions: Span 31.75m (104ft 2in);
  length 21.82m (71ft 7in); height 6.32m
  (20ft 9in)

Weight: 24,675kg (54,400lb) loaded

▲ **Handley Page Halton**
FLAMBOROUGH, BOAC, 1947

BOAC operated 12 Haltons, all of them conversions from Halifax military transports. *G-AHON* had been built as a Halifax C.Mk 8 for the RAF and was one of 10 converted by Short as Halton Mk I aircraft. Altogether, around 90 ex-RAF Halifax transports were converted for civil operations.

Specifications

Crew: 4–5

Passengers: 20–38

Powerplant: Four 634kW (850hp) Alfa Romeo
  128 RC.18 radial engines

Maximum speed: 361km/h (224mph)

Range: 2000km (1240 miles)

Service ceiling: 6350m (20,830ft)

Dimensions: Span 34.28m (112 ft 5.5in);
  length 24.77m (81ft 3in); height 5.25m
  (17ft 2.5in)

Weight: 21,655kg (47,641lb) loaded

▲ **Savoia-Marchetti SM.95**
Alitalia, 1948

The SM.95 flew for the first time in 1943. Just two aircraft were built initially, with production restarting soon after the first flight of the third in July 1945. Aerolinee Italiane Internazionali (Alitalia) was formed by a combination of Italian government interests, private investment and BEA, for services from May 1947. It used SM.95s on European routes, inaugurating a Rome–Northolt, London, service with the type on 30 April 1948.

▲ **Junkers Ju 52/3m**
JU-AIR, 1983

The Ju 52/3m remained a viable passenger-carrying possibility thanks to French and Spanish production, but was nowhere near as plentiful as the C-47. *HB-HOP* is one of four remarkable Ju 52/3m aircraft flown by Switzerland's JU-AIR. It remains fully operational with the airline in 2012, having been built in 1939.

Specifications

Crew: 3

Passengers: 17

Powerplant: Three 541kW (750hp) BMW-built
  Pratt & Whitney Hornet radial piston engines

Cruising speed: 250km/hr (180mph)

Range: 1290km (800 miles)

Service ceiling: 5900m (19,600ft)

Dimensions: Span 29.20m (95ft 11in);
  length 18.9m (62ft); height 5.55m (18ft 2in)

Weight: 9600kg (21,200lb) loaded

BERLIN AIRLIFT

While the Berlin Airlift was primarily a military effort, a large number of civilian aircraft from 25 British companies also became involved. Their contribution to the overall airlift effort, especially in terms of delivering more difficult cargoes, such as liquid fuels, is inestimable.

Operator	Aircraft types	Missions flown
Air Contractors	Douglas Dakota	386
Air Transport	Douglas Dakota	205
Airflight	Avro Tudor, Avro Lincoln	967
Airwork	Bristol Freighter	74
Aquila Airways	Short Hythe (salt transport)	265
BAAS	Handley Page Halton	661
BOAC	Douglas Dakota	81
Bond Air Services	Handley Page Halton	2577
British European Airways	Organizational role only	
British Nederland AS	Douglas Dakota	76
BSAA	Avro Tudor	2562
Ciros Aviation	Douglas Dakota	328
Eagle Aviation	Handley Page Halton	1504
Flight Refuelling Ltd	Avro Lancaster, Avro Lancastrian (both for liquid fuel transport)	4438
Hornton Airways	Douglas Dakota	108
Kearsley Airways	Douglas Dakota	246
Lancashire Aircraft Corporation	Handley Page Halton	2760
Scottish Airlines	Douglas Dakota, Consolidated Liberator	497
Silver City Airways	Bristol Freighter	213
Sivewright Airways	Douglas Dakota	32
Skyflight	Handley Page Halton	40
Skyways	Avro Tudor	2749
Transworld Charter	Vickers Viking	118
Trent Valley Aviation	Douglas Dakota	186
Westminster Airways	Douglas Dakota, Handley Page Halton	772
World Air Freight	Handley Page Halton	526

Specifications

Crew: 2–4

Passengers: 36

Powerplant: two 1492kW (2000hp) Pratt & Whitney Double Wasp twin-row radial piston engines

Maximum speed: 435km/hr (270mph)

Range: 5069km (3143 miles)

Service ceiling: 7470m (24,500ft)

Dimensions: span 32.91m (108ft); length 23.26m (76ft 4in); height 6.62m (21ft 8in)

Weight: 20,412kg (44,906lb) loaded

▲ Curtiss C-46 Commando

Pan American World Airways, 1950

N74171 was one of ten ex-USAAF C-46s leased by Pan Am for freight operations in the Caribbean and Central America from 1948 to 1955. The airline added 'World' to its title in January 1950. Most of the C-46s pressed into airline service were flown as freighters although the type was never as popular as the C-47.

US dominance
1945–53

World War II had a profound effect on the United States' airlines. They emerged stronger, fitter and ready to create a global route network, using experience gained on military contracts and a new class of long-range, high-performance aircraft.

IN THE UNITED STATES, as in many other countries, the wartime needs of the military consumed much of the country's aircraft production, while commercial transports were also pressed into service as freighters and troop carriers. Generally, the airlines served the nation's most important routes with the ubiquitous DC-3, at the same time satisfying the various and burgeoning needs of the military and other government organizations.

Pan American had established a wide-ranging network during the interwar years. Its services extended into Latin America and across the Pacific and, just before war broke out in Europe, the airline had begun transatlantic services using Boeing 314 flying boats. It was a natural candidate for long-range, international government contracts and these it undertook, although jointly with other carriers venturing beyond North America for the first time.

Ironically, the primary equipment used on these government contracts was the Douglas DC-4. Rejected by the airlines in its pre-war DC-4E form, it was now used by the airlines as the military C-54. The Douglas was joined by the Boeing Stratoliner –

flown across the North Atlantic by TWA – and the Sikorsky VS-44 flying boat – used to establish a New York–Foynes, Ireland route by American Export Airlines on 26 May 1942.

Gathering Experience

Airline crews also became involved in the so-called 'Hump' operation, flown from 1942 to lift supplies across the Himalayas from India to China in support of Chiang Kai-shek and US Army Air Force units based in the country. Pan American was instrumental in setting up the operation through the provision of DC-3s and experienced crews, the USAAF itself having little exposure to such difficult transport operations.

The 'Hump' operation finished in 1945 with the fall of Japan, releasing extremely experienced civilian and military crews into the airline system. Combined with the various transoceanic government contracts over the Atlantic and Pacific, it had greatly broadened the possibilities for the US carriers. They were left in a strong position, with a solid understanding of global routes and an extensive, hard-earned

Specifications

Crew: 4 (2–4 flight attendants)
Passengers: 60–81
Powerplant: Four 1864kW (2500hp) Wright
  R-3350-749C18BD-1 radial engines
Maximum speed: 555.22km/h (345mph)
Range: 4184.3km (2600 miles) max payload

Service ceiling: 7.34568km (24,100ft)
Dimensions: Span 37.49m (123ft);
  length 29.667m (97ft 4in); height 6.8326m
  (22ft 5in)
Weight: 48,534.4kg (107,000lbs) loaded

▲ **Lockheed C-69**
TWA, 1944

The military serial number gives this Constellation away as one of the military C-69s operated by TWA during World War II. The C-69 had been designed to satisfy military needs and even the L-049 was a compromise. Not until the L-649 entered service did the airlines have an optimized commercial Constellation variant.

knowledge base among their crews. At the same time, the military had been funding the development of long-range, four-engined transports. Clearly represented by the C-54, these advanced aircraft also included the Lockheed C-69, a machine better known as the Constellation.

Constellation Rises

TWA had ordered nine Model 49 Constellations before the war and Lockheed began building the prototype in 1940. But then the United States joined the war effort after the Japanese attack on Pearl Harbor on 7 December 1941, and in 1942 the Constellation prototype was requisitioned as the military XC-69 transport. By the time the aircraft was ready for its maiden flight on 9 January 1943, TWA had upped its order to 40, a figure matched by Pan Am, but neither carrier received a single aircraft, since

production was for military use only. In the event, the aircraft proved technically challenging and although its performance was exceptional, only 15 examples were built during the war and service trials could not begin in earnest until 1944.

Most of the Constellation's problems were caused by its Wright R-3350 radial engines, but even as Wright was working to fix these, Lockheed was devising new variants for the USAAF. In the event, the end of the war brought a mass cancellation of orders. Most of the C-69s were sold to civilian operators, and aircraft in an advanced state of build on the production line were completed as civilian L-049 airliners. The type was certificated as such on 11 December 1945 and Lockheed's brave decision to develop the model for commercial use gave it a huge lead in the emergent market for long-range passenger carriers.

▲ **Lockheed L-049 Constellation**

Pan American World Airways, January 1946

NC88838 was among the first L-049s delivered to Pan Am in 1946. The aircraft was also one of those that had been laid down on the production line as a military C-69 and completed post-war as an L-049 airliner.

Specifications

Crew: 4 (+ 2–4 flight attendants)	Service ceiling: 7.711km (25,300ft)
Passengers: 60–81	Dimensions: Span 37.49m (123ft);
Powerplant: Four 1640kW (2200hp) Wright	length 29.032m (95ft 3in); height 7.2136m
R-3350-745C18BA-1 radial engines	(23ft 8in)
Cruise speed: 503.72km/hr (313mph)	Weight: 39,122.3kg (86,250lbs) loaded
Range: 3685.4km (2290 miles) max payload	

Specifications

Crew: 5	Service ceiling: 7450m (24,442ft)
Passengers: 60–81	Dimensions: Span 37.49m (123ft);
Powerplant: Four 1864kW (2500hp) Wright	length 29.032m (95ft 3in); height 7.2136m
R-3350-749C18BD radial engines	(23ft 8in)
Cruising speed: 526.26km/hr (327mph)	Weight: 42,637.7kg (94,000lbs) loaded
Range: 3685km (2290 miles) max payload	

▲ **Lockheed L-649 Constellation**

Eastern Air Lines, March 1947

This Eastern machine was delivered to the airline in March 1947, equipped with a Speedpak for training work. The Speedpak provided the option of carrying cargo as well as a passenger load and could accommodate up to 3720kg (8200lb) of freight, albeit with an associated range penalty.

Specifications

Crew: 4–5	Service ceiling: 7225m (23,700ft)
Passengers: 95	Dimensions: Span 38.5m (126ft 3in);
Powerplant: Four 2423kW (3250hp) Wright	length 32.15m (105ft 4in); height 10.25m
972TC-18DA-3 radial engines	(33ft 7in)
Cruising speed: 570km/hr (355mph)	Weight: 65,775kg (145,000lb) loaded
Range: 8200km (5100 miles)	

▲ **Lockheed L-1049G Super Constellation**

TWA, March 1955

This L-1049G, or 'Super G', was one of the first delivered to TWA and was initially engaged in engineer training. It was equipped with weather radar and the longer nose cone associated with the installation. The aircraft was retired from TWA's internal network in 1964.

Lockheed's rivals had also realized that the world's post-war airlines were going to demand a new breed of aircraft. While Douglas was developing the DC-6 from the C-54/DC-4, Boeing was working on its Model 377 Stratocruiser, but neither aircraft would be available for service for at least a year and a half. Even though there were plenty of surplus C-54s available for conversion, there was nothing on the market that could rival the L-049's combination of speed and range.

In November 1945, Lockheed took orders from Air France, American Overseas Airlines (the successor to American Export Airlines), Eastern Airlines, KLM, Panagra, Pan Am and TWA, for a total of 89 aircraft. Ultimately, the company sold 103 L-049s. The first of the new-build aircraft emerged in 1947, but the first examples of modified C-69 airframes had been delivered to TWA in November 1945. Pan Am took its first Constellations in January 1946 and TWA began a regular New York–Paris schedule on 5 February. Journey time was typically between 16 and 17 hours, with technical stops for fuel at Gander and Shannon.

Lockheed Constellation – Civil Variants

Model	Notes	Number built
L-049 Constellation	First airliner variant; based on military C-69, Wright Cyclone R-3350-35 engines	74
L-649 Constellation	First variant built fully to commercial standards; also first compatible with Speedpak, R-3350-749C18BD-1 engines	14
L-649A Constellation	As L-649, but modified with more fuel in outer wings and higher weights	6 conversions
L-749 Constellation	Transoceanic version, more fuel, stronger undercarriage, higher weights	60
L-749A Constellation	L-749 with structural strengthening	59
L-1049 Super Constellation	Stretched fuselage, rectangular cabin windows, R-3350-956C18A engines	24
L-1049C Super Constellation	R-3350-872TC18DA-1 Turbo Compound engines	48
L-1049D Super Constellation	Convertible with twin cargo doors to port, reinforced floor and increased weights	4
L-1049E Super Constellation	L-1049C with L-1049D weights	28
L-1049G Super Constellation	Provision for tip tanks, higher maximum take-off weight, R-3350-972TC18DA-3 Turbo Compound engines	102
L-1049H Super Constellation	L-1049G with features of L-1049D	53
L-1649A Starliner	Lengthened L-1049G fuselage with new, longer-span, higher-aspect ratio wings, revised nacelles, increased fuel, R-3350-988TC18EA-2 Turbo Compound engines	44

Development work on the R-3350 engine, which increased both power and reliability, allowed Lockheed to re-engineer the L-049 into the L-649, the first truly commercial Constellation variant. First delivered to Eastern in May 1947, the L-649 introduced the optional Speedpak cargo pannier, generally improved performance and more luxurious accommodation.

Providing the L-649 with more fuel capacity allowed Lockheed to market the L-749 with the possibility of making non-stop New York–Paris flights, although a technical stop could still be forced by inclement weather or other factors. The manufacturer now also offered optional weather radar for the L-649 and L-749, as a retrofit or factory option.

Serious Rival

In September 1947, Douglas began flying its DC-6A freighter, an aircraft whose passenger derivative, the DC-6B, had already been ordered by United and American. TWA's mercurial owner, Howard Hughes, had prevented the airline's major rivals from acquiring Constellations, leaving the way clear for Douglas. Now Lockheed had to recognise the company as a major rival, since the DC-6B carried 23 more passengers than the L-749 and offered comparable performance.

In response, it inserted fuselage plugs fore and aft of the Constellations wings, increasing its fuselage length and capacity. Power was again increased, as were weights, and the new L-1049 made its first flight on 13 October 1950. By the time of the first L-1049 airline service, by TWA on 15 December 1951, the aircraft had been named Super Constellation, but the faster DC-6B had already been operating since April.

The Douglas easily outsold the L-1049, even though Lockheed developed its aircraft through a

Specifications

Crew: 4	Range: 4025km (2500 miles)
Passengers: 44–86	Service ceiling: 6795m (22,300ft)
Powerplant: Four 1081kW (1450hp) Pratt & Whitney Twin Wasp 14-cylinder radial engines	Dimensions: Span 35.81m (117ft 6in); length 28.6m (93ft 10in); height 8.38m (27ft 6in)
Cruising speed: 365km/hr (227mph)	Weight: 33,113kg (73,000lb) loaded

▼ Douglas DC-4

Scandinavian Airlines System, 1948

OY-DFI was one of the very few DC-4-1009 airliners built for commercial use post-war, rather than DC-4s converted from ex-military C-54 standard. It was delivered to DDL, but is shown here in SAS livery after the latter was formed by the amalgamation of airlines from Denmark, Norway and Sweden.

Specifications

Crew: 3	Range: 4835km (3005 miles)
Passengers: 54–102	Service ceiling: 7620m (25,000ft)
Powerplant: Four 1790kW (2400hp) Pratt & Whitney R-2800 Double Wasp 8-cylinder radial engines	Dimensions: Span 35.81m (117ft 6in) length 32.18m (105ft 7in); height 8.74m (28ft 8in)
Cruising speed: 507km/hr (315mph)	Weight: 48,534kg (107,00lb) loaded

▼ Douglas DC-6

Sabena, 1947

For airlines already using the DC-4, the DC-6 was an obvious choice of equipment as long-range routes proliferated. *OO-AWA* was one of three DC-6s ordered and delivered in 1947. The first DC-6B followed on 8 March 1953.

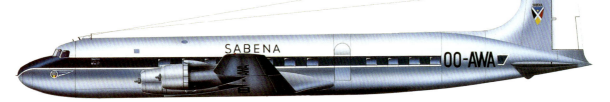

Post-war Douglas Commercials

Model	Notes	Number built
DC-4-1037	Only Douglas new-build commercial DC-4 variant; freighter based on military C-54, Pratt & Whitney R-2000 engines	79
Canadair DC-4M-2	Canadian-built commercial C-54 variant, Rolls-Royce Merlin 620 engines	20
Canadair C-4 Argonaut Aviation Traders	As DC-4M-2, but with more British equipment	22
ATL-98 Carvair conversions	Car/passenger transport	21
DC-6	Pratt & Whitney R-2800-CA15 Double Wasp engines	176
DC-6A	Freighter version, R-2800-CB16 Double Wasp engines	74
DC-6B	R-2800-CB16 or DB17 Double Wasp engines	288
DC-6C	Convertible/combi version, otherwise as DC-6A	74, including new build and conversion
DC-7	Wright R-3350-18DA-2 Cyclone 18 Turbo Compound engines	105
DC-7B	Similar to DC-7 but with more fuel	112
DC-7C	More fuel, longer fuselage, increased wing span, R-3350-18EA-1 Cyclone 18 Turbo Compound engines	120

range of variants. To make matters worse, the DC-7 was now threatening and was so superior to the L-1049 that another major re-engineering effort was required. Lockheed toyed with introducing a Pratt & Whitney T34 turboprop powerplant to its ultimate Constellation, but ultimately settled on further improved R-3350s, a slightly longer fuselage and a new wing. The result was the L-1649A Starliner, a machine so different that it was no longer called Constellation. Among the most advanced piston-engined aircraft ever built, it was easily outsold by the DC-7 and brought Lockheed's immediate involvement in the airliner market to an end.

The Douglas Commercials...

More than 1000 C-54s were built during the war, the Douglas transport completing 88,000 Pacific and Atlantic crossings,with just three machines being lost. The C-54 was clearly reliable, and easily available after the war, thanks to military surplus. With an eye to the future, the USAAF had commissioned Douglas to develop a larger version of the aircraft, designated XC-112A. This pressurized machine had obvious airliner qualities and Douglas began a parallel line of development that would lead to the DC-6. Against an order for 50 aircraft from American Airlines, which was unable to buy Constellations, Douglas prepared the DC-6 prototype for a first flight on 29 June 1946.

Specifications

Crew: 3 (+ 2 flight attendants)
Passengers: 189
Powerplant: Four 2535kW (3400hp) Wright
  Turbo-Compound radial piston engines
Maximum speed: 653km/hr (405mph)
Range: 7410km (4600 miles)

Service ceiling: 6615m (21,700ft)
Dimensions: Span 38.86m (127ft 5in);
  length 34.21m (112ft 3in); height 9.7m
  (31ft 10in)
Weight: 64,864kg (142,700lb) loaded

▼ Douglas DC-7C

Pan American World Airways, 1956

Pan Am introduced the DC-7C from April 1956 as a response to TWA's L-1049s and Starliners. The type was commonly known as the 'Seven Seas' in service, a play on its designation that also reflected its range performance. It was the last of the great piston airliners – in October 1955, Pan Am had ordered Boeing 707 and Douglas DC-8 jets.

The type entered service with American in April 1947 and sold well. With the basic DC-6 in production, Douglas began improving the design. First it produced the lengthened DC-6A freighter, and this set off warning bells at Lockheed because it clearly had the potential to become a fine airliner. And so, in fact, it did. When the DC-6B came to market, even the superlative Super Constellation struggled to compete with it – the Douglas may have lacked the good looks of the Lockheed, but it was faster and supremely reliable by the standards of the time.

The L-1049 was the Constellation competitor to the DC-6B, but only a few examples were actually available to the airlines until Lockheed introduced the L-1049C in 1953. At last it was able to offer a Turbo Compound version of the R-3350 to commercial operators; the engine had been restricted to military use thus far. The new engine allowed the Super Constellation to match the DC-6B for performance and better it for payload.

TWA introduced the L-1049C on the first ever non-stop transcontinental service in October 1953 and Douglas immediately responded by installing the Turbo Compound on its DC-6B. With funding and encouragement from American Airlines, Douglas also lengthened the fuselage and increased weights. The result was the DC-7, which Douglas developed through a handful of variants to dominate the final years of the piston era. So good was the DC-7, especially the ultimate DC-7C, that Lockheed had to develop the Starliner just to keep Douglas in sight. The latter built 120 DC-7Cs; Lockheed built just 44 Starliners.

Specifications

Crew: 2–3	Service ceiling: 7625m (25,000ft)
Passengers: 44	Dimensions: Span 32.1m (105ft 4in);
Powerplant: Two 1864kW (2500hp) Pratt	length 24.8m (81ft 6in); height 8.6m
& Whitney R-2800-CB16 radials	(28ft 2in)
Maximum speed: 480km/hr (298mph)	Weight: 22,500kg (49,600lb) loaded
Range: 2100km (1300 miles)	

▼ Convair CV-340

Lufthansa, 1955

Lufthansa flew its first post-war domestic service on 1 April 1955, using a Convair CV-340. The carrier also flew the CV-440, initially preferring the piston twins to the similarly ranged Vickers Viscount, but ultimately had to concede that it needed the British turboprop in order to be able to compete effectively in Europe.

▼ Boeing Stratocruiser

Pan American World Airways, November 1954

Pan Am equipped its Stratocruisers with auxiliary fuel tanks, allowing them to cross the Atlantic eastbound non-stop. Westbound, against the prevailing winds, a technical stop was still required. The big Boeing suffered with engine and propeller unreliability throughout its career, but remained popular with passengers and crews for its superior levels of comfort.

Specifications

Crew: 4 + 81	Range: 6760km (4200 miles)
Powerplant: four 2610kW (3500hp) Pratt	Service ceiling: 9755m (32,000ft)
& Whitney R-4360 Wasp Major 28-cylinder	Dimensions: Span 43m (141ft);
radial engines	length 33.6m (110ft); height 11.65m (38ft)
Cruising speed: 550km/hr (342mph)	Weight: 66,135kg (145,800lb) loaded

...and Boeing Stratocruiser

Boeing had produced two great airliners in the years immediately before the war: the Clipper and Stratoliner. Unfortunately, production of both had been curtailed by the outbreak of World War II. Boeing's wartime effort had focused on combat aircraft, among them the B-29 heavy bomber. Just as it had developed the Stratoliner from the B-17, the company then set about developing a transport from the B-29. The USAAF ordered three prototypes of the resulting XC-97 Stratofreighteron 23 January 1943, with four YC-97 aircraft following. These were based on the more advanced B-50, and the fourth was finished for VIP flying and featured airline-style seats. By this time, Boeing had already announced that it would build a commercial version of the C-97, and in 1945, Pan Am ordered 20 of the new Stratocruiser.

The Stratocruiser was introduced on Pan Am's transatlantic routes alongside the Lockheed airliner on 2 June 1949. Although it could carry more passengers than the Constellation, the Stratocruiser had shorter range. Orders for the Stratocruiser came in from Northwest, United and BOAC, but ultimately only 56 of them were built. Boeing's day had not yet come. But come it would, with the era of the jetliner.

Domestic Services

On their domestic operations, the United States' airlines faced a dilemma that would persist into the 1970s – how best to replace the DC-3. The airlines needed to offer similar levels of service domestically as they did internationally and the DC-3/C-47 simply was not up to the job. On the other hand, it was cheap to own and reliable, characteristics that made it difficult to replace. Ultimately, two manufacturers came forward with designs: Martin with its unpressurized 2-0-2, and Convair with its pressurized CV-240. First flown on 22 November 1946, the 2-0-2 entered service with Northwest in 1946, but Martin struggled to establish the aircraft in service. Technical difficulties and a crash caused more problems and although Martin produced a much more capable version as the 4-0-4, only 149 of its twins were built.

Convair fared much better with its piston line, which entered service in considerable numbers around the world. It flew the first CV-240 on 16 March 1947 and went on to build more than 1000 aircraft in a series of improved variants, some of them turboprop conversions. With DC-6s and DC-7s, Constellations, Stratocruisers and Convair-Liners in widespread service with US and European airlines, America's dominance of the airliner market had been established.

Convair propliners

Model	Notes	Number built
CV-240 Convair-Liner	40-seat airliner, Pratt & Whitney R-2800-S1C3G Double Wasp engines	566 for civil and military operators
CV-340	Longer fuselage, 44 passengers, increased wing area, higher weights, R-2800-CB16 or CB17 Double Wasp engines	311 for civil and military operators
CV-440	Maximum 52 passengers, exterior and interior improvements, R-2800-CB16 or CB17 Double Wasp engines	155 for civil operators
CV-540	CV-340 with Napier Eland NEl.1 turboprop engines	6 conversions
Canadair 540	Canadian CV-440 with Eland NEl.1 turboprop engines	3 conversions, 10 new build
PacAero CV-580 'Super Convair'	CV-340/440 with seating for 52 passengers, Allison 501-D13 turboprop engines	164 conversions
CV-240D/CV-600	CV-240 with seating for 48 passengers, Rolls-Royce RDa.10/1 Dart Mk 542 turboprop engines	38 conversions
CV-340D and CV-440D/CV-640	CV-340/440 with seating for 56 passengers, RDa.10/1 Dart Mk 542 turboprop engines	27 conversions
Kelowna Flightcraft Convair CV 5800	Stretched CV-580, or conversion package for CV-240/340/440 with fuselage stretch, cargo door and glass cockpit, Rolls-Royce 501-D22G turboprop engines	2 conversions

European struggles: UK and France
1945–55

The UK government applied itself to the problem of post-war commercial aviation in 1942, but came up with requirements that closely constrained its aircraft manufacturers. France continued the development of designs nurtured under Nazi rule.

BRITAIN BEGAN CONSIDERING the post-war needs of commercial aviation as early as 1942, when the so-called Brabazon Committee was formed under John Moore-Brabazon, 1st Baron Brabazon of Tara. In 1909, Moore-Brabazon had become the first Englishman to make a successful powered, controlled flight in a heavier-than-air machine, and he went on to become Minister of Transport and then Minister of Aircraft Production.

The committee was tasked with assessing the air transport needs of the British Empire and the Commonwealth. It worked steadily into 1945, before arriving at a list of four primary configurations, or 'Types'. Each Type was optimized for the particular needs of the Empire or Commonwealth, as well as the requirements of the airlines expected to operate it – BOAC and, later, its domestic and regional British European Airways Division. Type I called for a large, long-range transatlantic airliner; Type II for a DC-3 and Dragon Rapide replacement; Type III for a medium-haul airliner; and Type IV for a jet. All four were closely tailored to the needs of the British

airlines and in almost all cases this would hinder their sales prospects on the open market.

The Type I requirement was settled by the Bristol Brabazon, a behemoth powered by eight Bristol Centaurus piston engines driving four pairs of contra-rotating propellers. The aircraft was rendered useless by the passenger accommodation ordered by BOAC, whose management considered that transatlantic travellers would all be wealthy and demand the utmost in space and luxury. Brabazon facilities therefore included a cinema, cocktail bar, lounge, a central cabin with tables and chairs, and separate forward cabins for small groups of travellers. Total capacity was for 100 passengers, making the aircraft's operating costs per passenger per mile astronomical. Before it had left the ground for its delayed first flight on 4 September 1949, the Brabazon was doomed to failure. Nevertheless, work began on a turboprop-powered Mk II, but the machine was never completed, since BOAC quickly lost interest in the project. Both Brabazons were scrapped in 1953.

Specifications

Crew: 3

Passengers: 24–36

Powerplant: Two 1260kW (1690hp) Bristol Hercules 634 14-cylinder radial engines

Cruising speed: 338km/hr (210mph)

Range: 837km (520 miles)

Service ceiling: 7240m (23,750ft)

Dimensions: Span 27.20m (89ft 3in); length 19.86m (65ft 2in); height 5.97m (19ft 7in)

Weight: 15,422kg (34,000lb) loaded

▲ **Vickers Viking IB**

VERDANT, BEA, 1946

Delivered in 1946, *G-AHPL* was initially named *VERDANT* in BEA service, its name later being changed to *Lord Anson*. The Viking IB typically accommodated up to 36 passengers in BEA's so-called Admiral class, along with a crew of four.

Type II and Beyond

Britain had the dual requirement for a DC-3 and Dragon Rapide replacement. Some of the biplane Rapides flew throughout the conflict and the type remained in service for some years after the war. BEA pushed for a larger machine than that suggested by the Committee, while subsequent developments left turboprop power as an obvious choice. Fearing that this might be a technological step too far, the Committee split the category into Type IIA – piston power – and Type IIB – turboprop. Since BEA had requested a larger design and there was still a perceived need for the original smaller machine, a new Type V was also introduced.

The Type IIA specification was satisfied by the Airspeed Ambassador, a reliable, moderately successful type that served BEA well, but Type IIB proved to be among the most successful of all. Vickers' Viscount satisfied the needs of BEA, but also managed to achieve considerable export success and more than 400 were built.

The Type V requirement eventually morphed into Type VA, which produced the moderately successful Miles Marathon as a DC-3 replacement, and Type VB, which replaced the Dragon Rapide with the far more widely accepted de Havilland Dove.

Type III produced the unfortunate Avro Tudor. Ordered in 1944, the Tudor delivered C-54-like capability in an aircraft equipped with an anachronous tailwheel undercarriage. The Tudor I had been intended for transatlantic routes and its various design problems ultimately led BOAC to buy Stratocruisers. For Commonwealth routes, BOAC had intended to operate the Tudor II, alongside QANTAS and South African Airways (SAA). Once again the design disappointed, however, with BOAC buying Canadair C-4s, QANTAS ordering Constellations and SAA taking DC-4s.

The de Havilland Comet settled the Type IV requirement, as an aircraft built through incredible foresight, but once again tied too closely to the perceived needs of the UK airlines. It became the world's first operational jet airliner, but in sales terms was always overshadowed by the Boeing 707.

Other Options

On 1 August 1946, British European Airways and British South American Airways were set up to operate alongside BOAC. For the first time, Britain was planning routes to and within South America and these three associated airlines, along with several others attempting to build early post-war schedules or establish themselves as new operators, were eager to begin flying. Waiting for the Brabazon Committee designs was out of the question, so Britain's airlines inevitably leaned heavily on RAF-surplus C-47s. The Dragon Rapide also remained a reliable and numerous type, but there were other interesting options.

Avro had designed the York for wartime service by hanging a new, transport fuselage on Lancaster wings and tail surfaces, while the Lancastrian was a rather

Specifications	
Crew: 2	Range: 1296km (805 miles)
Passengers: 14	Service ceiling: 5639m (18,500ft)
Powerplant: Four 186.4kW (250hp) de	Dimensions: Span 21.79m (71ft 6in);
Havilland Gipsy Queen 30 Mk 2 piston	length 14.78m (48ft 6in); height 4.75m
engines	(15ft 7in)
Maximum speed: 266km/hr (165mph)	Weight: 5897kg (12,975lb) loaded

▲ **Riley Turbo Skyliner (de Havilland Heron)**
Sunflower Airlines

De Havilland developed the Heron as a four-engined, high-performance version of the popular Dove. The Heron sold well, providing sterling service with airlines including BEA and Sabena. It was also subject to powerplant conversions, Riley replacing the original Gipsy engines with Lycomings, as on this Fijian aircraft, and Saunders installing a pair of PT6A turboprops.

more modest conversion, adding streamlined nose and tailcones, and passenger seats, to the basic bomber design. Several ex-RAF Halifax transports were also modified for airline service as Haltons.

Vickers was a little more ambitious with its Viking, a short/medium-range aircraft ordered by the British Government in 1944. It combined an all-new airliner fuselage with the wings of the Wellington bomber. Entering BEA service in 1946, it replaced DC-3s on services to Europe. BEA continued Viking operations into 1954 and more than 160 aircraft were built in three versions. The type went on to serve faithfully with second line operators and the last examples were retired late in the 1960s.

The other interesting option was for flying boat operations using modified surplus Short Sunderlands. BOAC eventually used 24 demilitarized Sunderlands, taking the first of the rather basic machines in 1942. After the war, they were improved to Hythe standard and more were added to the fleet, while several others were used by airlines in South America, Australia and New Zealand. Later, a more luxurious conversion was completed for BOAC as the Sandringham, and several more of these aircraft were created for the carrier, as well as Tasman Empire Airways Ltd (TEAL), which used them to connect New Zealand and Australia.

BOAC also took the Short Solent, a commercial derivative of the Seaford, itself a wartime improvement on the Sunderland. TEAL and others became Solent customers as the aircraft was gradually improved, and although the days of flying boat operations were numbered, the type proved so alluring that the final examples served with Antilles Air Boats in the Virgin Islands between 1974 and 1978.

French Airliners

France had boasted a thriving pre-war aviation industry and although its activities had been hampered by war, essential skills had at least been maintained by war production for the German invader. Several 1930s prototypes and designs were placed in abeyance at the beginning of the war, to be dusted off and further developed as soon as hostilities ceased. Inevitably, Air France took on DC-3s and DC-4s and, later, Constellations, but it was also served by indigenous industry.

A major reorganization and nationalization of the aircraft manufacturers had been accomplished in 1941 and from within this new structure, three notable types emerged. Back in 1935, Breguet had begun work on its 730 flying boat. Built to the extent of two examples, it spawned the civilian 731 and a 760 landplane derivative of this was developed from 1944 under German control. The huge, double-deck airliner that resulted from this work flew for the first time on 15 February 1949. Air France took 12 of the improved Breguet 763 Provence version, primarily for use on routes to Algiers, but by 1964 more economical aircraft were available and the 763 was relegated to freight duties. The last, flying privately in support of Concorde development, were retired in 1971 and 1972.

Specifications

Crew: 3	Service ceiling: 5700m (18,700ft)
Powerplant: Four 1081kW (1450hp) Pratt	Dimensions: Span 35.81m (117ft 6in);
& Whitney R-2000-7M2 Twin Wasp	length 31.27m (102ft 7in); height 8.38m
14-cylinder radial engines	(27ft 6in)
Cruising speed: 342km/hr (213mph)	Weight: 33,475kg (73,800lb) loaded
Range: 3700km (2300 miles)	

▲ **Aviation Traders ATL.98 Carvair**
British Air Ferries, 1960s

Among the more unusual of Europe's post-war commercial aircraft designs, Bristol produced the Model 170 Freighter. Its bulbous proportions allowed airlines to serve a niche market, carrying mostly holidaymakers, and their cars, over the Channel to France. When the Bristols became due for retirement, Aviation Traders produced a C-54/DC-4 conversion known as the Carvair (Car-via-air) to replace them.

French Industry Consolidation

In 1936, the many French aircraft manufacturers were amalgamated to form a nationalized aircraft industry. Further consolidation occurred in 1941, with more changes after the war.

Nationalized company	Constituent companies
Société Nationale de Constructions Aéronutiques de l'Ouest, also known as SNCAO	Breguet and Loire-Nieuport
Société Nationale de Constructions Aéronutiques du Nord, also known as SNCA du Nord, SNCAN, or Nord	Amiot, Breguet, CAMS, Les Mureaux and Potez
Société Nationale de Constructions Aéronutiques du Sud-Est, also known as SNCA du Sud-Est, SNCASE, or Sud-Est	CAMS, LeO, Potez, Romano, Société Provençale de Constructions Aéronutiques; also Société Nationale de Constructions Aéronutiques du Midi (Dewoitine) from 1941
Société Nationale de Constructions Aéronutiques du Sud-Ouest, also known as SNCASO or Sud-Ouest	Blériot-SPAD, LeO, Bloch; also SNCAO from 1941

The giant Latécoère 631 flying boat had been designed to a 1936 requirement for a transatlantic airliner and flew for the first time on 4 November 1942. The prototype was then taken by the Germans, but destroyed by Allied bombing, while a second machine was completed and successfully flown on 6 March 1945. A spectacular aircraft seating just 46 passengers, the 631 was very much of its time and obsolete when Air France placed it into service on routes between Biscarosse and the French West Indies. After two crashes in 1948, the surviving machines were modified as freighters, but another accident in 1955 saw them withdrawn.

A rather more capable aircraft, the Sud-Est Languedoc combined much of the technical quality of the L-049 Constellation, with an old-fashioned 'tail-dragger' undercarriage. It origins lay in the Bloch SO.160, designed as a 20-seater for Air Afrique services. First flown in 1939, the machine was built for operations from austere airfields, but was clearly too small. A redesign to SO.161 standard allowed 33 passengers to be carried and although a prototype was flown late in 1939, the programme was stalled until the first production SE.161 took flight in 1945. The Languedoc replaced Ju 52/3ms on Air France services from June 1946 and a re-engining programme to replace the aircraft's Gnome-Rhône radials with Pratt & Whitney Wasps made it an altogether more practical proposition.

Languedocs served Air France and Poland's LOT into the 1950s, when retired aircraft passed to several smaller operators. The last Languedoc in commercial service was probably an Air Liban machine, which was retired in 1963.

Specifications

Crew: 3

Passengers: 107

Powerplant: Four Pratt & Whitney R-2800-CA18 radial piston, 2400hp (1790kW) each

Maximum speed: 390km/h (242mph)

Range: 2290km (1430 miles)

Dimensions: Span 42.96m (140ft 11in); length 28.94m (94ft 11in); height 9.56m (31ft 4in)

Weight: 50,000kg (111,000lb) loaded

▼ Breguet 763 Provence

Air France, 1953

Known officially as the Provence, the Breguet 763 was more commonly referred to as the 'Deux-Ponts', in reference to its double decks. The aircraft was not particularly lucrative in operation for Air France and saw out its days as the Universal freighter, or in military service.

Other contenders
1945–55

Across Europe the DC-3 dominated airline fleets, but the continent's manufacturers added other types to the mix. Italy brought wartime designs to fruition, while the Soviet Union emerged as a major force in civil aviation.

ELSEWHERE IN EUROPE, the first few years after the end of World War II saw very little in the way of airline development or aircraft production. In the Netherlands, Fokker was a shadow of its former self, having already been overtaken by new technology in the 1930s.

Italy retained the vestiges of its pre-war industry, however, and Alitalia was able to introduce Fiat G.12 tri-motors on its domestic routes on 5 May 1947, with the Savoia-Marchetti SM.95 following the Fiat into service in 1948. These aircraft allowed Alitalia to fly the Italian flag on Italian-built aircraft internationally, but they had almost no impact on the wider airliner market. Indeed, the efforts of the combined British, French and Italian industries trailed far behind those of the United States.

Specifications

Crew: 3	Range: 1500km with 26 passengers (932 miles)
Passengers: 21–32	Service ceiling: 6500m (21,325ft)
Powerplant: Two ASh-82FNV 14 cylinder	Dimensions: Span 31.7m (104ft);
2-row air cooled radial engine, 1380kW	length 21.31m (69ft 11in); height 8.07m
(1850hp) each	(26ft 5in)
Maximum speed: 407km/h (253mph)	Weight: 17,250kg (38,029lb) loaded

▼ Ilyushin Il-12 'Coach'
Aeroflot, 1947

Ilyushin pre-dated the Convair CV-240, Martin 2-0-2 and Saab Scandia with the tricycle undercarriage configuration of its Il-12, but the type was otherwise generally outdated. In an open market it would almost certainly not have had the economy in operation to compete with the Western types.

Specifications

Crew: 5	Range: 1100–2500km (685–1550 miles)
Passengers: 24	Dimensions: Span 28.81m (94ft 6in);
Powerplant: Two Shvetsov ASh-62IR 4-bladed	length 19.65m (64ft 5in);
VISh-21, 746 kW (1000 hp) each	height 5.15m (16ft 11in)
Maximum speed: 300km/h (186mph)	Weight: 10,700kg (23,589lb) loaded

▼ Lisunov Li-2
Czechoslovak air force

The Li-2 served widely with the USSR's client states. Aeroflot's Li-2s wore schemes similar to that of this Czech machine during the Great Patriotic War. As well as regular schedules, they flew troops to the frontline during major engagements.

Specifications

Crew: 4

Passengers: 24 or 32

Powerplant: Two Pratt & Whitney R-2180 Twin
Wasp E 14-cylinder radial engine, 1825hp
(1361kW) (with water injection) each

Maximum speed: 450km/h (280mph)

Range: 2650km (1432 nmi, 1647 miles)

Service ceiling: 7500m (24,605ft)

Dimensions: Span 28m (91ft 10in);
length 21.3m (69ft 10in);
height 7.4m (24ft 3in)

Weight: 15,900kg (35,053lb) loaded

▼ **Saab Scandia**

SAS, 1951

Ordered by ABA, the Scandia entered passenger service with SAS in 1951. *SE-BSB*
was the second aircraft delivered and it later served
with VASP. The highest-time Scandia, this
machine amassed 20,670 flying hours. VASP
retired its last Scandias in 1965.

Specifications

Crew: 4

Passengers: 24–28

Powerplant: Two Shvetsov ASh-82T 14-cylinder
air-cooled radial engines, 1417 kW (1900 hp)
each

Maximum speed: 417km/h (259mph)

Range: 1305km (705 nmi, 811 miles)

Service ceiling: 7400m (24,280ft)

Dimensions: Span 31.70m (104ft);
length 22.3m (73ft 2in);
height 7.9m (25ft 11in)

Weight: 18,000kg (39,683lb) loaded

▼ **Ilyushin Il-14 'Crate'**

LOT, 1955

LOT replaced its Il-12B equipment with Il-14s in 1955. Both the Il-12 and Il-14
were subject to Air Standards Co-ordinating Committee (ASCC) codenames,
becoming the 'Coach' and 'Crate', respectively.

Interestingly, another manufacturer produced a
notable airliner in the effort to replace the DC-3. In
November 1946, Sweden's Saab flew the first example
of its twin-engined Scandia. Ordered by Sweden's
ABA, and Brazil's VASP and Aerovias do Brasil, the
Scandia failed as a commercial venture as Saab
struggled to find capacity to build it, and turboprop
airliners began to appear. Just 18 were built.

With the post-war realignment of Europe, Soviet
airliners became more widespread as the Eastern Bloc
grew. They never offered any real competition to the
established European and US manufacturers, but were
the only option for countries under Soviet influence.

Ilyushin became the design bureau of choice in
the immediate pot-war years, its first task being to
build a replacement for the Lisunov Li-2, which was
itself no more than a Soviet-built DC-3. Flown for
the first time on 9 January 1946, the Il-12 was
Ilyushin's first attempt. It was based on much of the
Li-2's structure, but with tricycle landing gear and
seating for up to 27 passengers. It was succeeded by
the improved Il-14, which was a basically similar
aircraft with a new wing and increased power. Some
2200 Il-14s were built for civilian and military use,
and the type was also manufactured in East
Germany and Czechoslovakia.

Chapter 4

The Modern Era Begins (1949–92)

By the late 1940s, airlines were flying regular transatlantic schedules in pressurized aircraft. The United States' carriers were expanding rapidly, with global intentions, while Europe's airlines were rebuilding their pre-war networks with new reach, thanks almost entirely to US equipment. On the other hand, air travel was in many ways still less than ideal. It was often uncomfortable, with aircraft forced to fly 'through the weather' and it was undoubtedly noisy. It was also slow and relatively inefficient. But work was well advanced on the next major leap forwards – the jet airliner.

◀ **Boeing 727**

Boeing was not the first to market with any of its jet airliners until it flew the 727 in 1963. The foundation of its phenomenally successful commercial line has always been to produce the correct aircraft for any particular market at the right time, as well as its willingness to talk to customers and adapt aircraft to their needs. The short/medium-haul 727 is a prime example, selling 1831 examples, compared to the 117 of its closest rival, the Hawker Siddeley Trident.

Europe's jet pioneers
1949–60

Britain established an early lead in jet airliner development, but quickly lost out through tragic circumstances. The Soviet Union worked hard on its own jet transport, while France produced a short/medium-haul twinjet.

WITH CONSIDERABLE INPUT from Geoffrey de Havilland, the 1942 Brabazon Committee included plans for a turbojet airliner in its recommendations for the UK's post-war air transport system. Its Type IV requirement resulted in the de Havilland Comet I, flown for the first time on 27 July 1949. Powered by four de Havilland Ghost engines, the Comet entered service with BOAC on 2 May 1952, initially serving its London–Johannesburg route. Undoubtedly a fine performing aircraft – it cut BOAC's London–Tokyo schedule from 86 hours to 33 hours 15 minutes – the Comet was hamstrung by its limited accommodation, for just 36 passengers. To return a profit, long-haul jet operations would require aircraft of much greater capacity.

Comet Catastrophe

The world's first jet airliner had barely entered service when it suffered its first accident. Pilot error – probably relating to a general lack of appreciation

of the differences in take-off behaviour between large tail-dragger, piston-powered aircraft and the tricycle-undercarriage Comet – led a BOAC jet to crash at Rome-Ciampino on 26 October 1952. Another crash, in similar circumstances, destroyed a Canadian Pacific Comet I on 3 March 1953.

Of greater concern, however, was the loss of another BOAC aircraft, which fell into the sea off Elba, Italy, from a height of 7925m (26,000ft) on 10 January 1954. The most comprehensive air-crash investigation to date established the cause of the accident to have been failure of the fuselage structure at the corner of an air direction-finding antenna window.

De Havilland responded with a redesigned, improved, Rolls-Royce Avon-powered Comet 4. BOAC began the first transatlantic jet services with the type on 4 October 1958, but the Boeing 707 – an altogether more suitable jet airliner – had already entered service. With its name tainted by early accidents and faced with competition from the

Specifications

Crew: 7	Service ceiling: 11,500m (37,730ft)
Passengers: 50–100	Dimensions: Span 34.54m (113ft 4in);
Powerplant: Two Mikulin 95.1kN (21,400lbf)	length 40.05m (131ft 5in); height 11.90m
AM-3M-500 turbojets	(39ft 0in)
Maximum speed: 950km/h (590mph)	Weight: 76,000kg (167,550lb) loaded
Range: 2650km (1650 miles)	

▼ **Tupolev Tu-104A 'Camel'**
Aeroflot, 1958
The Tu-104A replaced the basic Tu-104 in production from about the 11th aircraft. The A-model seated 70 passengers, 20 more than the Tu-104. Provisions for the USSR's severe winter weather included heavy-duty hangers for the passengers' overcoats.

superior 707, the Comet never sold in significant numbers and Britain's advantage was lost.

Tu-104

Air transport suited the vast tracts of the Soviet Union well, but aircraft like the Li-2, for example, took 33 hours for the journey from Moscow to Vladivostok, including nine stops for fuel. A modernization plan was put in place and work began on the USSR's first jet transport during 1953.

With a wing and empennage based on that of the Tu-88 bomber, the Tupolev Tu-104 was ready for its first flight on 17 June 1955. The prototype visited London-Heathrow on 22 March 1956, its swept wings immediately marking it out as a far more advanced aircraft than the Comet. Aeroflot services began on 15 September 1956 and although the type was initially uneconomical in service, developed Tu-104A and B variants were very successful.

Caravelle

In France, Sud-Aviation addressed the market for a short/medium-haul jetliner with its SE.210 Caravelle. Powered by Avon turbojets and establishing a new powerplant installation design by mounting its engines in nacelles attached to the rear fuselage, the Caravelle flew for the first time on 27 May 1955.

Comet forward fuselages were installed in the first two prototypes to speed their construction and the testing was successful, although full French and US certification was not achieved until 6 May 1958.

The Caravelle entered service with SAS on its Copenhagen–Beirut schedule on 26 April 1959 and the type became well established with the airlines, even in the United States. In total, some 280 of the type were built in several variants, with Air France retiring its last example in 1981.

de Havilland Comet production variants		Number built
Model	Notes	Number built
Comet 1	44-seat airliner; de Havilland Ghost 50 Mk 1 turbojet engines	10
Comet 1A	More fuel; Ghost 50 Mk 2 engines	10
Comet 2	More fuel; stretched fuselage; Rolls-Royce Avon Mk 503 turbojet engines	15 for BOAC & Royal Air Force
Comet 4	Additional wing fuel tanks; stretched fuselage; 78 passengers; Avon Mk 524 engines	27
Comet 4B	Wing fuel tanks deleted; stretched fuselage; reduced wing span; 99 passengers; Avon Mk 524 engines	18
Comet 4C	Comet 4B fuselage; Comet 4 wing; Mk 524 engines	31 for civil and military customers

Specifications

Crew: 4

Passengers: 56–81

Powerplant: Four 46.8kN (10,500lbf) Rolls-Royce Avon Mk 524 turbojets

Maximum speed: 846km/h (526mph)

Range: 5190km (3225 miles)

Service ceiling: 12,000m (39,370ft)

Dimensions: Span 34.3m (112ft 6in); length 32.71m (107ft 4in); height 8.69m (28ft 6in)

Weight: 54,000kg (119,050lb) loaded

▼ De Havilland Comet 4C

Middle East Airlines, 1960s

Middle East Airlines (MEA) used the Comet in 4, 4B and 4C variants, alongside the Caravelle. OD-ADT was sold to Dan-Air as a spares source in 1973, the British airline having become one of the last bastions of Comet operations.

Second generation jets
1960–82

The UK responded to the superiority of Boeing's 707 by building the VC10, a superior aircraft of little appeal to the airlines. Britain struggled to build a truly successful second-generation jet, while in the Soviet Union, Tupolev mastered the art of export success with its Tu-134.

ALTHOUGH THE COMET had been comprehensively overtaken by the Boeing 707, the UK was not ready to give up on the long-haul, 'big jet' market, especially since US dominance was being further secured by Douglas with its DC-8. Britain's response was the Vickers VC10, another very fine aircraft tied too closely to the unusual requirements of BOAC.

Powered by technologically advanced Rolls-Royce Conway turbofans, mounted in podded pairs beneath its T-tail, the VC10 was optimized for hot-and-high operations off the shorter runways on BOAC's route network. This made it expensive to operate, but allowed the carrier to use jet equipment in existing airports whose runways were too short for the US types. Unfortunately for BOAC, many of these airports simply extended their runways, and unfortunately for Vickers, the VC10 was tarnished with a reputation for being too expensive to operate.

The VC10 entered BOAC service on its London–Lagos route on 29 April 1964 and was followed by the Super VC10 – with more power and seating up to 163 passengers – on the London–New York service on 1 April 1965. The VC10 proved especially popular with the passengers of the few airlines that flew it, often achieving a transatlantic load factor 20 per cent higher than that of its US rivals. This alone should have enabled it to operate profitably, but its higher fuel consumption overshadowed its passenger appeal in the minds of airline executives and only 54 were built.

Medium- and Short-Haul

Europe's aircraft manufacturers were in no position to take on Boeing and Douglas, but opportunities existed in the medium- and short-haul segments. In 1956, BEA issues a requirement for a jet transport to service its short and medium haul routes. De Havilland's DH.121 Trident was selected and development went ahead under the auspices of Hawker Siddeley, into which de Havilland had been absorbed in January 1960. BEA revised its requirements several times, eventually settling on an aircraft seating up to 103 passengers. De Havilland worked hard to meet BEA's demands and ceased its overseas advertising campaign for the Trident until they were met. The result was an airliner perfect for the unique requirements of BEA, but very unattractive to other carriers.

Specifications

Crew: 3	Service ceiling: 11,582m (38,000ft)
Passengers: 139–174	Dimensions: Span 44.55m (146ft 2in);
Powerplant: Four 100.1kN (22,500lb) Rolls-	length 52.32m (171ft 8in); height 12.04m
Royce Conway Rco.43 Mk.550 turbofans	(39ft 6in)
Maximum speed: 935km/h (581mph)	Weight: 151,953kg (335,000lb) (max take-off)
Range: 7600km (4725 miles)	

▲ **Vickers Super VC10**
BOAC, 1965

The Super VC10 offered better operating economics than the VC10. It was also among the fastest commercial aircraft of its era and offered impressive passenger appeal. Unfortunately, the entire VC10 programme had been tied too closely to BOAC's requirements and the Super came too late to make an impression on Boeing 707 sales.

The Trident I began revenue services for BEA on 11 March 1964 and although Hawker Siddeley attempted to improve the type by providing it with more power and greater passenger capacity, only 117 Tridents were built.

BAC was rewarded with much greater success for its One-Eleven. A twinjet fitting into the market below the Trident, the Rolls-Royce Spey-engined One-Eleven was built without interference from BEA or BOAC. As a result it was attractive to a wide range of airlines and inherently more suitable for development. First flown on 20 August 1963, the One-Eleven was developed through a series of variants and remained in production in the UK until 1982. Nine aircraft were also built in Romania, for a total run of 245 aircraft.

Two More Tupolevs

Aeroflot had also recognized the need for a smaller-capacity, short-range jet and Tupolev scaled down the Tu-104. The resulting Tu-124 flew for the first time on 24 March 1960 and although it performed well, its structure and powerplant installation were old-fashioned, making it expensive to operate. Tupolev therefore designed the Tu-134 'Crusty', a thoroughly capable aircraft with rear-mounted engines and a T-tail. Evolved through a series of variants, it was exported to 21 airlines and 853 were built.

Specifications

Crew: 3–5 + 3–4 flight attendants	Service ceiling: 12,100m (39,040ft)
Passengers: 72–84 passengers	Dimensions: Span 29.00m (95ft 1in);
Powerplant: Two 66.68kN (14,990lbf) Soloviev	length 37.10m (121ft 8in); height 9.02m
D-30-II turbofans	(29ft 6in)
Maximum speed: 950km/h (559mph)	Weight: 47,600kg (104,940lb) loaded
Range: 3000km (1180 miles)	

▲ **Tupolev Tu-134 'Crusty'**
Balkan Bulgarian Airlines, 1973
The joint Bulgarian–Soviet airline TABSO took its first jet – a Tu-134 – in 1967. Renamed Balkan Bulgarian Airlines on 1 February 1968, the carrier eventually took 16 of the Tupolevs. The glass nose of this early aircraft accommodated the machine's navigator.

Specifications

Crew: 4 + 3	Service ceiling: 13,105m (43,000ft)
Passengers: 151	Dimensions: Span 44.55m (146ft 2in);
Powerplant: Four 100.1kN (22,500lbf) Rolls-	length 48.36m (158ft 8in); height 12.04m
Royce Conway Mk. 301 Turbofan engines	(39ft 6in)
Maximum speed: 933km/h (580mph)	Weight: 151,900kg (334,878lb) (max take-off)
Range: 9412km (5850 miles)	

▲ **Vickers VC10**
British Caledonian, 1970
G-ASIX was built for British United Airways (BUA), which merged with Caledonian Airways in 1970 to become British Caledonian (BCal). The ex-BUA VC10s served BCal only briefly, since Boeing 707s were already on order, and they were all sold in 1974.

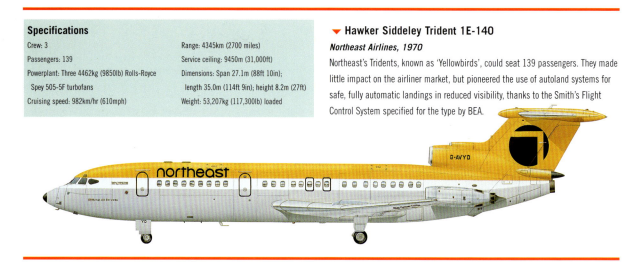

Specifications

Crew: 3

Passengers: 139

Powerplant: Three 4462kg (9850lb) Rolls-Royce
Spey 505-5F turbofans

Cruising speed: 982km/hr (610mph)

Range: 4345km (2700 miles)

Service ceiling: 9450m (31,000ft)

Dimensions: Span 27.1m (88ft 10in);
length 35.0m (114ft 9in); height 8.2m (27ft)

Weight: 53,207kg (117,300lb) loaded

▼ Hawker Siddeley Trident 1E-140

Northeast Airlines, 1970

Northeast's Tridents, known as 'Yellowbirds', could seat 139 passengers. They made little impact on the airliner market, but pioneered the use of autoland systems for safe, fully automatic landings in reduced visibility, thanks to the Smith's Flight Control System specified for the type by BEA.

Boeing builds a dynasty
1954–84

Boeing's groundbreaking 707 became available when the Comet was grounded and the Douglas DC-8 was the only serious rival. Ever ingenious and able to satisfy the market, Boeing then adapted elements of the basic design to create the 720, 727 and 737 airliner families.

BOEING TOOK ITS TIME time before forging ahead with its first jet transport. It had huge orders for the B-47 and B-52 bombers and therefore a wealth of experience with large swept-wing aircraft and turbojet engines. Taking the Model 367 Stratocruiser as its starting point, the company worked through several design evolutions, before deciding upon a configuration with a 35° swept wing, powered by four turbojets in separate underwing nacelles. As the 80th variant in the design study, the project was designated Model 367-80. It retained the 'double-bubble' fuselage design of the Model 367, albeit faired into a smooth oval cross-section, but was actually an entirely new aircraft.

The new jet was ready for its maiden flight on 15 July 1954. It came while the Comet was grounded and the world's airlines were receiving the latest, most advanced piston-engined models. Wary of jet technology after the Comet debacle, the

Specifications

Crew: 3

Powerplant: Four 44.5kN (10,000lbf) Pratt &
Whitney JT3 turbojet engines

Maximum speed: 937km/h (582mph)

Range: 5683km (3530 miles)

Service ceiling: 13,110m (43,000ft)

Dimensions: Span 39.88m (129ft 8in);
length 39.97m (127ft 10in); height 11.59m
(38ft)

Weight: 86,360kg (190,000lb) loaded

▲ Boeing Model 367-80

Boeing, 15 July 1954

Boeing built the Dash 80 using $16 million of its own money. The aircraft was initially unattractive to airline customers and the Dash 80 is more closely related to the military Model 717 or C-135. The Dash 80 is on permanent display at the National Air & Space Museum's Steven F. Udvar-Hazy Center, Washington, DC.

Boeing 707 production variants

Model	Notes	Number built
707-120	179-seat airliner; Pratt & Whitney JT3P turbojet engines	56 for civil and military customers
707-138	Shortened fuselage; JT3P engines	7 for QANTAS
707-220	Pratt & Whitney JT4A-3 turbojet engines	5 for Braniff
707-320	189 passengers; longer wing span; revised fuselage; more fuel; Pratt & Whitney JT4A-3 turbojet engines	69
707-120B	707-120 with Pratt & Whitney JT3D turbofan engines and optional wing of Boeing 720	72 new-build and conversions
707-138B	JT3D engines	6 conversions for QANTAS
707-320B	219 passengers; longer span, revised wing; JT3D-3 engines	174 (2 for US Air Force)
707-320C	Convertible with cargo door; strengthened cabin floor and undercarriage; longer span, revised wing; JT3D-3 engines	337 for civil and military customers
707-420	707-320B with Rolls-Royce Conway 508 turbofan engines	37

carriers initially saw little need to replace their DCs and Constellations. Boeing had invested its own funds in building the 367-80, or Dash-80, and although it was keen to gain airline interest, it also realized that the US Air Force would need to replace its KC-97 tankers with a jet type. Initially therefore, it focused on military orders, of which the first of very many was placed in September 1954.

Turning its attention back to the airlines, Boeing learned that the fuselage of its new aircraft was too narrow for the six-abreast seating they desired. Boeing therefore widened it, at great expense.

First Orders

After much lobbying by Boeing, Pan Am eventually placed the first order for what was now the Model 707, introducing the type into service across the

Atlantic in October 1958. The aircraft's range was too limited for regular non-stop operations, a problem soon fixed as developed versions appeared, but otherwise its performance, capacity and futuristic design marked almost as great a leap over the capability of the Comet I as the de Havilland type had over its piston rivals.

Boeing continued to struggle for orders as maintenance problems were overcome and airports struggled to modify their infrastructures to support the runway requirements of the 707, but soon American Airlines, Braniff and Continental had come on board. The first foreign orders then came in from Air France and Sabena, and Boeing was able to begin building what would become a jet dynasty.

Specifications

Crew: 3

Passengers: 147

Powerplant: Four 84.52kN (18,900lbf) Pratt & Whitney JTSD-7 turbofan engines

Maximum speed: 1009km/hr (625mph)

Range: 9262km (5742 miles)

Service ceiling: 11,890m (39,000ft)

Dimensions: Span 44.42m (145ft 8in); length 46.61m (152ft 10in); height 12.93m (42ft 5in)

Weight: 151,318kg (332,900lb) loaded

▲ **Boeing 707-320C**

Burlington Air Express, 1985

Boeing developed the 707 through a bewildering array of variants. The -320C was a convertible variant and Burlington Air Express was a major operator of the model. An express cargo and overnight parcels operator, it began replacing its 707s with DC-8s in 1991.

Specifications

Crew: 3

Passengers: 131

Powerplant: Three 6575kg (14,500lb) Pratt &
Whitney JT8D-1 turbofan engines

Maximum speed: 920km/h (570mph)

Range: 4000km (2485 miles)

Service ceiling: 11,900m (39,000ft)

Dimensions: Span 32.9m (108ft); length 40.6m
(133ft 2in); height 10.35m (34ft)

Weight: 77,110.7kg (170,000) loaded

▼ Boeing 727-100

SAHSA, 1980s

Servicio Aereo De Honduras SA operated a pair of 727-100s from 1981. The
airline had been established with assistance from Pan Am in 1945, becoming
independent in 1970. Its first jet was a 737-200 acquired in 1974, and which
remained operational until 1993.

Specifications

Crew: 3

Passengers: 189

Powerplant: Three 6575kg (14,500lb) Pratt &
Whitney JT8D-9A turbofan engines

Maximum speed: 920km/h (570mph)

Range: 4000km (2485 miles)

Service ceiling: 11,900m (39,000ft)

Dimensions: Span 32.9m (108ft); length 46.7m
(153ft 2in); height 10.35m (34ft)

Weight: 95,025kg (209,500lb) loaded

▼ Boeing 727-200

TAP Air Portugal, 1983

Transportes Aereos Portugueses (TAP) was a major 727 operator, using both
-100 and -200 aircraft. The type entered TAP service in 1967 and served into
the 1990s, when it was replaced by A320-series airliners. CS-TBW was TAP's
13th 727-200.

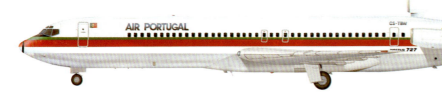

Specifications

Crew: 2

Passengers: 136

Powerplant: Two 6575kg (14,500lb) Pratt
& Whitney JT8D engines

Maximum speed: 876km/hr (544 mph)

Range: 4300km (2600 miles)

Service ceiling: 10,700m (35,000ft)

Dimensions: Span 28.35m (93ft);
length 30.53m (100ft 2in); height 11.23m
(36ft 10in)

Weight: 58,100kg (128,100lb) loaded

▼ Boeing 737-200 Advanced

Amberair, 1988

With the 737-200 Advanced, sales of Boeing's smallest airline really began to
flourish. G-BOSA was first registered in the UK as G-BAZI
in 1973, becoming B-BOSA with Amberair in 1988.
The airline existed for just a few months, while the
aircraft was withdrawn from the UK register and
leased abroad in 1994.

Boeing 737 Classic variants

Model	Notes	Number built
737-100	107-seat airliner; Pratt & Whitney JT8D-7 or -9 turbofan engines	30 (one for NASA)
737-200/737-200 Advanced	Stretched fuselage; 130 passengers; more fuel; Advanced had JT8D-15 engines; also available in High Gross Weight versions	991 for civil and military customers
737-200C/737-200QC	Convertible/Quick Change Convertible; also available in Advanced version	104
737-300	Stretched fuselage; CFM International CFM56-3 turbofan engines	1113
737-400	Stretched fuselage; 168 passengers; CFM56-3 engines	486
737-500	Shortened fuselage; 108 passengers; CFM56-3 engines	389

Specifications

Crew: 3

Passengers: 130

Powerplant: Two 7030kg (15,500lb) Pratt & Whitney JT8D-15-17 turbofans

Cruising speed: 925km/hr (575mph)

Range: 4265km (2650 miles)

Service ceiling: 11,900m (39,000ft)

Dimensions: Span 28.35m (93ft); length 30.5m (100ft); height 11.3m (37ft)

Weight: 52,390kg (115,500lb) loaded

▼ Boeing 737-400

British Airways, 2000s

The re-engined 737-300/400/500 aircraft easily outsold the -200s. The -300 was the first of the new 737s to fly, on 24 February 1984, after Boeing had solved considerable problems in accommodating the 'fat' CFM56 turbofan on the 737's low-slung wing.

New Models

Although Boeing had developed a shorter-ranged, lighter Model 720 version of the 707, it was not suitable for routes serving airports with shorter runways and the company saw a need for a more optimized airframe. It therefore took the upper fuselage of the 707 and combined it with a new lower fuselage and advanced high-lift wing. The three-engined powerplant of the new aircraft was mounted at the rear, in single nacelles to either side of the rear fuselage and with the third engine mounted above the fuselage and aspirated via an intake in the fin root, in much the same way as on the Trident.

The resulting Boeing 727 first flew on 9 February 1963. The major difference between it and its British rival was that the 727 was built to compete globally, while the Trident had been built for BEA.

Meanwhile, Douglas had created the DC-9, a twinjet aimed at the same market as the Caravelle and One-Eleven. With its maiden flight in 1965 it seemed as though Douglas had stolen a march on Boeing in this important market, since the latter could only announce its intention to build an aircraft of similar capacity.

Boeing's new Model 737 retained the established fuselage cross-section of the 707 and 727, and the forward fuselage and basic cockpit of the latter, but employed a new wing and twin turbofan engines in sleek nacelles attached close to the wing undersides. Several airlines had already ordered DC-9s and a few were committing to the One-Eleven, but some, critically Lufthansa and United, had not yet decided on their short-haul requirements. Boeing courted Lufthansa and won an order for 21 737s. Launching the programme on the strength of this order, it soon managed to secure interest from United – a Caravelle operator – and worked towards the 737's first flight on 9 April 1967.

Lufthansa took a handful of 737-100 aircraft, but United had ordered a longer 737-200, which instantly became the standard model. Boeing kept things competitive with its 737-200 Advanced and then, as the more capable DC-9 and MD-80 variants posed a threat, re-engined the type with the thoroughly modern CFM56 turbofan. The programme gained momentum and the 737 was on its way to becoming the world's best-selling jet airliner, a position it retains in 2012.

In Boeing's wake
1952–92

Douglas was keen to continue its dominance of the long-haul airliner market and worked hard to catch Boeing's lead. But the DC-8 was less advanced than the Boeing 707 and rarely competed on level terms. Douglas had more success with its short-haul DC-9.

DOUGLAS WAS UNDOUBTEDLY the dominant force in airliner production by the mid-1950s. Like Boeing, it could see the potential for jet-powered airliners and first offered such a design – designated DC-8 – in 1952. US carriers, still struggling to re-establish profitability after the war, showed no interest. By 1955, however, with the causes of the Comet crashes discovered and the announcement that the Comet 4 would be commencing transatlantic services, there was renewed interest.

Boeing had already flown its radical 367-80 and apparently had a major headstart over Douglas, which would be unable to fly its own, larger prototype until 1958. But Douglas had seen that the Boeing, like the Comet, would not be able to make the transatlantic crossing non-stop in both directions. By producing a larger airframe benefiting from the greater power becoming available as turbojet development continued, the DC-8 could be delivered with true transatlantic range.

Pan Am was tempted by the promise of longer range and although it launched the 707 with an order for 20, it also signed up for 25 DC-8s, planning to offer an alternative to BOAC's Comet service in 1958 and then a non-stop transatlantic service as soon as it could get its hands on the DC-8. The airlines had

also complained that the 707 was too narrow and on that basis the DC-8 had taken orders that Boeing might well have considered its own. When United ordered DC-8s in preference to 707s late in 1955, it stated that the decision had come down to cabin width. Boeing went away to widen its design, at huge expense, coming back to the market with a slight cabin width advantage over the DC-8.

Taking Flight

Much of the four-year advantage that Boeing had over Douglas therefore evaporated, as the former developed the 707 into the 717 for the military and redesigned it for the airlines. The 707 finally entered service in October 1958, the DC-8 having flown for the first time that May. Douglas worked hard on the initial DC-8-10 for United and had the model ready for service entry in September 1959. The developmental gap had been narrowed to just 11 months. But although the chronological gap had been closed, the developmental gap remained considerable. Douglas lacked Boeing's world-leading experience in the application of swept-wing technology to large aircraft and the DC-8's wing was considerably less

▲ Douglas DC-8-30
Pan Am, 1960

Pan Am had to wait until 7 February 1960 before receiving its first DC-8, the shorter-ranged DC-8-10 for United having taken precedence at Douglas. N800PA was the first -30 to fly and the fifth DC-8 built.

Specifications

Crew: 4

Passengers: 105–118

Powerplant: Four 7167kg (15,800lb) Pratt & Whitney JT43A turbojets

Cruising speed: 964km/hr (599mph)

Range: 7500km (4660 miles)

Service ceiling: 13,800m (45,300ft)

Dimensions: Span 43.41m (142ft 5in); length 45.87m (150ft 6in); height 13.21m (43ft 4in)

Weight: 125,192kg (276,000lb) loaded

Douglas DC-8 variants

Model	Notes	Number built
DC-8-10	150-seat airliner; Pratt & Whitney JT3C-6 turbojet engines	26
DC-8-20	DC-8-10 with more powerful Pratt & Whitney JT4A-3 turbojet engines	36
DC-8-30	Longer range; higher weights; JT4A-9 or -11 engines	57
DC-8-40	DC-8-30 with Rolls-Royce Conway Mk 509 turbofan engines	32
DC-8-50/DC-8-55	189 passengers; Pratt & Whitney JT3D-1 or -3 turbofan engines; DC-8-55 had JT3D-3B engines	89
DC-8-50C	Convertible version of DC-8-50	39
DC-8-50F/DC-8-55F/DC-8F Jet Trader	Freighter version of DC-8-50/DC-8-55	15
DC-8-61/DC-8 Super 61	Stretched DC-8-55, 250 passengers	78
DC-8-61C/DC-8 Super 61C	Convertible version of DC-8-61	10
DC-8-62/DC-8 Super 62	Stretched fuselage; increased wing span; more fuel; Pratt & Whitney JT8D-3B turbofan engines	51
DC-8-62C/DC-8 Super 62C	Convertible version of DC-8-62	10
DC-8-62F/DC-8 Super 62F	Freighter version of DC-8-62	6
DC-8-63/DC-8 Super 63	DC-8-61 fuselage with DC-8-62 wing; higher weights; JT8D-3B or -7 engines	47
DC-8-63C/DC-8 Super 63C	Convertible version of DC-8-63; higher weights	53
DC-8-63F/DC-8 Super 63F	Freighter version of DC-8-63; higher weights	7
Cammacorp DC-8 Super 71	DC-8-61 conversion; CFM International CFM56-1 or -2 turbofan engines	43
Cammacorp DC-8 Super 71F	DC-8-61 freighter conversion; CFM56-1 or -2 engines	10
Cammacorp DC-8 Super 72	DC-8-62 conversion; CFM56-1 or -2 engines	3
Cammacorp DC-8 Super 72CF	DC-8-62 convertible freighter conversion; CFM56-1 or -2 engines	3
Cammacorp DC-8 Super 73	DC-8-63 conversion; CFM56-1 or -2 engines	6
Cammacorp DC-8 Super 73F	DC-8-63 freighter conversion; CFM56-1 or -2 engines	36
Cammacorp DC-8 Super 73CF	DC-8-63 convertible freighter conversion; CFM56-1 or -2 engines	9

advanced than that of the Boeing. The more powerful engines that Douglas had for had also not become available, so that even the DC-8-10 was rather underpowered. Only 28 -10s were sold and most of them were re-engined. Douglas had concentrated on the transcontinental -10 for United and now turned to the longer-ranged, heavier DC-8 for Pan Am. In the meantime, however, Boeing had delivered its Intercontinental 707-320, an aircraft of true transatlantic capability and carrying more passengers than the DC-8. Boeing had won the 'big jet' race. Although the DC-8 sold well, Douglas never again presented a serious challenge in the long-haul jet market.

Short-Haul DC-9

By the late 1950s, jet technology was revolutionizing long-haul travel, but the many hundreds of aircraft flying domestic and regional services around the world were generally piston powered and represented the design philosophy of an earlier era.

Sud-Aviation had produced the Caravelle to satisfy the market, but since Vickers and Lockheed were working on turboprops, the French jet had no direct competition. Boeing and Douglas planned to build rivals, and Douglas was first off the mark, showing United and other airlines its plans for a four-engined DC-9 in 1959. After United and Eastern bought the Boeing 727 in 1960, Douglas began talking to Sud-Aviation and General Electric about re-engining the Caravelle, but when BAC announced its One-Eleven, Douglas responded with a new aircraft, which it began presenting to the airlines in 1962.

The new type emerged as the DC-9 twinjet, launched against a Delta order in April 1963. First flight came on 25 February 1965 and by the time Boeing could fly the 737 for the first time, Douglas was preparing its third DC-9 version for service. The DC-9 was larger and more economical than the One-Eleven and had serious competition only when the 737 finally entered service in 1968. Some 976 DC-9s were built.

Specifications

Crew: 4

Passengers: 131

Powerplant: Four 71.4kN (16,050lbf) General
Electric CJ805-23B turbofans

Maximum speed: 1000km/hr (621mph)

Range: 5785km (3595 miles)

Service ceiling: 12,495m (41,000ft)

Dimensions: Span 36.6m (120ft); length 42.5m
(139ft 9in); height 11m (39ft 6in)

Weight: 111,674kg (246,200lb) loaded

▲ Convair CV-990 Coronado

Swissair, 1962

Swissair was the first airline into service with the CV-990, debuting the type on
9 March 1962. Its Convairs served routes to the Middle and Far East, and India,
but were withdrawn during the mid-1970s. The last commercial CV-990s were
retired by Spain's Spantax in 1987.

Specifications

Crew: 2

Passengers: 90

Powerplant: Two 62kN (14,000lbf) JT8D-1 and
JT8D-7 engines

Cruising speed: 903km/hr (561mph)

Range: 2340km (1450 miles)

Service ceiling: 11,278m (37,000ft)

Dimensions: Span 27.25m (89.4ft);
length 31.82m (104.4ft); height 8.38m
(27ft 5in)

Weight: 41,100kg (90,700lb) loaded

▲ Douglas DC-9-10

Best Airlines, 1980s

Best was a small airline set up in the 1980s to serve US regional routes. It
operated just two aircraft, both DC-9s, during its short existence. The DC-9-10
was the first production DC-9 model, but Douglas was soon making use of the
designs inherent ease of 'stretching' to develop longer, higher-capacity versions.

Specifications

Crew: 2

Passengers: 172

Powerplant: Two 82kN (18,500lbf) Pratt &
Whitney JT8D-200 engines

Cruising speed: 811km/hr (504mph)

Range: 2910km (1810 miles)

Service ceiling: 11,278m (37,000ft)

Dimensions: Span 32.82m (107ft 8in);
length 45.01m (147ft 8in); height 9.02m
(29ft 7in)

Weight: 63,500kg (140,000lb) loaded

▲ McDonnell Douglas MD-81

Austral, 1980s

Douglas brought in DC-9 orders at an unprecedented rate during the 1960s, but
struggled to meet demand. Both the DC-8 and DC-9 were costly to develop and
skilled workers were being lost to the Vietnam War effort. The result was that
DC-9 costs rose and the company began losing money. McDonnell took Douglas
over in 1967, going on to revitalize the DC-9 as the MD-80 series, typified by
this MD-81 of Argentine domestic operator Austral.

Douglas DC-9, McDonnell Douglas MD-80 and Boeing 717 variants

Model	Notes	Number built
DC-9-10/DC-9-15	90-seat airliner; Pratt & Whitney JT8D-5 turbofan engines; more powerful JT8D-1 engines on DC-9-15	113
DC-9-10C	Convertible version of DC-9-10	24
DC-9-20	Increased wing span; JT8D-9 engines	10
DC-9-30	Stretched DC-9-20; 119 passengers; JT8D-7 engines	585
DC-9-30C	Convertible version of DC-9-30	30
DC-9-30F	Freighter version of DC-9-30	6
DC-9-40	Stretched DC-9-30; 132 passengers	71
DC-9-50	Stretched DC-9-30; 139 passengers	96
DC-9 Super 80/ MD-80/MD-81	Stretched DC-9-50; 172 passengers; JT8D-209 engines	132
MD-82	MD-81 with JT8D-217 engines	539
CATIC MD-82T	MD-82 built by SAIC in China from McDonnell Douglas kits	30
MD-83	MD-81 with more fuel; JT8D-219 engines	265
MD-87	MD-81 shrink; 130 passengers; taller fin; JT8D-217B engines	75
MD-88	Upgraded MD-82; increased weights; EFIS cockpit; JT8D-217C engines	150
MD-90-30	Stretched MD-80 with MD-87 fin; EFIS cockpit; IAE V2500-D5 turbofan engines	113
MD-90-30ER	MD-90-30 with more fuel; higher weights; BMW Rolls-Royce BR715 turbofans	1
CATIC MD-90-30T TrunkLiner	MD-90-30 built by SAIC in China from McDonnell Douglas kits	2
MD-95/717-200	Stretched; modernized DC-9-30; 106 passengers; BR715 engines	155

Convair's Also-Rans

Convair presented an unexpected challenge to Boeing and Douglas in the 'big jet' market, when it flew its CV-880 for the first time in January 1959. Many company insiders were keen to develop a jet successor to the CV-240 series, a design that would have had at least a five-year advantage over the DC-9, but Convair was a subsidiary of Hughes, and Howard Hughes owned TWA. He was determined that his airline should fly long-haul Convairs.

The CV-880 was very fast but inefficient, and its narrow cabin seated only five abreast, rather than the six of the 707 and DC-8. Just 65 were built – Convair needed to sell 120 to cover development costs. Nevertheless, it pressed on with the lengthened CV-990. Powered by the CJ805-21 turbofan derivative of the CV-880's General Electric CJ805-3 turbojet, the CV-990 was even faster, but suffered extensive aerodynamic problems. These were eventually overcome, but they delayed service entry – with American, TWA ironically being unable to finance a purchase – until March 1962. Just 47 CV-990s were sold and Convair withdrew from the long-haul market.

Specifications

Crew: 2

Passengers: 269

Powerplant: Two 88.78kN (19,950lbf) Pratt & Whitney JT8D-217C turbofan engines

Maximum speed: 922km/hr (573mph)

Range: 4385km (2725 miles)

Service ceiling: 11,286m (37,028ft)

Dimensions: Span 32.92m (108ft); length 36.27m (119f); height 9.14m (30ft)

Weight: 63,370kg (139,706lb) loaded

▼ McDonnell Douglas MD-87

Finnair, 1980s

McDonnell Douglas developed several MD-80 variants, but the first to significantly change the type's dimensions was the shortened MD-87. It was aimed at the short-fuselage DC-9 replacement market, and 75 were delivered between 1987 and 1992. Aero OY began marketing itself as Finnair in 1953, officially changing its name on 25 June 1968.

Europe falls behind
1961–92

Europe had neither the means nor, apparently, the foresight to build jet airliners to rival those of Boeing and Douglas. Meanwhile, in the Soviet Union, Ilyushin and Tupolev quietly built thoroughly competent jetliners by the hundred.

OTHER THAN THE COMET, there were no attempts to create a European long-haul jet airliner until well into the 1970s. Given the large number of short inter-city routes across the continent, the short-haul market remained attractive, however. Two companies made serious attempts at producing jets to replace the piston and turboprop aircraft used on such routes. They also intended to offer viable alternatives to the US and British jets on offer.

Fokker's Fellowship

Observing BEA's requirement for a short-haul jet to replace its turboprop equipment and an industry belief that the day's of propeller-driven aircraft were numbered, Fokker began working on a jet replacement for its own Friendship turboprop in the early 1960s. Mindful of BAC's One-Eleven, the Dutch company opted to produce a smaller aircraft with exceptional short-field capability, allowing it to operate

into airports otherwise unavailable to jets – a similar marketing strategy to that which served the VC10 so badly.

The F28 Fellowship flew for the first time on 9 May 1967 and received Dutch certification in 1969. It was thus some way behind the One-Eleven, DC-9 and 737 in coming to market, although it satisfied a sufficiently distinct requirement that considerable sales might still have been forthcoming. As it happened, Fokker never managed to achieve large individual orders. Its sale team worked hard to win orders for handfuls of aircraft and, although the Fellowship was developed through a series of variants, still only 241 were built.

Dassault's Mercure

The other significant Western European short-haul programme produced Dassault's Mercure. The manufacturer began work on a 737 competitor in 1967, just as the 737 was making its first flight. Dassault's faith in the Mercure was considerable, given that it had no global support network in place for commercial aircraft and that it was likely only to

Specifications

Crew: 2–3	Range: 2100km (1300 miles)
Passengers: 85	Service ceiling: 10,670m (35,000ft)
Powerplant: Two 4468kg (9850lb) Rolls-Royce	Dimensions: span 23.58m (77ft 4in); length
Spey Mk 555 15 turbofans	27.40m (89ft 11in); height 8.5m (27ft 10in)
Maximum speed: 843km/hr (524mph)	Weight: 29,485kg (65,000lb) loaded

▲ **Fokker F28-1000 Fellowship**

Aviaction, 1971

Germany's Aviaction took four Mk 1000 Fellowships, but ceased trading in 1973. Fokker initially built the F28 in standard Mk 1000 (65 seats), 5000 (shortened) and 6000 (stretched) variants. Later it produced the improved short-fuselage Mk 3000 and stretched Mk 4000.

Specifications

Crew: 5

Passengers: 175

Powerplant: Four 10,985kg (24,200lb) Soloviev
D-30KU turbofan engines

Maximum speed: 900km/hr (560mph)

Range: 7800km (4850 miles)

Service ceiling: 12,800m (42,000ft)

Dimensions: Span 43.20m (141ft 9in);
length 53.12m (174ft 3in); height 12.35m
(40ft 6in)

Weight: 165,000kg (363,762lb) loaded

▼ Ilyushin Il-62M 'Classic'

Linhas Aereas de Angola, 1971

Linhas Aereas de Angola, or TAAG, operated the Il-62M into the 2000s, although by 2012 it was flying an all-Boeing fleet. The airline was established in 1938, but operations were limited until 1948, when it took DC-3s on strength. It took its first jet, a 737, in 1976.

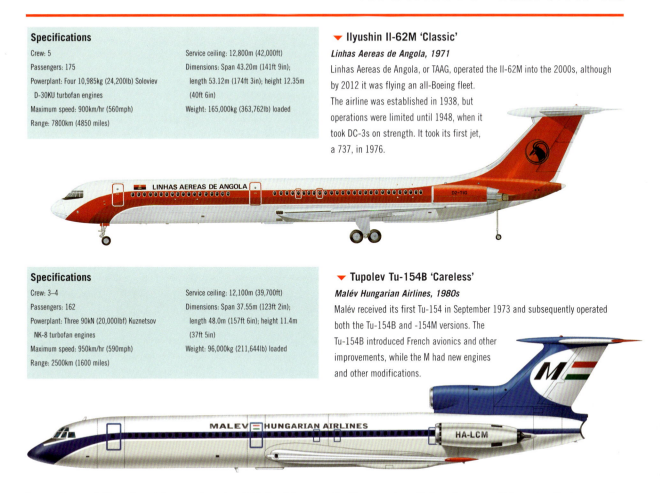

Specifications

Crew: 3–4

Passengers: 162

Powerplant: Three 90kN (20,000lbf) Kuznetsov
NK-8 turbofan engines

Maximum speed: 950km/hr (590mph)

Range: 2500km (1600 miles)

Service ceiling: 12,100m (39,700ft)

Dimensions: Span 37.55m (123ft 2in);
length 48.0m (157ft 6in); height 11.4m
(37ft 5in)

Weight: 96,000kg (211,644lb) loaded

▼ Tupolev Tu-154B 'Careless'

Malév Hungarian Airlines, 1980s

Malév received its first Tu-154 in September 1973 and subsequently operated both the Tu-154B and -154M versions. The Tu-154B introduced French avionics and other improvements, while the M had new engines and other modifications.

be ready to deliver its airliner after the 737 had been in service for four or five years.

As it was, the Mercure, using the same engines as the 737-200 and seating up to 140 passengers, entered service in 1973, by which time the 737 was well established and the DC-9 available in several iterations. The Mercure might still have offered some competition to the Americans, but it was blighted by short range. This was tolerable on shorter European sectors, but unsuited to operations in the United States. In effect, Dassault had created a large, short-ranged 737, an aircraft for which the global market had no use. Just 12 Mercures were built, the type serving only with French domestic carrier Air Inter.

Soviet Developments

The USSR had settled on turboprop power for its long-haul needs, with Tupolev's Tu-114 in service from 1961, but a pure jet design was clearly needed for the future. Ilyushin therefore began work on the

Il-62, an aircraft bearing a striking similarity to the VC10, but built to very different requirements. The Il-62 flew for the first time in January 1961. Aeroflot began scheduled service with the type on 10 March 1967, initially on domestic routes, but soon began flying it internationally. Several airlines in the Soviet sphere of influence bought Il-62s and the type was improved as the Il-62M for service from 1974. Altogether, 287 Il-62s were built and the type remained in limited commercial service in 2012.

Aeroflot also had a large fleet of medium-range turboprops and first-generation jets to replace, and for this it turned to Tupolev and its Tu-154 trijet. Similar in concept to the 727-200, but much more powerful to allow for operation from short runways at austere airports, the Tu-154 had much in common with the Tu-134. First flown in 1968, the Tu-154 began passenger services in 1971. Considerably improved during a production run that lasted until 1992, the Tu-154 was widely exported and 996 aircraft were built.

First-generation turboprops
1947–88

In a stark contrast to the 'big jet' market, Europe came to dominate sales of first-generation turboprops, primarily through the efforts of Fokker, with its excellent F27 Friendship.

THE BASIC ECONOMICS of the turboprop compared to the pure jet are as sound today as they were in the late 1940s. Arranging a turbine, or jet engine, to drive a propeller through a gearbox produces a much more efficient source of motive power, especially over shorter ranges, but results in a considerably slower aircraft. There is always a delicate balance to be struck between fuel economy, range, speed and operating altitude.

The Brabazon Committee had recognized the advantages of the turboprop over the piston engine – higher aircraft speeds and much reduced vibration and noise – and recommended the production of such a machine under its Type IIB specification. The result was the Vickers Viscount, which first flew on 16 July 1948. The type flew the world's first turbine service on 29 July 1950, between London and Paris, but was too small for economical use. It was therefore redesigned to seat up to 60 passengers, in which form it conquered not only the European market, but also achieved sales in America. Indeed, the Viscount became one of Britain's most successful airliners, with 438 sales.

BOAC had issued a specification for a larger, medium-range airliner in 1947. Designed for its Empire routes, the Bristol machine was switched from piston to turboprop power before its first flight in 1952. It entered service as the Britannia, flying London–Johannesburg from February 1957 and London–New York from December, but it was soon overshadowed on the transatlantic routes by the Boeing 707.

Vickers also produced a larger turboprop, the four-engined Vanguard, for BEA. It proved only moderately successful, but several of the 43 built were modified for continued service as Merchantman freighters.

Handley Page flirted briefly with the turboprop, producing the Herald as a rival to the Fokker F27, having stuck doggedly to piston power long enough to lose any chance of competing. The company sold 48 Heralds; Fokker sold 582 F27s. Hawker Siddeley and, later, British Aerospace (BAe), had more success with the HS.748. Designed by Avro, the 748 entered service in 1962 and found favour with civilian and military customers. It enjoyed a new lease of life in the 1990s as the Advanced Turboprop (ATP).

Specifications

Crew: 2

Passengers: 75

Powerplant: Four 1030kW (1381hp) Rolls-Royce Dart RDa.7/1 Mk 525 turboprop engines

Maximum speed: 566km/hr (352mph)

Range: 2220km (1380 miles)

Service ceiling: 7620m (25,000ft)

Dimensions: Span 28.56m (93ft 8in); length 26.11m (85ft 8in); height 8.15m (26ft 9in)

Weight: 30,617kg (67,500lb) loaded

▼ **Vickers Viscount 708**

Air France, 18 May 1953

The first of 12 Viscounts for Air France and the first export Viscount delivered, F-BGNK was delivered on 18 May 1953. The Viscount 708 generally seated 40 passengers in service, but could be configured for up to 59. Air France flew the Viscount until 1961, when its fleet passed to Air Inter.

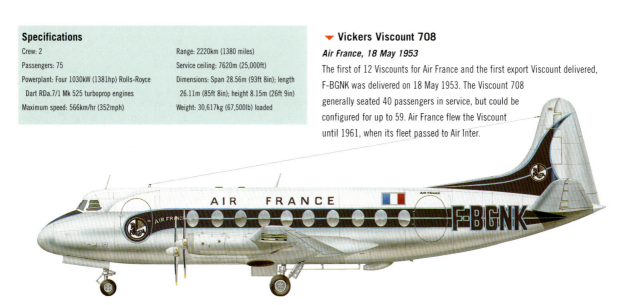

Specifications

Crew: 3

Passengers: 98

Powerplant: Four 2800kW (3750hp) Allison
501-D13 turboprop engines

Maximum speed: 721km/hr (448mph)

Range: 3540km (2200 miles)

Service ceiling: 8665m (28,400ft)

Dimensions: Span 30.18m (99ft 0in);
length 31.85m (104ft 6in); height 10.00m
(32ft 10in)

Weight: 7257kg (16,000lb) loaded

▼ Lockheed L-188C Electra

KLM, September 1959

Lockheed built the L-188C with higher weights and increased power for longer-range operations. KLM ordered 12 of the 90-seaters, taking its first, PH-LLA, named *Mercurius*, in September 1959.

Specifications

Crew: 2

Passengers: 56

Powerplant: Two 1715kW (2300hp) Rolls-Royce
Dart RDa.7 Mk 532-7L turboprop engines

Maximum speed: 473km/hr (294mph)

Range: 2660km (1655 miles)

Service ceiling: 8540m (28,000ft)

Dimensions: Span 29.00m (95ft 2in);
length 25.50m (83ft 8in); height 8.41m
(27ft 7in)

Weight: 19,730kg (43,500lb) loaded

▼ Fairchild F-27A Friendship

Hughes Airwest, 1970s

Hughes Airwest flew the F-27 and F27 on US regional routes throughout the 1970s. The F-27A featured more powerful Rolls-Royce Dart engines than the original F-27 and was generally equivalent to the Fokker-built F27 Mk 200.

Specifications

Crew: 5

Passengers: 84–110

Powerplant: Four 3983kW (4000hp) Ivchenko
AI-20M turboprop engines

Maximum speed: 685km/hr (388mph)

Range: 3700km (2295 miles)

Service ceiling: 9250m (30,000ft)

Dimensions: Span 37.40m (122ft 8in);
length 35.90m (117ft 9in); height 10.17m
(33ft 4in)

Weight: 64,000kg (93,500lb) loaded

▼ Ilyushin Il-18 'Coot'

CAAC, 1960s

Ilyushin exported at least 100 Il-18s, to customers, including the Chinese state airline, the Civil Aviation Administration of China (CAAC). A handful of Il-18s remains in commercial service in 2012 and the type also provided the basis for military Il-20 and Il-38 variants.

Specifications

Crew: 2

Passengers: 24

Powerplant: Two 1484kW (1990hp) Rolls-Royce
Dart Mk 529-8X turboprop engines

Maximum speed: 556km/hr (345mph)

Range: 838km (520 miles)

Service ceiling: 11,245m (36,900ft)

Dimensions: Span 23.88m (78ft 4in);
length 22.96m (75ft 4in); height 7.01m (23ft)

Weight: 16,329kg (35,924lb) loaded

▼ Grumman Gulfstream I

TAS, 1990s

Grumman designed the Gulfstream I as a pioneer turboprop business aircraft, but it also appealed to commuter airlines requiring a small, efficient airliner. Several European airlines employed the Gulfstream as such, including Italy's TAS, which later re-equipped with the BAe 146.

I-TASO

▼ Hawker Siddeley HS.748 Series 2A

Bahamasair, 1979–93

Bahamasair used five HS.748 Series 2A aircraft on inter-island services between 1979 and 1993. The Series 2A offered increased power and higher weights. Bahamasair was established in 1973 and continued trading in 2012, with two 737-200s and five Bombardier Q300 turboprops.

C6-BEE

Specifications

Crew: 2

Passengers: 58

Powerplant: Two 1700kW (2280hp) Rolls-Royce
Dart RDa.7 Mk 535-2 turboprop engines

Maximum speed: 462km/hr (286mph)

Range: 1891km (1176 miles)

Service ceiling: 7600m (25,000ft)

Dimensions: Span 30.02m (98ft 6in); length
20.42m (67ft); height 7.57m (24ft 10in)

Weight: 20,182kg (44,400lb) loaded

Fokkers and Fairchilds

Fokker became the undisputed champion of the first-generation turboprop with its F27 Friendship. First flown on 24 November 1955, the Friendship entered service with the United States' West Coast Airlines on 28 September 1958 and in Europe, with Aer Lingus, in December. It sold well worldwide, but its penetration of the US market was greatly assisted by a licence-building arrangement with Fairchild, which built the type as the F-27. Later, Fairchild became Fairchild Hiller, continuing with a stretched variant known as the FH-227. The F27 also enjoyed a 1990s' resurgence, as the basis of the evolved Fokker 50.

Lockheed attempted to enter the short/medium-haul turboprop market with its L-188 Electra, which first flew in 1957. It offered high cruising speeds, excellent field performance and advanced powerplant and airframe design, but suffered a series of early accidents. The cause was ultimately identified and a fix developed, but by that time the Boeing 727 was available and the Electra's market had disappeared.

Other Contenders

The Soviet Union produced its first long-range turbine aircraft just as it had produced its first jetliner, by installing an airliner fuselage between bomber wings. The Tu-114 added such a fuselage to the flying surfaces and powerplant of the Tu-95 bomber. The result was a phenomenal, if somewhat short-lived, unique turboprop airliner with swept wings. Ilyushin's Il-18 was more ambitious – a completely new, optimized design for an efficient, modern, 75-passenger airliner. Entering service in 1959, 565 were built, in several variants; production ceased in 1979. Japan, meanwhile, formed a consortium to design and build its first-generation turboprop, the YS-11. Capable and well built, it sold reasonably well in North America, Europe and Asia, but was always expensive in an already crowded market.

Specifications

Crew: 2–3

Passengers: 56

Powerplant: Two 1570kW (2105hp) Rolls-Royce
Dart Mk 527 turboprop engines

Cruising speed: 445km/hr (277mph)

Range: 2834km (1761 miles)

Service ceiling: 8504m (27,900ft)

Dimensions: Span 28.9m (94ft 9in); length
23m (75ft 6in); height 7.34m (24ft 1in)

Weight: 19,505kg (43,000lb) loaded

▼ Handley Page Herald

Air UK, 1980–85

Handley Page developed the Herald from the Miles Marathon, a product of the
Brabazon Type VA requirement for a DC-3 replacement. Handley Page switched
the Marathon from its four-piston engined powerplant
to twin turboprops, but lost out comprehensively to
the F27. Air UK was formed in 1980, inheriting
Heralds from British Island Airways.

Specifications

Crew: 5

Passengers: 220

Powerplant: Four 11,033kW (14,784hp)
Kuznetsov NK-12MV turboprop engines

Maximum speed: 880km/hr (545mph)

Range: 6200km (3853 miles)

Service ceiling: 12,000m (39,500ft)

Dimensions: Span 51.10m (168ft);
length 54.10m (177ft); height 13.31m (44ft)

Weight: 179,000kg (393,800lb) loaded

▼ Tupolev Tu-116

Aeroflot, 1958

Two Tu-116 aircraft were created by basic conversion of Tu-95 airframes,
for route-proving, training and publicity purposes, while the
Tu-114 was under development. Only one, CCCP-76462, was
handed over to Aeroflot.

Specifications

Crew: 3

Passengers: 64

Powerplant: Two 2282kW (3060hp) Rolls-Royce
Dart Mk 502-10K turboprop engines

Maximum speed: 471km/hr (293mph)

Range: 3218km (2000 miles)

Service ceiling: 6980m (22,900ft)

Dimensions: Span 32m (105ft);
length 26.3m (86ft 3in); height 9m (29ft 6in)

Weight: 24,500kg (54,013lb) loaded

▼ NAMC YS-11A

Mid Pacific Air, 1981–88

Mid Pacific Air flew several YS-11A turboprops between 1981 and 1995,
N114MP serving the airline at various times between 1981 and 1988.
The Nihon Aeroplane Manufacturing Company
(NAMC) was a consortium of Fuji, Kawasaki,
Mitsubishi, Nippi, Shin Meiwa and Showa.

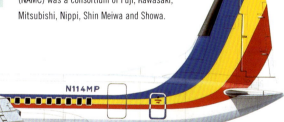

Chapter 5

Widebodies, Regionals and SSTs (1966–2012)

As the worldwide demand for air travel grew, the airlines looked to expand their capacity. There was always the option of buying more jets, but only so many aircraft movements could serve any one route – and thus the era of the high-capacity widebody airliner began. At the other end of the scale, smaller airliners began moving passengers form local hubs to regional airports, where regional aircraft often took them to the major hubs. While this great increase in travel options and sophistication was going on, the manufacturers were developing new airframe and cockpit technologies and even dabbled with the Holy Grail of commercial operations – supersonic flight.

◀ **Boeing 757**

Boeing developed a complementary pair of new airliners during the 1970s: the 757 narrowbody and the 767 widebody. The 757 was a new-technology replacement for the 727, while the 767 was Boeing's response to the product of a new manufacturer in a market previously unrecognized. Airbus Industrie, a European aerospace consortium, was offering the A300, a medium-range widebody, for 'short, fat routes' – that is, shorter routes with high passenger numbers.

Widebodies
1966–2007

A new generation of high-capacity airliners was built from the late 1960s, as the era of mass air travel dawned. Boeing continued its jetliner domination in this emerging widebody market.

ETWEEN 1960 AND 1966, the number of passengers carried by the world's airlines – excluding those of China and the USSR – almost doubled, from 106 million to 200 million. The airlines were delighted to be moving more people and making more profit, while the aircraft manufacturers were delighted to satisfy the need for larger fleets of commercial aircraft, but the growth rate had been very rapid and the basic infrastructure of air travel was becoming stretched.

The airways could only cope with a certain level of traffic, while the airports had limited ramp space and runway capacity, so that simply throwing more 707s or DC-8s at a popular route was becoming impossible – there just was not the infrastructure to support so many aircraft. It was also true that these early jets burned a great deal of fuel, especially when their turbojets and primitive turbofans were compared to the latest engines in development. They were very noisy and extremely dirty, since water injection was a common means of boosting take-off power, creating trails of thick black smoke in the process. With more aircraft movements, the noise and pollution levels at and around airports were

becoming intolerable, while the airlines themselves were keen on the increased profit that reduced fuel burn could bring.

Boeing Shocks the World

As the industry leader, Boeing delivered a major surprise in 1966, when it announced that Pan Am was the launch customer for its new Model 747. The airline had signed up for 25 of the giants, which offered long range, high capacity and reduced seat-mile costs for increased profitability.

Boeing, Douglas and Lockheed had been contesting the US Air Force's competition to find a new large transport aircraft using the modern high-bypass ratio turbofan engines then becoming available. Lockheed was the victor with its C-5 Galaxy, the losers retiring to lick their wounds and make best use of their investment. Boeing decided to take a radical leap forward and produce an airliner of twice the capacity then available. Douglas took a more conservative, medium-capacity approach. At first Boeing considered a double-deck machine similar in width to the 707, but this was rejected by the airlines. Working through many more iterations,

Specifications

Crew: 3–4	Service ceiling: 10,180m (33,400ft)
Passengers: 255–380	Dimensions: Span 50.39m (165ft 4in);
Powerplant: Three 22,226kg (49,000lb) General	length 55.35m (181ft 7in); height 17.7m
Electric CF6-50A turbofan engines	(58ft 1in)
Maximum speed: 924km/hr (574mph)	Weight: 251,744kg (555,000lb) loaded
Range: 7550km (4691 miles)	

▼ **McDonnell Douglas DC-10-30**

Wolfgang Amadeus Mozart, KLM, February 1973

KLM took PH-DTE on strength in February 1973, for service alongside the 747 on its long-haul routes. The airline received 10 DC-10-30s, all of them named after composers. The long-range -30 typically seated between 255 and 270 passengers.

Boeing 747 production variants

Model	Notes	Number built
747-100	490-seat airliner; Pratt & Whitney JT9D-3 or -3A; General Electric CF6-50, -45 or -80; or Rolls-Royce RB211 turbofan engines	167
747-100B	Strengthened 747-100, higher weights; JT9D-7A, CF6-50 or -45, or RB211-524 engines	9
747-100SR/747SR	High-density, Short Range variant for Japanese domestic market, reinforced undercarriage; JT9D-7A, or CF6-50 or -45 engines	29
747-200B	747-100B with more fuel, higher weights, wider choice of engine subvariants	225 (2 for US Air Force)
747-200C	Convertible version of 747-200B	13
747-200F	Freighter version of 747-200B with visor nose and optional cargo door	73
747-200M	Combi version of 747-200B	78
747-300	Stretched upper deck for 69 passengers; increased cruise speed; JT9D-7R4G2, CF6-50E2 or -80E2, or RB211-524D4 engines	56
747-300M	Combi version of 747-300	21
747-300SR	High-density, Short Range variant for Japanese domestic market; reinforced undercarriage; JT9D-7R4G2 engines	4 for Japan Airlines
747-400	Longer span wings with winglets; EFIS flight deck; revised structure; optional fuel increase; Pratt & Whitney PW4056; CF6-80C2; or RB211-524G turbofan engines	442 (2 for Japan Air Self-Defense Force)
747-400BCF /747BCF	Boeing Converted Freighter based on 747-400, produced by China's Taikoo Aircraft Engineering (TAECO)	50 aircraft in service 2012, in 'production'
747-400D	High-density, Short Range variant for Japanese domestic market; 568 passengers; reinforced undercarriage and fuselage; original wing span; no winglets; CF6-80C2 engines	19
747-400ER	Extended Range 747-400; CF6-80C2B5F engines	6 for QANTAS
747-400ERF	Freighter version of 747-400ER; Pratt & Whitney PW4062; or CF6-80C2B5F turbofan engines	40
747-400F	Freighter version of 747-400 with visor nose and short hump; PW4062; CF6-80C2B5F; or RB211-524H2-T engines	126 (1 for US Air Force)
747-400LCF Dreamlifter	Evergreen 747-400 Large Cargo Freighter conversion for Dreamliner programme; PW4062 engines	Four
747-400M	Combi version of 747-400; PW4062 or CF6-80C2B5F engines	61
747-400SF/747SF	Special Freighter conversion by Bedek Aviation	In 'production'
747-8/747-8I	Stretched fuselage; increased wing span; raked wingtips; more fuel; higher weights; General Electric GEnx-2B67 turbofan engines	36 orders by January 2012 (8 BBJs), in production
747-8F	Freighter version of 747-8 with visor nose and short hump; GEnx-2B67 engines	70 orders by January 2012, 10 delivered, in production
747SP	Special Performance version; shortened fuselage; taller fin; longer span tailplanes; JT9D-7A or Rolls-Royce RB211-524B2; C2 or D4 turbofan engines	45

it eventually settled on a single-deck machine considerably wider, indeed larger in all dimensions, than the 707. In fact, Boeing had arrived at little more than a very large 707, powered by four extremely powerful, fuel-efficient Pratt & Whitney JT9D turbofans. These engines were also considerably quieter and much cleaner than existing jet engines and combined with the large airframe to make a much more appealing proposition.

The new concept was presented to the airlines in January 1966 and Pan Am signed up on 13 April 1966. At $525 million, the order was then the largest ever in commercial aviation.

'Jumbo' in Service
The 747 flew for the first time on 9 February 1969 and was ready for Pan Am to inaugurate services with a New York–London flight on 22 January 1970.

Specifications

Crew: 3

Passengers: 269

Powerplant: Two 23,133kg (51,000lb) General
Electric CF6-50C turbofan engines

Maximum speed: 917km/hr (570mph)

Range: 4818km (2993 miles)

Service ceiling: 10,675m (35,020ft)

Dimensions: Span 44.84m (147ft 1in);
length 53.75m (176ft 4in); height 16.53m
(54ft 3in)

Weight: 157,000kg (346,125lb) loaded

▼ Airbus A300B4

Hapag-Lloyd, 1980s

Shipping company Hapag-Lloyd was the first customer for the A300C4 convertible freighter, introducing the type into service in 1980. It also took the A300B4, having begun passenger charters during the 1970s and continued independent airline operations until 1999.

Specifications

Crew: 2–4

Passengers: 40

Powerplant: Three 22,680kg (50,000lb) Rolls-
Royce RB211-524B turbofan engines

Range: 9655km (6000 miles)

Service ceiling: 12,800m (42,000ft)

Dimensions: Span 47.35m (155ft 3in);
length 50m (164ft); height 16.9m (55ft 3in)

Weight: 225,000kg (496,000lb) loaded

▼ Lockheed L-1011 TriStar 500

British Airways, 1980s

British Airways launched the long-range TriStar 500 with an order for six, the first of which entered service in 1979. They generally flew the airline's long thin routes, and all passed to the Royal Air Force at the end of their airline careers.

A last minute engine overheating problem delayed take-off, but the aircraft that the world's press had christened 'Jumbo Jet' had entered service.

Boeing was quick off the mark with improved versions, soon offering a choice of engines, a key option that would swing many airliner deals in the future. The 747-200B was the first of the truly successful variants and the company also developed the dedicated 747F freighter, but misjudged the long-range 747SP badly. Problems during development of the long-range Special Performance aircraft delayed its service entry, while at the same time Boeing began offering the -200B with increased weights. By the time the SP was ready, the -200B had almost as much range as the new version, but with all the capacity of a standard 'Jumbo'.

On 5 October 1982, the 747-300 completed its maiden flight, bringing greater passenger capacity to the line, but a far more radical improvement came with the 747-400 of 1988. Including the stretched upper deck of the -300, the -400 introduced an Electronic Flight Instrumentation System (EFIS) 'glass' cockpit with screens replacing traditional dials. It also featured an improved wing, with winglets, revised structure and a choice of three more modern engine variants from the manufacturers traditionally associated with the type – Pratt & Whitney, Rolls-Royce and General Electric.

Douglas and Lockheed

Both Lockheed and Douglas saw a market emerging for smaller, high-capacity widebody aircraft, suitable for the type of 'short-fat' route that typified US transcontinental travel. American Airlines had requested such an aircraft, with seats for 250 passengers, as early as 1966.

Douglas took its work on the USAF's transport programme and focused on developing this medium-sized aircraft, although development quickly became the responsibility of the new McDonnell Douglas concern. The DC-10 programme was launched in February 1968, for a first flight on 29 August 1970. First into service, with American and United, in August 1971, the DC-10-10 domestic version was followed by the longer-ranged DC-10-40, the transatlantic -30 and the hot-and-high DC-10-15. A series of unfortunate accidents and engine problems badly tainted the DC-10's reputation, but the type continued in production into the 1980s and 446 were built.

Lockheed's experience was less profitable, with both the airframer and its chosen engine manufacturer, Rolls-Royce, teetering on the brink of bankruptcy during development of the L-1011 TriStar. Although Lockheed had also reacted to American's requirement, interest in its product came primarily from Eastern and TWA. The TriStar programme was launched on 1 April 1968, with first flight on 16 November 1970. The parallels with the DC-10 were readily apparent, but Lockheed was struggling with cost overruns on the C-5, while Rolls-Royce had its own problems and failed on 4 February 1971. Lockheed limped

along with government backing and Rolls-Royce was reinstated as the nationalized Rolls-Royce (1971) Ltd, so the first deliveries – to Eastern – went ahead in April 1972, but by then Lockheed had lost ground to McDonnell Douglas. The TriStar was similarly developed through a number of versions, but the programme came to an end in 1983, after just 250 aircraft had been built.

European Competition

Having been decisively left behind as soon as Boeing flew the 707, Europe's airliner manufacturers realized that the only way forwards was as a consortium. Discussions began early in the 1960s and by October 1972, the Airbus Industrie group, with Sud-Aviation (soon to become Aerospatiale) taking design lead and Hawker Siddeley as privileged subcontractor on wings, was ready to fly its first A300B1 prototype.

The aircraft was the first in a new class of medium-range, high-capacity, twin-engined widebodies. Boeing and McDonnell Douglas were caught without anything to rival the Airbus, while Lockheed was in no position to build another commercial jet. As the A300B2, the Airbus entered service on 23 May 1974 and the manufacturer continued to develop new versions and rack up orders even as Boeing struggled to respond. The reaction eventually came in July 1978, just as Airbus announced that it was going ahead with a shortened, longer-ranged A310 version of the A300.

The 767 flew for the first time on 26 September 1981 and so began a game of Airbus–Boeing cat

Specifications

Crew: 3–4 (+ 11 cabin crew)	Service ceiling: 12.000m (39.370ft)
Passengers: 350	Dimensions: Span 48.06m (157ft 8in);
Powerplant: four 127.5kN (28,665lbf)	length 60.21m (197ft 7in); height 15.68m
Kuznetsov NK-86 two-spool turbofan engines	(51ft 5in)
Maximum speed: 950km/hr (590mph)	Weight: 215,000kg (458,560lb) loaded
Range: 3600km (2237 miles)'	

▲ **Ilyushin Il-86 'Camber'**

Aeroflot, 1980s

Ilyushin had been proposing an aircraft of Il-86 type since 1966 and revealed its first Il-86 design in 1971, but it was the 1980s that finally spurred the Soviet authorities to fund development. In service the aircraft proved noisy, short ranged and uneconomical.

Specifications

Crew: 2

Passengers: 200

Powerplant: Two 22,650kg (50,000lb) General
 Electric CF6-80C2A2 high bypass turbofans

Cruising speed: 965km/hr (600mph)

Range: 6800km (4225 miles)

Service ceiling: 12,500m (41,000ft)

Dimensions: Span 43.86m (143ft 10in);
 length 46.66m (153ft 1in); height 15.80m
 (51ft 10in)

Weight: 138,600kg (305,560lb) loaded

▼ Airbus A310-200

Thai Airways, 1988

Thai took the first of its two A310-200s in April 1988. Airbus
built the A310 as the -200 base model, -200C convertible,
-200F freighter and -300 versions, the latter for longer
ranges. Customers could chose between Pratt
& Whitney JT9D and General Electric
CF6 turbofans.

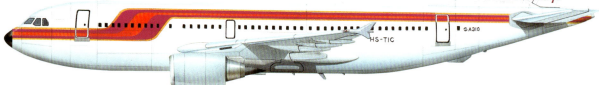

Specifications

Crew: 2

Passengers: 350

Powerplant: Two 266.9kN (60,042lbf) General
 Electric turbofan engines

Cruising speed: 913km/hr (567mph)

Range: 11,230km (6965 miles)

Service ceiling: 12,192m (40,000ft)

Dimensions: Span 47.57m (156ft);
 length 54.94m (180ft 3in); height 15.85m
 (52ft)

Weight: 181,437kg (399,161lb) loaded

▼ Boeing 767-200ER

Air Seychelles, 1989

Boeing developed ER (Extended Range) versions of both the 767-200
and stretched 767-300, with higher weights and additional fuel.
Air Seychelles leased S7-AAS from International Lease Finance
Corporation (ILFC), such arrangements having become a
popular means for airlines to vary their operational
fleets with relative ease.

Specifications

Crew: 2

Passengers: 410

Powerplant: three 27,360kg (60,300lb) Pratt &
 Whitney PW4460 turbofans

Cruising speed: 932km/h (579mph)

Range: 9270km (5760 miles)

Service ceiling: 9935m (32,600ft)

Dimensions: Span 51.66m (169ft 6in);
 length 61.21m (200ft 10in); height 17.60m
 (57ft 9in)

Weight: 273,300kg (602,500lb) loaded

▼ McDonnell Douglas MD-11

Swissair, 1990s

Swissair had built up a fleet of 19 MD-11s by 1999, but then sold
them to FedEx for freighter conversion. McDonnell Douglas
initially struggled to meet its range guarantees for the
MD-11 and was then taken over by Boeing in 1997,
effectively sealing the type's fate.

Specifications

Crew: 2

Passengers: 375–400

Powerplant: Four 151kN (34,000lbf) CFM56-5
  turbofan engines

Maximum speed: 913km/hr (563mph)

Range: 13,700km (8500 miles)

Service ceiling: 12,527m (41,099ft)

Dimensions: Span 60.30m (197ft 10in);
  length 63.60m (208ft 8in); height 16.85m
  (55ft 3in)

Weight: 276,500kg (610,000lb) loaded

▼ Airbus A340-300

Air France, 1990s

Air France was the first airline to receive A340-300s, taking the first
of the long-fuselage model on 26 February 1993. The short-
fuselage, long-range A340-200 had first been delivered to
Lufthansa, on 2 February, the two variants being
developed simultaneously.

Specifications

Crew: 3

Passengers: 300

Powerplant: Four 156.9kN (35,300lbf)
  Aviadvigatel PS-90A turbofan engines

Cruising speed: 850–900km/hr
  (525–5580mph)

Range: 9000km (5570 miles)

Service ceiling: 12,000m (39,360ft)

Dimensions: Span 60.11m (197ft 2in);
  length 55.35m (181ft 6in); height 17.57m
  (57ft 7in)

Weight: 216,000kg (475,000lb) loaded

▼ Ilyushin Il-96-300

Aeroflot, 1988

CCCP-96000 was the Il-96 prototype, flying for the first
time in 1988. Powered by PS-90A turbofans, the Il-96
has improved fuel economy and greater range
than the Il-86 and remained in limited
production in 2012.

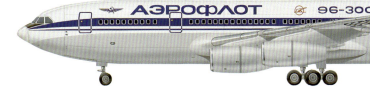

Specifications

Crew: 2

Passengers: 440

Powerplant: Two x 300kN (67,500lbf) General
  Electric CF6-80E1A2 turbofan engines

Maximum speed: 913km/hr (563mph)

Range: 8982km (5140 miles)

Service ceiling: 12,527m (41,100ft)

Dimensions: Span 60.3m (197ft 10in);
  length 63.69m (208ft 11in); height 16.83m
  (55ft 3in)

Weight: 235,000kg (520,000lb) loaded

▼ Airbus A330-300

Cathay Pacific, 1997

Airlines now expect a choice of engines, and powerplant competitions are almost
as hotly contested as those for the airframe itself. Cathay opted for
the Rolls-Royce Trent to power its A330-300s, having dismissed
the rival General Electric and Pratt & Whitney options.

Specifications

Crew: 2

Passengers: 440

Powerplant: Two x 327kN (73,548lbf) Pratt & Whitney PW4073/A turbofan engines

Cruise speed: 950km/hr (590mph)

Range: 9700km (6027 miles)

Service ceiling: 13,140m (43,100ft)

Dimensions: Span 60.9m (199ft 11in); length 63.7m (209ft 1in); height 18.5m (60ft 9in)

Weight: 247,200kg (545,000lb) loaded

▼ **Boeing 777-200**

United Airlines, 1995

United worked closely with Boeing on the 777's specification but was initially unhappy with the aircraft. The problems were eventually, if a little acrimoniously, solved and United flew the first 777 service on 7 June 1995, between London and Washington, DC.

and mouse that continues to this day, with the unfortunate MD-11, a high-tech general improvement on the DC-10, amounting to little more than a flash in the pan for McDonnell Douglas, since it entered an evolving market populated by twin-engined types and suffered performance shortfalls.

The Long Haul

In 1986, Airbus announced that it was proceeding with a natural progression of the A300, to take on the 747 and MD-11 in the longer-haul, high-capacity market. In fact, it took the unusual step of creating a four-engined, long-range airliner and a medium-haul twin as closely related variants of the same basic design. Not a company to be caught napping twice, Boeing immediately responded with its 777.

The A340 entered service with Lufthansa on 15 March 1993, the A330, with Air Inter, in January 1994. The 777 marked a step change in design philosophy for Boeing, introducing fly-by-wire technology to the company and being optimized for 180-minute Extended Range Twin-Engined Operations (ETOPS) from the outset. It entered service with United in June 1995. Competition remained fierce as both manufacturers developed their products, but the long-haul advantage eventually fell to Boeing, after an initial success for Airbus. The Europeans took the A340 and swapped its CFM56 engines for Rolls-Royces Trents.

The resulting 'hot rod' was available from 2002 as the high-capacity A340-600, or ultra-long-range

A340-500. The latter was briefly the world's longest-ranged aircraft, but Boeing developed two astonishing 777 variants in response. The 777-300ER emerged in 2004 to take on the A340-600, while the 777-200LR Worldliner entered service in 2007 and rendered the A340-500 obsolete at a stroke, achieving all that the Airbus had to offer with half the engines to fuel. The A340 quickly faded from production, although the A330, ironically, enjoyed a renaissance as operators looked for modern capacity to tide them over while they waited for their delayed Boeing 787 Dreamliners.

Soviet Widebodies

Fully aware of the strides being taken in airliner development by the West, the Soviet authorities ordered a prestige aircraft to be in service for the 1980 Moscow Olympics. The design and building tasks were assigned to Ilyushin, which came up with the four-engined Il-86. First flown on 24 October 1977, the type entered service in December 1980, missing the Olympics and soon proving disappointing. The Il-86 never had the range for transatlantic services and was generally expensive to operate.

With a panoply of weaknesses to correct, Ilyushin abandoned the Il-86 and produced the new, albeit similar in appearance, Il-96. Delivered to Aeroflot from 1995, the Il-96 is in every way a better aircraft, but even with optional Western engines it has been unable to compete on the open market with the A340/330 and 777, and consequently just a handful have been built.

Supersonic transports
1962–2003

Only two supersonic airliners have entered service, Concorde and the Soviet Tu-144. The latter's career was short lived, while Concorde was retired in 2003. There is no sign of any replacement SST.

IN 1962, BRITAIN AND FRANCE agreed to co-operate on the development of a supersonic transport (SST). Aerospatiale would take the lead on airframe development, working alongside BAC, while Rolls-Royce would head engine development, working closely with SNECMA (Société Nationale d'Etude et de Construction de Moteurs d'Aviation).

Work had been done on SST designs in both countries, while the new engine was based on the Olympus, already developed for the ill-fated TSR.2 strike aircraft.

The first Concorde prototype flew on 2 March 1969, after a remarkably short development for a project so complex (politically and technically). Orders flowed in from several airlines because it was clear that as soon as a rival offered supersonic travel, the only way to compete was with Concordes of your own. Unfortunately, while the four Concorde prototypes were still at work on the test programme, the 1973 oil crisis hit and airlines began cancelling orders for the thirsty SST. There had also been environmental protests over noise, especially in the United States, and these combined with rising fuel costs to drive away all but the BOAC and Air France orders.

In the event, British Airways and Air France began simultaneous services on 24 May 1976, subsequently proving that the aircraft could be flown at an operating profit, but with a production run of just 16 aircraft, Concorde's development costs could never be recouped. The aircraft continued to turn a profit into the 2000s, even as its systems became obsolete and special dispensation had to be made to allow it to operate outside strict noise controls. However, the 2000 crash of an Air France Concorde effectively sealed the type's fate and BA retired the last flying example on 26 November 2003.

Soviet Pretender

Tupolev began work on a Soviet SST in 1964, expecting to build at least 75 aircraft for internal use. Superficially similar to Concorde, the Tu-144 prototype had a kinked delta wing, but similar long,

▼ **Tupolev Tu-144 'Charger': nose section**

On the production Tu-144, retractable canards were extended from above the forward fuselage for landing and take-off. Providing forward lift, they allowed more efficient use of the elevons, for improved low-speed handling and reduced field length. The nose is shown in its cruise and landing/take-off positions.

▲ **Tupolev Tu-144 'Charger'**
Aeroflot, 1975

In its production form, the Tu-144 was larger, heavier and faster than Concorde. It could seat 140 passengers compared to Concorde's 100 and cruised at 2500km/h (1553 mph) or Mach 2.35. CCCP-77144 was the second production aircraft and visited the Paris air show in 1975.

Specifications

Crew: 3

Passengers: 140

Powerplant: Four Kuznetsov 12,983kg (28,660lb) NK-144 turbofan engines

Maximum speed: 2500km/hr (1553mph)

Range: 6500km (4030 miles)

Service ceiling: 16,000–18,000m (52,500–59,000ft)

Dimensions: Span 28.80m (94ft 6in); length 65.70m (215ft 6in); height 12.85m (42ft 4in)

Weight: 180,000kg (396,830lb) loaded

narrow fuselage and drooping nose. The latter improved visibility over the nose during landing and take-off at the high angles of attack demanded by deltas in the low-speed regime. Once airborne, as the crew prepared the aircraft to enter the cruise, the nose was raised.

The aircraft flew for the first time on 31 December 1968, beating Concorde into the air but, like the Anglo-French jet, then being subject to considerable redesign before a production aircraft could be built. In the case of Concorde, the first two prototypes had been built for short-range services to satisfy Air France and when the fallacy of that decision was realized, two more prototypes had to be built for long-range work. The Tu-144 underwent considerable airframe changes, including the installation of retractable canards above the forward fuselage, before entering service, as a cargo carrier, on 26 December 1975.

Passenger services began on 1 November 1977, but a fatal accident on 28 May 1978, which followed a very public inflight break-up at the Paris air show in 1973, brought an immediate end to operations on 1 June. Tupolev produced an improved Tu-144D, able to cruise supersonically without afterburner, but although the type was used for advanced flight tests – including work with NASA in the late 1990s – none entered airline service.

America Dabbles

America had begun dabbling in SST design during the late 1950s and eventually the Boeing 2707 concept was chosen for development, initially as a swing-wing design. Looking not unlike today's B-1B Lancer bomber, the Boeing had become a delta design by the time that it was cancelled on economic grounds in 1971.

Boeing tried the high-speed formula again in 2001, proposing a Sonic Cruiser that would fly in the high transonic regime, around Mach 0.98. The airlines preferred economy to a small gain in speed, however, and Boeing abandoned the Sonic Cruiser in favour of the 787, an aircraft of radical design concept delivering more traditional performance.

Specifications

Crew: 3	Range: 6228km (3870 miles)
Passengers: 144	Service ceiling: 18,290m (60,000ft)
Powerplant: Four 17,259kg (38,050lb) Rolls-Royce/SNECMA Olympus 593 Mk 601 turbojet engines	Dimensions: Span 25.55m (83ft 10in); length 62.10m (203ft 9in); height 11.40m (37ft 5in)
Maximum speed: 2179km/hr (1354mph)	Weight: 185,066kg (408,000lb) loaded

▼ Aerospatiale/BAC Concorde

British Airways, 1990s

British Airways found Concorde eminently profitable in service, especially on its prestigious transatlantic routes. It also found a ready and very lucrative market for special charters, offering the experience of 'going supersonic' at a fraction of the cost of a regular transatlantic schedule.

Concorde Milestones

Date	Milestone
25 October 1962	BAC and Sud Aviation signed the Anglo-French Supersonic Aircraft treaty
April 1966	Work began on Concorde 001
2 March 1969	Concorde 001 flew for the first time, at Toulouse, France
1969	Flight testing began; it continued into 1974
19 July 1974	The UK and French governments decided that just 16 aircraft would be built
21 January 1976	British Airways and Air France began services simultaneously
25 July 2000	An Air France Concorde crashed shortly after take-off from Paris Charles de Gaulle airport
7 November 2001	British Airways and Air France returned their Concordes to service after post-crash modifications
May 2003	British Airways and Air France began to wind down their Concorde fleets and the type was retired in October

Specifications

Crew: 3

Passengers: 100

Powerplant: Four 169.17kN (227hp) Rolls-
   Royce/SNECMA Olympus 593 Mk 610
   turbojets

Maximum speed: 2180km/hr (1355mph)

Range: 6250km (3880 miles)

Service ceiling: 18,300m (60,000ft)

Dimensions: Span 25.55m (83ft 10in);
   length 62.10m (203ft 9in); height 11.40m
   (37ft 5in)

Weight: 185,066kg (408,000lb) loaded

▼ **Aerospatiale/BAC Concorde**

Air France, 21 January 1976

F-BVFA was the fifth production Concorde and flew for the first time on 25 October 1975. It operated the inaugural Air France Paris–Dakar–Rio de Janeiro service on 21 January 1976.

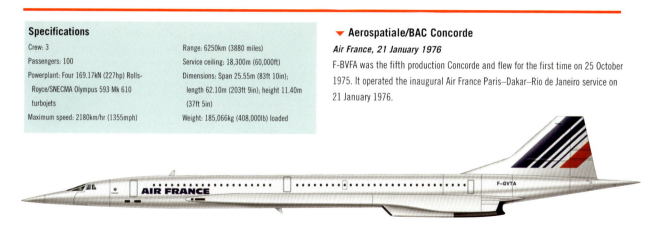

Regional reality
1947–2012

As the world's airlines began re-equipping with jets, so they lost their ability to serve many smaller airports. A new class of airliner therefore evolved, to uplift passengers from these local airfields and deliver them to the major hubs.

WHILE IT IS TRUE is true to say that the majority of the airline flying done during the early years of air transport would today be classed as regional, the concept of regional flying really became established with the dawn of the jet age. As aircraft began carrying hundreds rather than 10s of passengers, and as their airfield demands became greater, so smaller,

regional airports could no longer be served by mainline types. A new class of small, efficient airliner – a modern DC-3 in fact – was required.

Elsewhere, of course, air travel had become essential in maintaining modern communications with isolated communities, and smaller airliners had been serving such populations for many years.

Specifications

Crew: 1

Passengers: 9

Powerplant: Two 194kW (260hp) Lycoming
   0-540-E4C5 piston engines

Maximum speed: 257km/hr (159mph)

Range: 2032km (1260 miles)

Service ceiling: 4938m (16,200ft)

Dimensions: Span 14.93m (49ft);
   length 10.87m (35ft 7in); height 4.18m
   (13ft 8in)

Weight: 6600kg (14,520lb) loaded

▼ **Britten-Norman BN-2A-21 Islander**

Transeki Airways, 1980s

Built for rugged dependability, the Islander remains in production in 2012, after several changes of ownership since ZS-XGF was built in 1975. The aircraft has found its niche serving more isolated communities and is available in piston – as here – and turboprop versions.

Specifications

Crew: 2 (+ 1)

Passengers: 29

Powerplant: Two 1230kW (1650hp) Garrett
TPE331-14GR/HR turboprops

Maximum speed: 547km/hr (339mph)

Range: 1433km (890 miles)

Service ceiling: 7925m (26,000ft)

Dimensions: Span 18,29m (60ft);
length 19.25m (63ft); height 5.74m
(17ft 11in)

Weight: 10,886kg (23,949lb) loaded

▼ BAe Jetstream 31

Canadian Partner/Ontario Express, 1980s

Owned and operated by Ontario Express, this Jetstream 31 was
flown in Canadian Partner livery as a feeder for Canadian
Airlines' hub airports. The aircraft is fitted with the
optional underfuselage baggage pannier.

Specifications

Crew: 2 (+ 1)

Passengers: 19

Powerplant: Two 533kW (715hp) Allied Signal
(Garrett AiResearch) TPE331-5-252D
turboprop engines

Maximum speed: 440km/hr (273mph)

Range: 2704km (1676 miles)

Service ceiling: 8535m (28,000ft)

Dimensions: Span 16.97m (55ft 8in);
length 16.56m (54ft 4in); height 4.86m
(15ft 11in)

Weight: 5700kg (12,640lb) loaded

▼ Dornier Do 228-200

Air Guadeloupe, 1988

Delivered to Air Guadeloupe in 1988, F-OGOF is typical of the Do 228s serving
smaller operators in markets were passenger numbers are limited. The aircraft
remained with the airline when it became successively
Caribeanne Transport and then Air Caraibes in 2001.

Perhaps the best way to appreciate the nature of such
services is to consider the history of two disparate
examples: the UK's so-called 'Highlands and Islands'
routes; and the islands of French Polynesia.

On 1 February 1947, BEA absorbed the UK's
multifarious small domestic airlines. In so doing it
assumed responsibilities for previously independent
services linking the mainland with various island
groups, especially the Scottish, Scilly and Channel
Islands. The mainstay of these difficult routes was the
de Havilland Rapide. In 1950, the airline assembled
the survivors of the Rapides inherited from its
constituent carriers as the 'Rapide Class', this 18-
aircraft fleet then gradually dwindling as operations

continued into the 1950s. In 1955, BEA replaced the
Rapides of its Scottish Division with four-engined
Heron 1B aircraft, the latter maintaining not only the
links already established between mainland Scotland
and its various islands, but also the inter-island
connections so vital to island life.

Operating conditions are particularly harsh from
some of the region's less developed strips, which can
be short and unpaved, and in 1973 BEA began
operating a pair of Shorts Skyliner short take-off and
landing aircraft on these routes. With the creation of
British Airways in 1974, the Scottish Division
services passed to Loganair. Established in 1962,
initially as an air taxi operator, Loganair brought

de Havilland Canada commercial aircraft

Model	Notes	Number built
DHC-2 Beaver	Seven-seat light transport; Pratt & Whitney R-985-AN14B/16B Wasp Junior radial piston engine	Around 1657 (approximately 630 for civil use)
DHC-3 Otter	14-seat light transport; Pratt & Whitney R-1340-S1H1G Wasp radial piston engine	460 (approximately 167 for civil use)
DHC-6 Twin Otter	20-seat light transport (Series 300); two Pratt & Whitney Canada PT6A-27 turboprop engines; in production as the Viking Twin Otter Series 400	844 for civil and military customers; in production
DHC-7 Dash 7	50-seat airliner (Series 100); four Pratt & Whitney Canada PT6A-50 engines	113 for civil and military customers
DHC-8 Dash 8	39-seat airliner (Series 100); two Pratt & Whitney Canada PW120A turboprop engines; in production as Bombardier Q400	More than 1000 for civil and military customers; in production

Specifications

Crew: 2

Passengers: 17

Powerplant: Two 462kW (620hp) Pratt & Whitney Canada PT6A-27 turboprop engines

Maximum speed: 328km/hr (204mph)

Range: 1340km (832 miles)

Service ceiling: 7000m (23,000ft)

Dimensions: Span 17.24m (56ft 6½in); length 18.86m (48ft 9in); height 5.68m (18ft 7½in)

Weight: 5300kg (11,684lb) loaded

▼ Harbin Y-12 (II)

Harbin, 1990s

China's Harbin developed the Y-12 from its earlier, smaller, but generally similar Y-11. Available in several variants, the Y-12 is powered by the PT6A turboprop and provides seating capacity and performance roughly equivalent to that of the 'Twotter'.

Specifications

Crew: 2

Passengers: 50

Powerplant: Four 835kW (1120hp) Pratt & Whitney PT6A-50 turboprop engines

Maximum speed: 0km/hr (0mph)

Range: 328km (204 miles)

Service ceiling: 7000m (23,000ft)

Dimensions: Span 17.24m (56ft 6½in); length 18.86 m (48ft 9in); height 5.68m (18ft 7½in)

Weight: 5300kg (11,684lb) loaded

▼ de Havilland Canada DHC-7 Dash 7 Series 110

Brymon Airways, 1981

Just 114 Dash 7s were built, but the type offered a combination of capacity and short-field performance that remains unmatched. It was essential in pioneering inner-city commuter airport operations, especially at London-City, where Brymon was among the first carriers into the original 'STOLport'.

Specifications

Crew: 2

Passengers: 18

Powerplant: Two 486kW (650hp) Pratt & Whitney Canada PT6A-27 turboprop engines

Maximum speed: 338km/hr (210mph)

Range: 1297km (804 miles)

Service ceiling: 8140m (26,700ft)

Dimensions: Span 19.81m (65ft); length 15.77m (51ft 9in); height 6.05m (19ft 10in)

Weight: 5670kg (12,474lb) loaded

▼ de Havilland Canada DHC-6 Twin Otter Series 300

norOntair, 1980s

As the Twin Otter's popularity with commuter lines grew, de Havilland Canada added an extended nosecone to the Series 200 and 300 aircraft, providing additional baggage space. During the 1980s, DHC-6 and -8 machines were flown in norOntair colours by several smaller operators, feeding passengers into the larger carrier's North Bay, Ontario, hub.

Specifications

Crew: 2

Passengers: 18

Powerplant: Two 559kW (750hp) Pratt & Whitney Canada PT-6A-34 turboprop engines

Maximum speed: 411km/hr (255mph)

Range: 2010km (1246 miles)

Service ceiling: 6550m (21,500ft)

Dimensions: Span 15.32m (50ft 3in); length 15.10m (49ft 6in); height 4.91m (16ft 1in)

Weight: 5900kg (12,980lb) loaded

▼ Embraer EMB-110P1 Bandeirante

Dolphin Airways, 1983

By no means a spectacular aircraft in itself, the Bandeirante did everything that was asked of it very well, helping establish Embraer as a major player in the airliner market. Florida's Dolphin Airways flew a maximum of eight Bandeirantes before falling foul of financial difficulties in 1983.

Specifications

Crew: 2

Passengers: 37

Powerplant: Two 1395kW (1870hp) General Electric CT7-9B turboprop engines

Cruising speed: 522km/hr (325mph)

Range: 1810km (1125 miles)

Service ceiling: 9449m (31,000ft)

Dimensions: Span 21.45m (70ft 4in); length 19.75m (64ft 8in); height 6.89m (22ft 6in)

Weight: 12,928kg (28,500lb) loaded

▼ Saab 340A

Continental Express, 1989

Saab made considerable progress in the US market, having a modern product available as the demand for second-generation turboprop feederliners grew. Leased new to Bar Harbor Airlines in 1986, a series of take-overs saw N401BH flying in Continental Express colours from 1988–89.

Embraer commercial aircraft

Model	Notes	Number built
EMB-110 Bandeirante	15-seat airliner; two Pratt & Whitney Canada PT6A-34 turboprop engines	498 for civil and military customers
EMB-120 Brasilia	30-seat airliner; two Pratt & Whitney Canada PW118A turboprop engines	352 for civil and military customers
ERJ 135	37-seat airliner; two Rolls-Royce AE3007 turbofan engines	See below
ERJ 140	44-seat airliner; reduced range; two Rolls-Royce AE3007 engines	See below
ERJ 145	50-seat airliner; reduced range; two Rolls-Royce AE3007 engines	See below
ERJ 145XR	50-seat airliner; increased range; two Rolls-Royce AE3007 engines	Around 900 of ERJ series for civil and military customers
E170	78-seat airliner; two General Electric CF34-8E turbofan engines	See below
E175	88-seat airliner; reduced range; two General Electric CF34-8E engines	See below
E190	114-seat airliner; increased range; two General Electric CF34-10E engines	See below
E195	124-seat airliner; two General Electric CF34-10E engines	Around 1000 E-Jets ordered by 30 September 2011; in production

Britten-Norman Trislanders to the island services, but subsequently replaced them with the classic de Havilland Canada DHC-6 Twin Otter, an aircraft popularly known as the 'Twotter' and designed for low-volume air services into austere strips. It also introduced the Britten Norman Islander and continued to use these types through changes of livery and ownership for more than three decades.

In 2012, Loganair serves the Scottish islands with a pair of Twin Otters and two Islanders. The Twin Otters operate in flybe livery, although Loganair enjoys the traditional and essential government subsidy on routes considered to be vital but impossible to operate profitably by commercial means. The airline continues to fly the world's shortest scheduled air service, the journey from Westray to Papa Westray forming part of the Orkney Island service and taking a little under two minutes. The Twotter is also still flown to the island of Barra, which is served at low tide, since services operate off the beach.

French Polynesia

The 118 islands of French Polynesia present all the challenges of Scottish islands flying, but on a dramatically larger scale; the most distant island is 1100km (684 miles) from the capital Tahiti. At the same time, the region's population is just 264,000, roughly equivalent to that of a large British city. Air services are clearly the key to modern communications in such an area, but small islands can bear only short, basic airfields, while aircraft capacity is limited not only by the available runways, but also by passenger demand.

The first of the nation's runways was built in 1942, remaining the only airfield facility until 1961. In the meantime, local air services were run using flying boats, but when the global use of such machines fell into decline, a programme of airfield construction was begun. By 1970, Air Polynesie was flying Fokker F27s between six airfields and continued to expand as new facilities were open. Air Tahiti took responsibility for services from 1986 and in 1987 began replacing the F27s with ATR turboprops.

Today, the airline serves French Polynesia's 47 airports with a fleet of 11 ATR72s and a single Twotter. The ATRs are flown under ETOPS 120 regulations, allowing more direct overwater routes to be taken between islands. They provide essential travel for local people, but also form the backbone of the region's tourism. Traditionally, the airline has been able to serve loss-making, thin routes, because its profitable tourist routes provide sufficient funds to make good the losses. Indeed, some of its destinations are islands with fewer than 200 inhabitants, for whom the weekly schedule brings in and takes out essential goods, as well as exchanging passengers. Like Loganair, Air Tahiti has a very short Twin Otter route, operating a government-owned aircraft on a six-minute, 18km (11-mile) flight from Papeete to Moorea.

Regionals and Feeders

Air Tahiti and Loganair are typical of many smaller operators in that they provide both essential local services and feed passengers into regional international hubs. International passengers arrive and depart from Tahiti airport and Air Tahiti is their primary option for onward travel. It also serves to return them at the end of their stay and 'deliver' local people to the airport for international departures. Loganair feeds passengers into and out of the major regional international hubs of Glasgow and Edinburgh, from where passengers can chose to fly into Europe, domestically, or across the Atlantic. The airline operates in flybe colours, in association with the large UK regional airline and a passenger picked up off the beach at Barra, for example, in a flybe-liveried Twin Otter, might soon find themselves on a mainline flybe Bombardier Q400 turboprop or Embraer 195 regional jet, winging their way to destinations further afield.

Just as flybe uses Loganair to feed passengers into its regional hubs, many of the world's largest airlines have agreements with operators of smaller aircraft to feed passengers into their international hubs. These so-called hub-and-spoke operations emerged in the United States during the 1960s and 1970s. Airlines that had for many years been serving smaller airlines with their primary DC-3, DC-4 and Constellation equipment, for example, re-equipped with early jets and found themselves unable to service the smaller airports in their networks.

Large numbers of enterprising commuter airlines sprang up in response. Often flying piston-twins of 10 or so seats, these carriers delivered passengers from local airports to the major facilities where flights from the likes of American and TWA could be picked up. As the demand for air travel increased, so 'commuter liners' increased in size, typically becoming 'feederliners' seating at least 19 passengers and most often powered by turboprops. The major airlines soon realized the benefits in having a system of feederlines flying passengers along 'spokes' from local airports and into their major 'hub' airports. If the feeder line were franchised and flew aircraft in a similar livery to the mainline equipment, the passenger could feel that they were being taken care of by the larger airline throughout their journey, experience a consistent level of service and book through-tickets with the one airline direct from their home destination.

Soon, dedicated feederlines began appearing, American Eagle serving American Airlines, for example, while United Express fed United's hubs. Larger and more efficient aircraft were demanded and were soon

Specifications

Crew: 2
Passengers: 36
Powerplant: Two 875kW (1173hp) Pratt & Whitney Canada PT6A-67R turboprop engines
Cruising speed: 393km/hr (244mph)
Range: 1697km (1055 miles)

Service ceiling: Not known
Dimensions: Span 22.8m (74ft 9in); length 21.6m (70ft 10in); height 7.3m (23ft 10in)
Weight: 11,793kg (26,0000lb) loaded

▼ **Shorts 360-100**

Manx Airlines, 1984

The Shorts 360 proved very popular with the UK's regional airlines, including Isle of Man-based Manx. Created by Air UK and British Midland, Manx fed passengers into both larger airlines' hubs, becoming part of the British Regional Airlines Group in 1988. When the Group was sold to BA in 2002, the individual airline brands within it disappeared.

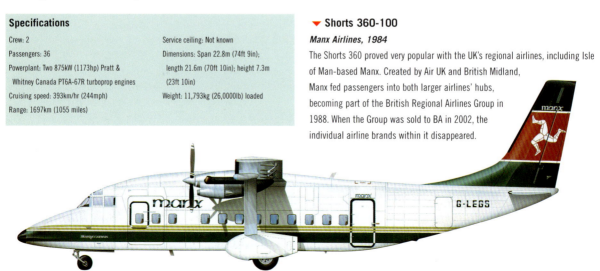

Specifications

Crew: 2

Passengers: 36

Powerplant: Two 1491kW (2000hp) Pratt & Whitney Canada PW120A turboprop engines

Cruising speed: 500km/hr (310mph)

Range: 2010km (1250 miles)

Service ceiling: 7620m (15,000ft)

Dimensions: Span 25.9m (85ft); length 22.5m (73ft); height 7.5m (24ft 6in)

Weight: 15,650kg (34,500lb) loaded

▼ de Havilland Canada DHC-8 Dash 8-100

City Express, 1985

Delivered to City Express on 5 September 1985, C-GGTO has led a varied service life and in 2012 was current with Queensland Regional Airlines in Australia. City Express focused its operations on linking primary business centres in Canada and the northern United States.

Specifications

Crew: 2

Passengers: 19

Powerplant: Two 559kW (750hp) Motorlet Walter M-601E turboprob engines

Cruising speed: 380km/hr (236mph)

Range: 1380km (855 miles)

Service ceiling: 6320m (20,700ft)

Dimensions: Span 19.98m (65ft 6in); length 14.42m (47ft 4in); height 5.83m (62ft 9in)

Weight: 6400kg (14,080lb) loaded

▼ LET L-410UVP-E

Aeroflot, 1980s

The Czech-built L-410 satisfied similar requirements to the DHC-6 and smaller feederliners, but for airlines under Soviet influence, and especially Aeroflot. Still offered for production in 2012, the type has latterly found favour for Third World operations thanks to its low acquisition costs, relative simplicity and rugged dependability.

---

able to operate regional routes in their own right. The era of the feederliner and regional airliner had arrived.

Turboprops for All

The ideal powerplant for this new generation of aircraft was the turboprop, the piston engine having been outmoded for larger aircraft, and the jet engine using too much fuel for the greater speed it provided to be economical over shorter sectors. In fact, over the relatively short ranges typically flown between local and hub airports, the jet's greater speed barely made any difference in total flight time.

It quickly emerged that a range of aircraft in the 19- to 50-seat bracket would be required, ironically a category into which the DC-3 might easily have fallen,

and so in many ways the aircraft manufacturers found themselves again looking to build a DC-3 replacement. De Havilland Canada was among the first companies to respond to the new demand, although its DHC-6 Twin Otter was something of a niche aircraft, being a 19-seater, but especially suited to rough, short-field operations. First flown in May 1965, the DHC-6 was followed in December by the prototype of the Model 99 Airliner from Beech. The Model 99 used much of the existing Queen Air 80 twin, combining it with a new fuselage to create a 15-passenger feederliner available for service from 1968.

The Model 99 sold well, but was perhaps more important in pushing Beech to develop the 19-seat Model 1900, a very successful machine built in several variants and continuing in service today. De Havilland Canada was also spurred on by the success of its Twin Otter, producing another niche airliner, the DHC-7 Dash 7. A four-engined machine, the 48-seat Dash 7 offered STOL performance. It was aimed at operators looking for a higher-capacity aircraft with DHC-6 performance and which the Fokker F27 would therefore not satisfy. The Dash 7 was moderately successful, but allowed de Havilland Canada to remain in the airliner business and develop the DHC-8 Dash 8. A high-technology twin turboprop, the Dash 8 was developed through four primary versions and remains in production in 2012 as the Bombardier Q400, seating up to 78 passengers.

In 1973, the first of a new airliner from a manufacturer new to the sector was delivered. Transbrasil Airlines took the first Embraer EMB-110 Bandeirante in March 1973 and the 21-seater was soon selling well in North America. So well, in fact, that Fairchild Swearingen, whose 20-seat Metro had become available around the same time, lobbied to have tariffs placed on the Embraer product, claiming unfair competition. Meanwhile, the Brazilian Empresa Brasileira de Aeronautica SA (Embraer) concern began work on its EMB-120 Brasilia, launching the 30-seater onto a ready market in 1979, before going on to dominate the regional jet market.

European Entrants

Europe's airframers were keen to have their slice of the feederliner pie, especially as the first generation of

regional turboprops became due for replacement. Dornier entered the market from 1981, with the 15-seat Do 228-100 and 19-seat Do 228-200, developing the basic airframe into the 30-seat Do 328 for delivery from 1993.

In the UK, British Aerospace rolled out the first production example of its Jetstream 31 on 25 January 1982. A development of the successful twin-turboprop business aircraft, the Jetstream 31 was offered as the 19-seat Corporate and later upengined as the Jetstream 32. As a final step in Jetstream evolution, BAe lengthened its fuselage to allow provision for 29 passengers in the Jetstream 41. Shorts achieved very little with its Skyliner version of the successful Skyvan, but went on to do well with the similar, but larger, 330 and 360, both of which sold in the United States as well as Europe.

Another European feederliner/regional aircraft came from an unexpected source, when Saab-Fairchild entered the market in 1983 with its 35-seat SF340. The US company soon abandoned the arrangement, leaving Saab to enjoy great success with the 340 and the more advanced, but generally similar, 2000. It was joined briefly by CASA-Nurtanio, with its high-wing, twin-turboprop CN235, which also flew for the first time in 1983, but ultimately appealed more to the military. It remains in production in 2012 as the Airbus Military CN235.

A final and most significant contender in the regional/feederliner market flew for the first time on

Specifications	
Crew: 2	Service ceiling: 7620m (25,000ft)
Passengers: 42–50	Dimensions: Span 24.5m (80ft 4in);
Powerplant: Two 1342kW (1800hp) Pratt &	length 22.6m (74ft 3in);
Whitney Canada PW120 turboprop engines	height 7.3m (23ft 11in)
Cruising speed: 560km/hr (348mph)	Weight: 18,600kg (41,000lb) loaded
Range: 1950km (1212 miles)	

▼ **ATR 42-300**

Air Mauritius, 1986

Delivered new to Air Mauritius in 1986, 3B-NAH passed to Air Madagascar in 1997, and in 2012 was serving Overland Airways. Air Mauritius began flying operations with a 707 in 1977. By 2012 it was flying the A330 and A340 medium/long-haul airliners, with the A319 and ATR 72 serving its short-haul/regional routes.

▲ **Fokker 50**

Fokker reinvented the F27 as the F50, replacing the latter's legacy engines with the new PW120, installing an EFIS cockpit and revising the airframe with extensive use of weight-saving composites. First flown on 28 December 1985, the Fokker 50 sold to the extent of 214 aircraft.

16 August 1984. Aerospatiale and Italy's Aeritalia joined forces to create Avions de Transport Régional (ATR), to develop an aircraft outwardly very similar to the CN235. The ATR 42 used new technology engines and offered accommodation for 42 passengers, and was joined in the air by the 72-seat ATR 72 on 27 October 1988. Both types have undergone continuous development, and the latest -600 variant was first delivered in August 2011 in ATR 72 form.

Specifications

Crew: 2	Range: 2778km (1726 miles)
Passengers: 19	Service ceiling: 10,058m (33,000ft)
Powerplant: Two 954kW (1280hp) Pratt &	Dimensions: Span 17.67m (58ft);
Whitney Canada PT6A-67D turboprop engines	length 17.63m (57ft); height 4.72m (15ft 6in)
Cruising speed: 533km/hr (331mph)	Weight: 7688kg (16,949lb) loaded

▲ **Beech 1900D**

US Air Express, 1986

Mesa Airlines took delivery of N163YV in 1996, operating the aircraft as a feeder for US Airways' services. Beech deepened the fuselage of the 1900D compared to the earlier 1900 models, to provide stand-up cabin headroom. It was then obliged to install various aerodynamic devices to restore directional stability.

Rise of the regional jet
1978–2012

British Aerospace, Fokker and even, to a degree, Airbus and Boeing, all dipped toes into the regional jet market. But the undisputed champions of the sector have emerged as Bombardier and Embraer.

HAWKER SIDDELEY PROCRASTINATED over the design of a new airliner for almost two decades from the late 1960s. The intention was to create a quiet, fuel-efficient short-haul airliner providing comfortable transport from smaller airfields. The decision was eventually taken to power the aircraft with four new-generation Lycoming ALF502 turbofans, a configuration that came in for criticism but promised to offer reduced operating costs compared to the twin jets of similar capacity then in service. As the economic situation of the early 1970s bit and with the UK Government making plans to nationalize Hawker Siddeley as British Aerospace, the airliner, known as the HS.146, was cancelled, reinstated with limited funding and, eventually, relaunched into a favourable market by BAe in 1978.

The 146 was developed in three primary versions, each offering greater passenger capacity, and enjoyed a resurgence in the 1990s as the improved, rebranded Avro RJ (Regional Jet), designated to compete in the burgeoning regional jet market. The BAe 146 matured as an economical, quiet jet, with a short-field performance that made it popular for operators flying from smaller airports. Like the Dash 7, it was a pioneer of operations into London-City and by pure good fortune arrived on the market in time to take advantage of the rise in jet regional and feeder operations.

Renewed Fellowship

Fokker announced its intention to create a 100-seat, upgraded version of the F28 Fellowship in 1983. It had found airlines wary of its late-1970s proposals for a regional jet, but with the availability of the efficient Rolls-Royce Tay turbofan and new-technology cockpit systems, it was able to return to the upgraded F28 formula. The first prototype F100 completed its maiden flight on 30 November 1986 and the type was soon picking up orders. Fokker flew the shortened F70 in 1993 and both types remained in production while Fokker faced increasingly stiff competition in a market that it had been early to recognize. By early 1996, the relatively high cost of the Fokkers, in competition

▲ BAe 146-200

Continental Express, 18 March 1987

Presidential Airways took delivery of N406XZ on 18 March 1987, for use on behalf of Continental Airlines in Continental Express colours. The 146-200 could be configured for 112 passengers, the -100 for 88 and the -300 for 128.

Specifications

Crew: 2	Service ceiling: 6005m (19,700ft)
Passengers: 9	Dimensions: Span 14.94m (49ft);
Powerplant: Two 194kW (260hp) Lycoming O-	length 10.87m (35ft 8in);
540-E4C5 6-cylinder air-cooled engines	height 4.16m (13ft 8in)
Cruising speed: 257km/hr (160mph)	Weight: 2857kg (6300lb) loaded
Range: 670km (425 miles)	

◀ **Fokker 100**
The F100 was Fokker's lead aircraft in the campaign to revitalize its F28 line. It sold well, Fokker delivering 280, plus 45 of the shorter F70, although at the time of the company's bankruptcy it had amassed orders for 351 and 77 aircraft, respectively.

with the Airbus A319 and Boeing 737-500/600, and the Canadair and Embraer regional jets, saw Fokker declared bankrupt.

Canadair Regional Jet

Canadair was enjoying considerable success with its Challenger business jet when it launched a Regional Jet derivation of the type on 31 March 1989. Bombardier had bought the Canadian aerospace and transportation group in 1986 and by the late 1990s the Regional Jet (RJ) was being marketed as the Bombardier CRJ.

In effect, the CRJ was an enlarged Challenger, its initial variant offering accommodation for 50 passengers. Canadair argued that the fuel efficiency of the most modern small turbofans – its jet was powered by the General Electric CF34-3A – at last allowed jet equipment to compete economically with turboprops over shorter routes with small passenger loads. It also claimed that passengers would always chose a jet over a 'prop', given the opportunity, since propeller-driven aircraft were perceived as old fashioned and therefore not as safe.

The first RJ100 was delivered to Lufthansa Cityline on 19 October 1992 and this initial model was replaced in production by the improved CRJ200 in 1996. Bombardier found that the type was eminently 'stretchable', going on to produce the 70-seat CRJ700, 90-seat CRJ900 and 100-seat CRJ1000 NextGen. First flown in 2008 and delivered from late 2010, after Bombardier had been obliged to resolve flight control issues, the CRJ1000 represents the last of the line. With global recession and increasing fuel costs, airlines began asking for more fuel-efficient aircraft in the late 2000s, and Bombardier once again turned its attention to satisfying the smaller end of the regional market with turboprops, while beginning work on the clean-sheet CSeries for the larger end of the market.

Embraer Regional Jet

Reaching the same conclusions as Canadair with regard to regional jet economics, Embraer launched its own aircraft into the sector on 12 June 1989. After considerable design revision, the EMB-145 flew for the first time on 11 August 1995. It used a stretched EMB-120 fuselage for 50 passengers and was powered by a pair of rear-mounted Allison GMA3007 turbofans.

Continental Express began EMB-145 operations on 6 April 1997 and as Embraer continued to develop and market the type it redesignated it as the ERJ145. Smaller ERJ135 and 140 variants were developed and altogether around 1100 airframes were sold, compared to more than 1600 CRJs, before Embraer turned its attention to a new generation of regional aircraft, the EJet.

Powered by underwing CF34 engines, the EJets continue in production and have proven phenomenally successful, serving the market from 70 to 100 seats through E170, E175, E190 and E195 variants.

Specifications

Crew: 2 (+ 1)

Passengers: 50

Powerplant: Two 34.68kN (7800lbf) Rolls-Royce
AE 3007-A1 or 36.9kN (8300lbf) Rolls-Royce
AE 3007-A1P engines

Maximum speed: 828km/hr (515mph)

Range: 2873km (1785 miles)

Service ceiling: 11,278m (37,000ft)

Dimensions: Span 20.04m (65ft 9in);
length 29.87m (98ft 0in);
height 6.76m (22ft 2in)

Weight: 22,000kg (48,501lb) loaded

▼ Embraer ERJ145

British Airways, 2002

Brymon Airways took delivery of G-EMBS in 2000. The aircraft became part of the British Airways Connect fleet in 2002, when Brymon became part of British Regional Airlines, a wholly owned subsidiary of British Airways.

Specifications

Crew: 2

Passengers: 228

Powerplant: Two 82.3kN (18,500lbf) GE CF34-
10E turbofan engines

Maximum speed: 890km/hr (553mph)

Range: 3334km (2072 miles)

Service ceiling: 12,500m (41,000ft)

Dimensions: Span 28.72m (94ft 3in);
length 38.65m (126ft 10in);
height 10.28m (34ft 7in)

Weight: 48,970kg (107,600lb) loaded

▼ Embraer E195

flybe, 2007

Flybe was launch customer for the E195, the largest of the EJet series. It received its first example in September 2006 and employs the aircraft on its longer routes into Europe. In spring 2012, Embraer announced plans to re-engine the EJet for future competition with the Bombardier CSeries.

New technology
1978–2012

Boeing began to consider a replacement for the 727 during the 1970s and developed the 757 alongside the 767. It could not have foreseen that Airbus would then create an airliner so efficient and so flexible that it would force a major 737 upgrade and encroach on the lower end of the 757's market.

BOEING SOON BECAME aware that the A300B offered a very attractive modern, quiet, fuel-efficient alternative to its 727. Operators of early 727s were very likely to look seriously at the Airbus when it came to renewing their fleets and although the trijet was still selling, Boeing needed a new product. Early design studies used the 727 flight deck area, but eventually Boeing decided to use a common section with the 767, developing the two types roughly in parallel.

British Airways and Eastern Airlines became the 757 launch customers in 1978, but sales were disappointing. Boeing nevertheless pushed on and flew the first 757 on 19 February 1982. Launched, unusually for an American type, with a foreign engine, the Rolls-Royce RB211-535C turbofan, the

757 caused some surprise with the ease of its flight test programme. The aircraft entered service with Eastern on 1 January 1983, introducing electronic displays to the short/medium-haul sector. Like the 767, its cockpit was something of a hybrid of new and old, but its primary systems were EFIS-based. Established in service, the 757 began to excel and Boeing was well pleased with its efforts.

A320

While Boeing was busy with the 757, Airbus Industrie was laying plans for a new short-haul jet to challenge the 737 and MD-80. Announced at the 1981 Paris air show, the aircraft was of generally conventional configuration, but featured fly-by-wire controls for the first time on a civil aircraft. Engine choice eventually fell to the CFM International CFM56 and International Aero Engines V2500. The A320's fuselage was wider than that of the 737 and MD-80 and, surprisingly, the 757.

The first A320-100 entered service with British Airways and Air France in 1988. The A320-100 was little more than an interim machine, however, soon replaced in production by the baseline A320-200. With rather more range than was strictly necessary for short-haul operations, the -200 was an ideal short/medium-range aircraft that was also suitable for longer thin routes. The A320-200 also introduced what Airbus refers to as 'wingtip fences', auxiliary vertical surfaces extending above and below the wing tip to increase efficiency by preventing tip vortices that otherwise cause drag.

Airbus Industrie began studying A320 derivatives in 1985, the first such aircraft emerging as the A321

Specifications

Crew: 2	Service ceiling: 11,900m (39,000ft)
Passengers: 231	Dimensions: Span 38m (125ft);
Powerplant: Two 18,950kg (41,780lb) Pratt &	length 46.96m (154ft);
Whitney PW2040 engines	height 13.6m (44ft 6in)
Cruising speed: 965km/hr (600mph)	Weight: 100,000kg (220,462lb) loaded
Range: 7315km (4545 miles)	

▼ Boeing 757-200

Royal Air Maroc, 1986

Royal Air Maroc, Morocco's flag carrier, or national airline, took CN-RMT on lease in 1986. A Pratt & Whitney PW2037-powered machine, it remained with the airline in 2012.

Specifications

Crew: 2 (+ 4)	Range: 5460km (3400 miles)
Passengers: 179	Service ceiling: 12,000m (39,000ft)
Powerplant: Two 111.0kN (20,000lbf) IAE	Dimensions: Span 33.91m (111ft 3in);
V2525 or two 117.98kN (26,500lbf) CFM56	length 37.57m (123ft 3in);
turbofans	height 11.8m (38ft 8in)
Maximum speed: 960km/hr (600mph)	Weight: 73,000kg (161,000lb) loaded

▼ Airbus A320-100

British Airways, 1987

Never a supporter of Airbus in terms of orders, British Airways acquired its A320s by default, since the aircraft were already on order with British Caledonian when the national carrier took its rival over. BA was deeply impressed with the aircraft and in late 2011 its fleet included 40 A320s (with three on order), two A318s, 33 A319s and 11 A321s.

Stretch. Launched in 1989, the A321 can accommodate up to 220 passengers, compared to the 180 of the A320, which places it firmly in 757 territory. Boeing had been obliged to re-engine its 737 to compete with the A320 – the first 737-300 flying on 24 February 1984 – and now its 757 was also under threat.

With the A320 and A321 taking customers in all of Boeing's traditional stamping grounds, Airbus decided that it was time to take on the lower end of the 737 market and the replacement market for the smaller DC-9/MD-80 machines.

In June 1993, it launched the A319 'shrink', an aircraft ideally suited to loads of up to 124 passengers. Much of the A319 is the same as the A320, and the variant is blessed with usefully long range, as well as the cross-qualification that allows

crews to qualify across the A320 series without extensive retraining. The A319 flew for the first time in March 1995 and entered service with Swissair on 22 May 1996.

With A320-series airliners in production to challenge all of Boeing's line from the smallest 737-500 to the 757-200, the European manufacturer made an attempt on the regional jet market. It further shrank the basic design to produce an aircraft suitable for 107 passengers in a two-class layout. Designed for high-frequency, low-density routes, the A318 was initially blighted by serious development problems with its alternative Pratt & Whitney PW6000 engines. In its CFM56-powered form, it entered service with Air France in 2002 and its exceptional range characteristics enabled BA to begin all-business class London City–New York flights with the A318

Specifications

Crew: 2	Range: 5600km (3500 miles)
Passengers: 220	Service ceiling: 12,000m (39,000ft)
Powerplant: Two 133–147kN	Dimensions: Span 34.10m (111ft 11in);
(30,000–33,000lbf) IAE V2500 series or CFM	length 44.51m (146ft 0in);
International CFM56-5 series engines	height 11.76m (38ft 7in)
Cruising speed: 828km/hr (511mph)	Weight: 93.5t (206,000lb) loaded

▼ Airbus A321

Alitalia, 1995

I-BIXB was delivered in 1995, Alitalia being the first customer to receive A321s. The aircraft remains with the airline in 2012 as one of 23 in its fleet. In 1998, the three primary Airbus Industrie partners, Aerospatiale, CASA and DASA, merged to form the European Aeronautic Defence and Space Company, or EADS. Airbus was then 80 per cent owned by EADS and 20 per cent by BAE Systems, and the 'Industrie' part of its title was dropped.

Specifications

Crew: 2	Range: 6700km (4100 miles)
Passengers: 156	Service ceiling: 12,000m (39,000ft)
Powerplant: Two 98–120kN (22,000–27,000lbf)	Dimensions: Span 34.10m (111ft 11in);
IAE V2500 series or CFM International	length 33.84m (111ft 0in); height 11.76m
CFM56-5 series engines	(38ft 7in)
Maximum speed: 871km/hr (537mph)	Weight: 75.5t (166,000lb) loaded

▼ Airbus A319

easyJet, 2011

EasyJet represents one of the most successful of the new generation of low-cost carriers that proliferated during the 1990s. The airline has a majority Airbus fleet, which at the end of 2011 included 142 A319s, with 13 on order.

Specifications

Crew: 2

Passengers: 189

Powerplant: Two 116.5kN (26,200lbf) CFM
  International CFM56-7B turbofan engines

Maximum speed: 876km/hr (544mph)

Range: 5665km (3520 miles)

Service ceiling: 12,500m (41,000ft)

Dimensions: Span 35.7m (117ft 5in);
  length 39.5m (129ft 6in);
  height 12.5m (41ft 2in)

Weight: 79,010kg (174,200lb) loaded

TUIfly, 2010

The merger of Hapag-Lloyd Express and Hapagfly formed TUIfly in 2007, to serve the needs of the TUI tour company. The airline flies only the 737-700 and -800, with 10 and 29 examples, respectively, in service late in 2011.

Boeing 737 Next Generation variants

Model	Notes	Number ordered (February 2012)
737-600	132-seat airliner; CFM International CFM56-7 turbofan engines	69 (last delivery 2006)
737-700	Stretched fuselage; 149 passengers; CFM56-7 engines; also available in Extended Range and Convertible versions	1397
737-800	Stretched fuselage; 189 passengers; CFM56-7 engines	4001
737-900	Stretched fuselage; 220 passengers; CFM56-7 engines	52
737-900ER	Stretched fuselage; 220 passengers; Extended Range; CFM56-7 engines	446

in 2009. Unfortunately for Airbus, A318 sales have been disappointing, but by March 2012 the manufacturer had taken 8380 orders for A320-series aircraft, with 5051 delivered.

Next Generation 737

Airbus was able to continuously improve its A320 range and while the CFM-engined Boeing 737s remained competitive, the airlines began to see real advantages in the Airbus types as the 1990s wore on. While there was still very little fundamentally wrong with the 737, it needed to offer higher levels of technology, a more aerodynamically efficient airframe and lower fuel burn if it was to continue competing effectively.

Boeing addressed its requirements by hanging the established 737 fuselage lengths between newly designed wings. The wings carried the latest CFM56-7 engines with full-authority digital engine control (FADEC) for optimum fuel efficiency. After some structural issues had been overcome, they also mounted elegant winglets. The passenger cabin was redesigned using cues from the 777, and the EFIS flight deck was designed for cross-qualification as well as retaining similarity with that of the previous generation 737. The first of what became the 737

New Generation, or 737NG, aircraft, a 737-700. It flew for the first time on 9 February 1997.

Overnight, all previous 737s became 'Classic' aircraft. Southwest took first NG delivery, in December 1997, and Boeing has subsequently gone on to develop a range of 737NGs, generally in keeping with the capacities of the Classic aircraft, but also introducing the stretched 737-900 and Extended Range 737-900ER.

The baseline 737-700 seats a maximum 149 passengers, the 737-800 up to 189, the 737-600 up to 132 and the -900 up to 189 in more spacious accommodation limited by emergency exit requirements. In two classes, the -900 aircraft seat 177 passengers, compared to the 162 of the -800 in a similar configuration. Like Airbus, Boeing created a generation of high-technology airlines covering all the traditional 737 passenger capacities and encroaching into the market that previously belonged to the 757. Also like Airbus, Boeing has seen very disappointing sales of the smallest member of its short/medium-haul airliner family, the 737-600 having sold just 69 copies by March 2012 compared to 4047 737-800s. Total 737 sales by March 2012 were 9788, making the 737 by far the world's the bestselling airliner.

Chapter 6

Twenty-first Century Developments (1988–2017)

The driving factors of the most recent airliner developments have been communications and cockpit technologies, structural techniques and materials and, perhaps most importantly, the vital necessity to reduce fuel burn and minimize the environmental impact of air travel. Airbus and Boeing followed very different strategies for their new airliner development plans, initially addressing different markets, before aligning themselves for renewed competition. Elsewhere, the Chinese ARJ21 and the Russian Superjet perhaps ushered in a new era in airliner manufacturing, while Bombardier's CSeries and Mitsubishi's MRJ are setting the standard for the regional jets of the future.

◀ **Airbus A350**

Airbus has always been a multinational concern, with components and subassemblies for its aircraft being built at widely dispersed sites. The first A350 forward fuselage section was delivered to the assembly line at St Nazaire, France, from the company's facility at Hamburg, Germany, on 23 December 2011. Final assembly of the first aircraft began in April 2012.

Boeing pushes on
2003–2017

Boeing struggled to bring the revolutionary 787 Dreamliner to service, but such trials are to be expected when a manufacturer pushes airframe and aeroengine technology to its limits. Its product line for the twenty-first century also includes the 747-8 and 737 MAX.

DURING THE LATE 1980s, and through the 1990s, Boeing and Airbus expressed very different philosophies in airliner development. Boeing believed that the future of air travel lay in large fleets of medium-capacity aircraft capable of covering medium- to long-haul routes at high speed and great efficiency. It proposed that such aircraft would provide 'point-to-point' services, eliminating connecting flights and some regional travel.

Airbus was of a contrary opinion. It saw a need for an airliner much larger even than the 747-400, to satisfy the growing demand for air travel, especially in the Middle East and Asia-Pacific regions. Boeing offered the Sonic Cruiser as its answer to these future requirements, while Airbus created the A380. Discouraged by airline reaction to the Sonic Cruiser, Boeing turned to a new design that would revolutionize large aircraft structures, introduce a new concept in powerplant and power systems, and offer a step change in economy.

Dreamliner

Launched on 16 December 2003, the 7E7 was described as being constructed primarily from composites. It would be powered by a new generation of engines, powering aircraft systems through electrical generation rather than the high-pressure bleed air normally used, for considerable fuel savings. In another first for Boeing, the aircraft would be produced in subassemblies by a global supplier network, for final assembly in the United States. Maturing as the 787 Dreamliner, the design was ambitious, groundbreaking and, as it turned out, fraught with risk. It was initially to be built in 223-seat 787-8 and 259-seat 787-9 variants.

Boeing struggled with its supply chain, even going to the extreme of buying some of its subcontractors so that it could ensure the quality and timeliness of their work. First flight was delayed time and again, but after major remedial structural work, the first 787 finally became airborne in December 2010, powered by Roll-Royce Trent 1000 engines. As test airframes continued to fly, the first General Electric GEnx-1B powered machine flew in July 2010, but then an inflight fire caused further delays. Boeing was finally able to deliver its first customer 787-8 to ANA late in 2011, albeit a slightly inferior aircraft as the company works to meet all of its range promises.

747-8

Boeing belatedly decided to enter the market for a high-tech,

Specifications

Crew: 2	Service ceiling: 13,000m (43,000ft)
Passengers: 467 (three-class confifuration)	Dimensions: span 68.45m (224ft 7in);
Powerplant: 4 x GEnx-2B67 296kN (66,500lbbf)	length 76.25m (250ft 2in); height 19.35m
Maximum speed: 917km/hr (570mph)	(63ft 6in)
Range: 4390km (5050 miles)	Weight: 340kg (757,000lb) loaded

▲ **Boeing 747-8**

Lufthansa, 2012

Lufthansa was the first customer for the 747-8I, or now simply 747-8, passenger version of the latest 747. The carrier's aircraft will be configured for 386 passengers in three classes.

◀ Boeing 737 MAX

In keeping with the nomenclature established for the 787, the 737 MAX will be offered in 737-7, 737-8 and 737-9 variants. The aircraft will feature the noise-reducing scalloped engine nacelle trailing edges of the 787 and 747-8.

▲ Boeing 787 Dreamliner

The Dreamliner has not been in service long enough for any real appraisal of its performance to be made, although Boeing admitted that the initial aircraft would fall short of the promised 14,825km (8000-nautical mile) range. Boeing had 851 Dreamliner orders on its books in March 2012.

high-capacity airliner, announcing a major redevelopment of the 747-400 as the 747-8 in 2004. With a stretched fuselage and revised wings, featuring the raked wing tips of the advanced 777 variants, the aircraft would be powered by GEnx-2B67 turbofans and available in 747-8I (Intercontinental) and 747-8F (Freighter) versions.

Forging ahead against the backdrop of disappointing orders, Boeing overcame unforeseen problems with the 747-8 to fly the first -8F in February 2010. Cargolux became the first 747-8 operator in October 2011, while Lufthansa was preparing to become the type's first passenger operator in April 2012.

737 MAX

Having invested hugely in the 787/747-8 and A380 programmes, respectively, neither Boeing nor Airbus had the stomach for designing a new single-aisle narrowbody to replace the world's 737 and A320 fleets. However, under intense pressure from the airlines, Airbus announced its re-engined A320neo in December 2010 and Boeing was eventually forced to respond.

Boeing's 737 MAX combines the CFM LEAP-B engine with an aerodynamically refined wing and other improvements, to offer an 18 per cent reduction in fuel burn compared to the most efficient single-aisle in service today. It will be available for service from 2017.

Airbus steals a march
1988–2015

Airbus proceeded with its A380 'super jumbo', but then had to abandon plans for an upgraded A330 and design the all-new A350 XWB to compete with Boeing's Dreamliner.

AIRBUS HAD ADDRESED the medium- and short-haul markets by the late 1980s and work was in progress on a new long-range airliner, but it had never challenged Boeing's monopoly of the very large airliner market. In 1988 it therefore began examining the possibilities for a high-capacity machine and in 1994 these possibilities were transformed into detailed planning for a future A3XX.

Work continued so that Airbus was able to launch the new type on 19 December 2000, as the A380. With double-deck cabins, it was immediately stunning and the scope of Airbus's ambition was further revealed when details of the aircraft's advanced part-composite construction and modular avionics systems were revealed. It was also clear that the new aircraft would help fuel a revolution in inflight entertainment (IFE) facilities, as Airbus set about creating exciting cabin concepts for the leviathan.

The first A380, a Rolls-Royce Trent-powered machine, flew on 18 January 2005, followed by the first Engine Alliance GP7000-engined aircraft on 25 August 2006. Airbus was able to deliver the first production aircraft to Singapore Airlines on 27 October 2007, but was struggling to build the A380 at anything like the rates it had promised.

Expensive and time-consuming changes had to be implemented, not only to the production line, but also to the company's management structure. Eventually, Airbus was able to bring the A380's weight issues and problems with its wing wiring looms under control, and by 2011 it was able to begin approaching the production rates it had hoped for from the outset.

The A380 has suffered continuing bad publicity with an inflight engine failure on a Qantas aircraft, plus a series of minor cracks in wing structural members, but by April 2012 fixes for all the aircraft's issues were in hand. In general, the airlines and their passengers are extremely happy with the A380.

A350 XWB

With the majority of its design effort focused on the A380, Airbus was content to allow an upgraded A330, designated A350, to compete with Boeing's promised 787. When it presented the new machine

▲ **Airbus A380**

Singapore Airlines, 27 October 2007

Singapore Airlines began A380 operations in 2007, attracting worldwide media interest. The carrier chose Rolls-Royce Trent 970 engines for its fleet and has been affected by the international directives concerning both these engines and the aircraft's wing structure.

Specifications

Crew (cockpit): 2

Passengers: 644 (two-class configuration)

Powerplant: 4 x Trent 970/B 310kN (70,000lbf)

Maximum speed: 945km/h (587mph)

Range: 15,400km (9500 miles)

Service ceiling: 13,115m (43,028ft)

Dimensions: span 79.75m (261ft 7in);
length 72.73m (238ft 7in); height 24.45m (80ft 3in)

Weight: 386,000kg (850,000lb) loaded

▲ **Airbus A350 XWB**

In March 2012, Airbus had 555 orders for the A350 XWB, with customers eagerly awaiting progress, since the airframer was forced to push its development schedule back in 2011. The initial A350-800 will seat up to 250 passengers.

to the airlines, however, their reaction was lukewarm at best. Airbus was therefore forced to go back to the drawing board, ultimately arriving at the A350 XWB – Extra Wide Body. Offering a little more cabin width than the 787, the new A350 uses a majority of composites in its structure, and it will seat between 270 and 350 passengers in three variants.

Powered by the Rolls-Royce Trent XWB engine, the A350 XWB has suffered delays, but should achieve first flight in the 2013–14 timeframe, with deliveries from 2014–15 onwards. The first airframe entered assembly for static test in 2012, with assembly of the first flying A350 XWB scheduled to begin in summer 2012.

A320 range

Airbus finally bowed to pressure from the airlines and major leasing outfits for an improvement in A320 efficiency late in 2010. The 'neo' improvements will be applied across the A320/A321/A319 range, and principal among them is the option of two new-generation powerplants. CFM has been chosen to supply its LEAP-X derivation of the CFM56, while Pratt &Whitney is offering its PW1100G PurePower geared turbofan. The aircraft will also dispense with the traditional wing tip fences, replacing them with tall winglets, which Airbus refers to as 'sharklets'.

Airbus claims a 15 per cent reduction in fuel burn for the A320neo over the current-build aircraft and aims to deliver the first neo in 2015.

Worldwide challengers
2005–2016

Bombardier has been joined by a handful of new companies in the race to produce not only the next generation of regional jet, but also a new breed of mainline aircraft.

THE 2000S SAW THE EMERGENCE of several new airliner designs. With the exception of Bombardier, none of the manufacturers involved would have readily sprung to mind as builders of jet airliners, and industry opinion remains divided on whether all or any of them will survive long enough to achieve commercial success.

Sukhoi Superjet

Sukhoi took the brave step not only of entering into an unfamiliar market, but also of introducing a new engine on its new aircraft. The company came to an agreement with Italy's Alenia Aermacchi to help it avoid the lack of international marketing expertise, customer service and maintenance facilities that have traditionally afflicted Russian airliner designs. It also chose a Russo-Italian engine, the SaM146 turbofan, developed by the Snecma/Saturn PowerJet consortium to power the 98-seat aircraft.

The first Sukhoi Superjet 100 (SSJ100) completed its maiden flight on 19 May 2008 and although the test schedule suffered delays, the first production aircraft entered service with Armavia early in 2011, with Aeroflot receiving its first aircraft in June that year.

Russia's Irkut is also working on a new airliner design, its MS-21 taking its first orders in 2010 and being firmly aimed at the Tu-154/Tu-204 and 737/A320 replacement markets. The popular PW1000G engine has been chosen to power the design and a number of Western contractors selected to provide systems and equipment. First flight is tentatively scheduled for 2014, with customer deliveries pushed back from 2016 to 2017.

COMAC ARJ21

The Commercial Aircraft Corporation of China flew its first ARJ21 prototype on 28 November 2008. Already delayed, the programme then suffered further problems and a particularly difficult 2011. The certification effort was continued into 2012. Some industry commentators have suggested that the ARJ21 is little more than a modernized MD-80, based on airframe technology acquired when the American type was built under licence in China, but the proliferation of modern

▲ **Bombardier CSeries**

In 2009 Lease Corporation International (LCI) ordered three CS100 and 17 CS300 jets, worth US$1.44 billion. The aircraft will operate in lessor liveries, rather than the LCI colours of this computer-generated image. Like the 787 and A350, the CSeries makes extensive use of composites in its airframe.

◄ COMAC ARJ21

COMAC continued to struggle with the ARJ21 into 2012, but was quoting a much delayed and revised certification date of later in the year. Meanwhile, at least one respected industry commentator has suggested that, delays aside, the ARJ21 is seriously overweight and will be unable to operate economically.

systems and the aircraft's CF34 engines show how far the 90-seat aircraft has progressed. COMAC is also investing heavily in the C919 'trunk liner', a 168-seat mainline aircraft that the company sees as a challenger to the A320neo and 737 MAX. It will be powered by LEAP-X1C engines and make extensive use of Western systems. Bombardier has announced that it is working closely with COMAC on the C919 and some systems and technologies are being co-developed for the CSeries. First flight has been scheduled for around 2014, with first deliveries in 2016, but given the delays suffered by the rather less ambitious ARJ21, these dates must be seen as optimistic.

Mitsubishi Regional Jet

Mitsubishi chose the PW1000G PurePower engine for its regional jet, which adheres to the 'new' regional jet formula of mounting its engines underwing. The aircraft is designed to carry between 70 and 90 passengers in some comfort, with great efficiency and with minimal emissions. Marketing efforts for the MRJ began in 2007 and the company soon began

amassing orders. However, the type's first flight, which had been scheduled for April 2012, was postponed early that month to an unconfirmed future date, while at least one industry expert has suggested that the programme has 'stalled'.

Bombardier CSeries

Bombardier's CRJ struggled in the regional jet market as soon as Embraer launched its EJets and in 2005 the Canadian company began offering its CSeries to the airlines. It then abandoned the project for lack of a suitable powerplant. Pratt & Whitney came to its rescue with the PW1500G geared turbofan, however, and in 2008 the programme was relaunched. Orders have been slow to materialize and some pundits remain convinced that the 100-seat CS100 and 130-seat CS300, plus planned larger derivatives, will be unable to compete against the A320neo and 737 MAX models. First flight is planned for late 2012 to early 2013, with service entry late in 2013.

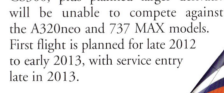

Specifications	
Crew: 2	Service ceiling: 12,500m (41,000ft)
Passengers: 68 (two-class, standard)	Dimensions: span 27.80m (91ft 2in);
Powerplant: PowerJet SaM146 69kN (15,400lbf)	length 26.44m (86ft 9in); height 10.28m
Maximum speed: 870km/hr (541mph)	(33ft 9in)
Range: 4550km (2830 miles)	Weight: 35,000kg (77,000lb) loaded

▲ Sukhoi Superjet 100

Aeroflot, 2012

Sukhoi has made great progress with the Superjet 100 and the type appears to be working well in Armavia and Aeroflot service. However, the manufacturer has still to break into the mainstream Western market – an essential step if the programme is to be commercially successful.

Chapter 7

General Aviation (1924–Present)

General aviation is a perhaps the aerospace section most familiar to the public at large, even though very few people are aware of the categorization. Light aircraft, used for club training, touring or simply pleasure flying, are the cornerstone of the general aviation world, but larger utility aircraft also fall into the category. The world's large fleet of piston, turboprop and jet business aircraft is perhaps the most glamorous sector of general aviation, while aerobatic and competition flying are its most exciting.

◀ **Beechcraft 400**

The Beech 400 typifies the international nature of general aviation and the typical business jet configuration. The design originated in Japan as the Mitsubishi Diamond, with airframes finished in the United States. In 1983, Beech bought full rights to the design and began building it as the Model 400.

Inter-war lightplanes
1925–2012

Barnstorming and joyriding brought aviation to a wide audience and soon private pilots began demanding light aircraft designed for leisure, touring and training purposes.

IN THE YEARS immediately after World War I, there were surplus military trainers to be had at minimal cost and plenty of enthusiastic, young and recently demobbed pilots to fly them. The larger and more capable machines were favoured by the airlines, but aircraft like the Avro 504 were generally suitable only for a pilot and passenger.

Such machines quickly became a foundation of the barnstorming and joyriding scene, where a pilot, or group of pilots, would land in a suitable field close to a town and set up shop. Barnstorming displays of aerobatics and daring manoeuvres were put on, while adventurous members of the public could pay for a short joyride. So general aviation (GA) was established in the UK and elsewhere, but especially in the United States, a nation soon to become the world's GA heartland.

de Havilland's Moths
Regardless of the military surplus, some more wealthy individuals began looking for light aircraft for their own leisure and touring purposes. Geoffrey de Havilland realized the potential for civil aviation very early on and

after the failure of a 1923 *Daily Mail*-sponsored competition to find an aircraft affordable 'by the man in the street', de Havilland set about designing a rather more capable machine than the low-powered ultralights inspired by the *Daily Mail*. The result was the DH.60 Moth, flown for the first time on 22 February 1925.

Although it was by no means generally affordable, the DH.60 was chosen to equip five government-sponsored flying clubs, and civilian flying became a reality. De Havilland developed the Moth through several variants, but most famously as the DH.60G, chosen by Amy Johnson, among others, for record-breaking long-distance flights. The association with these adventurers did de Havilland no harm at all and it continued building light aircraft for training and touring right up to the outbreak of World War II.

The de Havilland DH.75 Hawk Moth of 1928 was the first of the company's monoplane cabin tourers, which culminated in the DH.85 Leopard Moth of 1933, while the DH.83 Fox Moth (1932) and DH.87 Hornet Moth (1934) were its ultimate cabin biplanes.

▲ **Avro 504K**

The Cornwall Aviation Company Ltd, 1924

This 504K joined The Cornwall Aviation Company on joyriding duties in 1924. The company had five Avro 504Ks and was co-owned by the proprietor of a St Austell garage, where the aircraft were maintained. G-EBIZ remained on the UK civil register until 1935.

Specifications

Crew: 2

Powerplant: One 82kW (110hp) Le Rhône Rotary engine

Maximum speed: 145km/hr (90mph)

Range: 402km (250 miles)

Service ceiling: 4875m (16,000ft)

Dimensions: Span 10.97m (36ft); length 8.97m (29ft 5in); height 3.17m (10ft 5in)

Weight: 830kg (1829lb)

▲ **De Havilland DH.60 Moth**

1925–present

Built in 1925, G-EBLV is powered by an ADC Cirrus III engine. It was the installation of de Havilland's own Gipsy engine, beginning with the DH.60G in 1928 that made the Moth so successful, although this machine remains airworthy with the Shuttleworth Collection, under BAE Systems ownership.

Specifications

Crew: 1	Service ceiling: 3965m (13,000ft)
Passenger: 1	Dimensions: Span 8.84m (29ft);
Powerplant: One 44.7kW (60hp) ADC Cirrus I	length 7.16m (23ft 6in);
engine	height 2.68m (8ft 7in)
Cruising speed: 137km/h (85mph)	Weight: 611kg (1350lb) loaded
Range: 515km (320 miles)	

▲ **Focke-Wulf A 43 Falke**

Norddeutsche Luftverkehr, 1930s

The A 43 was a wood and fabric monoplane three-seater designed in 1931. General aviation, especially gliding, but also powered sport flying, was crucial to Germany's covert inter-war policy of nurturing a generation of young and idealistic pilots.

Specifications

Crew: 1	Service ceiling: 16,730ft (5100m)
Passengers: 2	Dimensions: Span 10.00m (32ft 10in);
Powerplant: One 164kW (200hp) Argus As 10	length 8.30m (27ft 3in);
engine	height 2.30m (7ft 7in)
Maximum speed: 255km/h (158mph)	Weight: 1125kg (2480lb) loaded
Range: 1050km (652 miles)	

Other Contenders

With the huge success of the de Havilland Moths, there was little space left on the UK market for other manufacturers, although Avro made a bold attempt with its Avian biplane, which was built in considerable numbers. Percival addressed the needs of customers wanting higher performance or wishing to enter air racing competitions, producing a series of related monoplanes in its Gull series, which was completed by the diminutive Mew Gull.

Meanwhile, manufacturers across Europe also made attempts at entering the lightplane market, including Focke-Wulf with its Falke, the Belgian Stampe concern with its excellent biplane trainers, and Poland's RWD, which developed a series of outstanding designs.

As the market recovered from the initial glut of war surplus types, light aircraft manufacturers also began operating in the United States. Throughout the inter-war period, several notable companies, including Bellanca, Cessna, Curtiss, Luscombe and Taylorcraft, all manufactured light aircraft, with Taylorcraft's Cub being developed into the legendary Piper Cub.

▲ **de Havilland DH.85 Leopard Moth**

1946–present

G-AIYS joined the UK civil register in December 1946 and remained airworthy in private hands in 2012. Testament to the utility and longevity of de Havilland's tourers, it also represents the many inter-war lightplanes and trainers still enjoyed on a regular basis by general aviation pilots the world over.

Specifications

Crew: 1	Service ceiling: 6557m (21,500ft)
Passengers: 2	Dimensions: Span 11.43m (37ft 6in);
Powerplant: One 97kW (130hp) de Havilland	length 7.47m (24ft 6in); height 2.66m
Gipsy Major	(8ft 9in)
Maximum speed: 191km/h (119mph)	Weight: 1008kg (2222lb) loaded

Specifications

Crew: 1	Service ceiling: 4145m (13,600ft)
Passengers: 1	Dimensions: Span 8.94m (29ft 4in);
Powerplant: One 96.9kW (130hp) de Havilland	length 7.29m (23ft 11in);
Gipsy Major I in-line engine	height 2.69m (8ft 10in)
Cruising speed: 145km/hr (90mph)	Weight: 828kg (1825lb) loaded
Range: n/a	

▲ **de Havilland DH.87 Hornet Moth**

1938

Perhaps the ultimate expression of the de Havilland tourer, the Hornet Moth became popular not only with private pilots but also as a club and executive transport aircraft. De Havilland Canada built 11 DH.87s, designing a seaplane undercarriage for the type using Fairchild floats.

Cessna domination
1928–2012

From humble origins, Cessna has come to dominate the general aviation market, with aircraft ranging from the Model 162 two-seat piston trainer to the transonic Citation Ten bizjet.

KANSAS FARMER CLYDE V CESSNA bought a Blériot-type monoplane in February 1911. By June he had crashed and rebuilt his aircraft several times, but had also taught himself how to fly. Cessna began exhibition flying in the summer months, before moving to Kansas in 1916 and taking space in the facilities of the Jones Motor Car Company, in exchange for carrying the firm's advertising on his aircraft. In his new facilities Cessna built another Blériot-type machine, plus the semi-enclosed 'Comet' of his own design and another 12 aircraft of various forms. The 'Comet' took the US speed record in July 1917, at 200.5km/h (124.6mph), but when the United States entered World War I, Cessna temporarily returned to farming.

In February 1925 he was invited to become president of the Travel Air Manufacturing Company by Walter Beech and Lloyd Stearman, both men to become giants of the general aviation and training worlds. They believed that the biplane was the key to future success, while Clyde Cessna's faith was in the monoplane. He left Travel Air in 1926, establishing the Cessna-Roos Aircraft Company with Victor Roos in September 1927. Roos departed in December and Cessna continued alone with his Cessna Aircraft Company Inc.

Into Production
The new company's first design, the Model A, was an enclosed four-seat, high-wing monoplane. At a stroke, Cessna had fallen upon the basic configuration that would ensure the future of his company. Several variants of the Model A taildragger were built, even as Cessna was working on the six-seat CW-6. First flown in November 1928, the CW-6 was basically similar to the Model A, but Cessna abandoned the design in favour of a four-seat derivative powered by a Curtiss engine. Curtiss had

offered to become a sales agent for the aircraft in this configuration, but in the event its performance was disappointing and the onset of the Depression saw to it that sales were limited.

As the 1930s' financial depression eased, production switched to the Model C. Basically similar to the Model A, the new model was considerably more advanced and refined. It flew for the first time in June 1935 and some 42 of the baseline model were built, before many more Model Cs were delivered to the US military in several variants.

Once again, however, Cessna's ambitions were thwarted by war, but this time the company was well positioned to make the most of the manufacturing opportunity that conflict offered, building in excess of 3000 examples of its twin-engined T-50 trainer and utility aircraft.

Post-War Models
On 28 June 1945, Cessna flew the prototype of its Model 120. A thoroughly modern design, albeit with

▼ **Reims Cessna F172F Skyhawk**

Cessna not only managed to produce a product accepted globally for its excellence, it also exploited local markets to the full, appointing manufacturers to build its models locally. In some cases these makers introduced their own variants and in all cases they allowed Cessna to optimize its products. This aircraft was built in France by Reims, as an F172. The Skyhawk name has been applied to various 172 models over the years, but is now Cessna's preferred designation for the type.

Specifications

Crew: 1 + 1

Powerplant: One 74.6kW (100hp) Continental
O-200A 4-cylinder air-cooled engine

Maximum speed: 188km/hr (117mph)

Range: 767km (475 miles)

Service ceiling: 3850m (12,630ft)

Dimensions: Span 9.97m (32ft 8in);
length 7.01m (23ft); height 2.77m (9ft 1in)

Weight: 726kg (1600lb) loaded

▼ Cessna 150

Late 1950s

This aircraft shows the original Model 150 configuration, with unswept fin and high-backed rear fuselage. Later the fuselage was 'cut down', with Cessna's Omnivision rear window installed in the aft cabin to improve the view upwards and to the rear.

Specifications

Crew: 1

Passengers: 5

Powerplant: One 213kW (285hp) Continental
IO-520-A 6-cylinder air-cooled engines

Maximum speed: 303km/h (188mph)

Range: 2011km (1250 miles)

Service ceiling: 4724m (15,500ft)

Dimensions: Span 11.20m (36ft 9in);
length 8.61m (28ft 3in);
height 2.95m (9ft 8in)

Weight: 1723kg (3800lb) loaded

▼ Cessna C210 Centurion

Mid-1960s

The Model C210 began as a retractable-undercarriage version of the Model 182, flying for the first time on 25 February 1957. A swept fin was added to the six-seat design before production began and, in Cessna's usual practice, it was then developed through multiple variants with revised equipment, avionics, powerplant and even annual variations in cabin trim and finish.

Specifications

Crew: 1

Passengers: 3

Powerplant: One 213kW (300hp) Continental
IO-520-D 6-cylinder air-cooled engine

Cruising speed: 272km/hr (169mph)

Range: 1384km (860 miles)

Service ceiling: 5229m (17,150ft)

Dimensions: Span 11.02m (36ft 2in);
length 7.85m (25ft 9in);
height 2.36m (7ft 9in)

Weight: 1519kg (3350lb) loaded

▼ Cessna 185 Skywagon

Cessna, 1960s

The Model 180 of 1972 added a new fuselage to all-metal Model 170 wings, creating a rugged six-seat utility aircraft. The strengthened Model 185 was aimed squarely at the 'bushplane' market and featured a large fin fillet for directional stability when operating on floats. This aircraft has an underfuselage Cargo-Pack pannier.

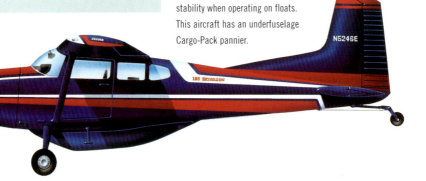

Post-war Cessna piston singles

Model	First flown	Description; original powerplant	Number built (all versions)
120		Economy version of 140; Continental C-85-12 piston engine	2172
140	28 June 1945	Two-seat tourer; Continental C-85-12 engine	4432
150	12 September 1957	Two-seat trainer; Continental O-200A piston engine	23,938
152	16 July 1976	Improved 150; Lycoming O-235-L2C piston engine	7584
162 Skycatcher	13 October 2006	Two-seat trainer; Teledyne Continental O-200-D piston engine	100 by September 2011; in production
170	5 November 1947	Four-seat tourer; Continental C-145 piston engine	7174
172	12 June 1955	Improved 170 with tricycle undercarriage; Continental O-300-C piston engine	More than 43,000 for civil and military customers; Skyhawk and Skyhawk SP in production
175	23 April 1956	More powerful 172; Continental GO-300-A engine	2118
177	15 July 1966	Re-engined, improved 172; Lycoming O-320-E2D piston engine	4294
180	26 May 1952	Improved 170; Continental O-470-A piston engine	6193
182		180 with tricycle undercarriage; O-470-R engine	More than 23,237 for civil and military customers; Skylane and Turbo Skylane in production
185	19 February 1965	Strengthened, six-seat/utility 180 with tricycle undercarriage; Continental IO-470-F engine	3978
188		Agricultural aircraft; Continental O-470-R engine	1528
190	7 December 1945	Five-seat tourer; Continental W670-23 piston engine	1083
195		More powerful 190; Jacobs R755-A-2 radial piston engine	100 for civil and military customers
205		Six-seat 210 with fixed tricycle undercarriage; Continental IO-470-S engine	577
206		More powerful 205; Continental IO-520-A piston engine	More than 8697; Stationair and Turbo Stationair in production
207		Stretched, seven-seat 206; IO-520-F engine	788
210	January 1950	Re-engined, re-designed 195; IO-470-E engine	9337
400 Corvalis	2004	Low-wing tourer acquired from Columbia Aircraft in 2007; Teledyne Continental TSIO-550-C piston engine	More than 180; Corvalis TTX in production

a wood and fabric wing and tailwheel undercarriage, the 120 managed to compete against large numbers of surplus military lightplanes to firmly establish the manufacturer. The Model 140 'de luxe' version also sold well and Cessna remained faithful to the four-seat configuration when it flew the Model 170 for the first time in November 1947. The 170's aluminium wing was fabric-covered, but the 170A of 1949 introduced an all-metal wing to the range.

Cessna's future success with piston singles owed much to the clean lines made possible by its faith in the inline engine layout, but it deviated from this theme with the Model 190/195 series. Powered by radial engines and first flown in Model 190 form on 7 December 1945, these aircraft were four/five-seat tourers. Built in considerable numbers, they introduced Cessna's distinctive spring-steel main undercarriage leg arrangement. The Model 170 and derivatives took their place in the range.

The Model 170 was further refined as the Model 170C of January 1955, which introduced a tricycle undercarriage to the Cessna range and led immediately to a Model 172 prototype. The latter has continued in production and, in terms of numbers built, dominates this sector of the market. In 1957, Cessna returned to the two-seat formula of the 120, this time applying it to the all-metal tricycle undercarriage Model 150. It had established another cornerstone of its range.

Subsequent production has centred around building new designs based on the sound basic principles of the 172/150. The 172 has evolved into a superb tourer, most recently with a Garmin G1000 EFIS cockpit and optional diesel engines. The Model 162 Skycatcher continues the legacy of the Model 150, and related 152, while Cessna has even managed to expand on the high-wing, single-engine theme to produce a powerful turboprop utility aircraft.

The PT6A-powered Cessna Caravan, Caravan Amphibian, Grand Caravan and Cargomaster have in many ways become the modern replacement for the de Havilland Beaver and Otter, but with considerable sophistication, making them suitable for commuter and business travel applications. The Caravan has also found considerable favour with the military, as a training, utility, special missions and attack aircraft.

Cessna was also able to use its single-engined business as the springboard to an extensive range of highly successful piston twins and internationally recognized business jets.

Specifications

Crew: 2	Service ceiling: 4480m (14,700ft)
Powerplant: One 82kW (110hp) Lycoming	Dimensions: Span 10.2m (33ft 4in);
0-235-L2C flat-4 engine	length 7.3m (24ft 1in);
Maximum speed: 204km/hr (126mph)	height 2.6m (8ft 6in)
Range: 7680km (477 miles)	Weight: 757kg (1670lb) loaded

▲ **Reims Cessna FA152 delivered 1977**

Denham Flight Training School, 1977

Based on the Model 150, the A152 was optimized for aerobatic training, with full three-point harnesses, rather than conventional seat belts, skylights in the cabin roof and other modifications. The Reims-built machines were designated FA152. The configuration of this machine makes an interesting comparison with the early Model 150.

▲ **Cessna 162 Skycatcher**

Cessna, 2008

Cessna designed the Skycatcher to suit the US Federal Aviation Administration's new Light Sport Aircraft (LSA) classification. Having launched the programme in 2007, Cessna struggled with the aircraft during flight testing but was able to deliver the first production machine in 2009. The aircraft is built for Cessna by Shenyang in China.

Specifications

Crew: 1	Service ceiling: 47270m (15,500ft)
Passengers: 1	Dimensions: Span 9.14m (30.0ft);
Powerplant: One 74.6kW (100hp) Continental	length 6.95m (22.8ft);
0-200D flat-four engine	height 2.53m (8.53ft)
Maximum speed: 218km/hr (136mph)	Weight: 598.7kg (1320lb) loaded
Range: 870km (541 miles)	

North American diversity
1922–2012

North America has always been fertile ground for the leisure and business lightplane operator. Several manufacturers have addressed the market, with today's pilots served by a selection of traditional companies and one or two newcomers.

SINCE THE EARLIEST DAYS days of general aviation in North America, several aircraft manufacturers have come and gone. Among those that thrived, the most famous names include Grumman American, Spartan, Stinson and Travel Air. All of these companies achieved some degree of success: Spartan, Stinson and Travel Air all achieving their measure of fame in the inter-war period, while Grumman America built a series of low-wing monoplane tourers post-war. Beech, Maule, Mooney and Piper have become firmly entrenched alongside Cessna as the mass providers of aircraft for the GA market, while in recent years two new North American organizations have successfully brought lines of modern piston aircraft into production.

Beechcraft
Beech, variously also known as Beechcraft and today part of Raytheon's Hawker Beechcraft, owes its origins to Walter and Olive Beech, a husband and wife team who established Beech Aircraft Co at Wichita, Kansas, literally just down the road from Clyde Cessna, in April 1932. Like Cessna, Beech had come from Travel Air, but unlike his colleague, Beech was determined to follow the biplane formula. His Beech 17 Staggerwing was a truly beautiful design, but his only biplane and only piston single until the first example of the unorthodox V-tailed Bonanza was flown in 1946. On the basis of modified versions of the Bonanza and a series of other designs, the Beech dynasty was founded.

Maule and Mooney
Belford D. Maule flew his first aircraft in 1957 and began aircraft production in 1962. Always renowned for its high-performance tail draggers, Maule celebrated its 50th anniversary in March 2012 by

Piper piston singles			
Model	First flown	Description; original powerplant	Number built (all versions)
J-3 Cub to 1937 PA-20 Pacer		Two-seat tourer; Continental A-65 piston engine	38,222 for civil and military customers
PA-22 Tri Pacer		PA-20 with tricycle undercarriage; Lycoming O-290-D piston engine	9490
PA-24 Commanche	24 May 1956	Four-seat, low-wing tourer with retractable undercarriage; Lycoming O-360-A1A piston engine	4867
PA-25 Pawnee PA-28 Cherokee, Warrior, Challenger, Archer, Pathfinder,		Agricultural aircraft; Lycoming O-320-A1A piston engine	5169
Dakota and Arrow	10 January 1960	Four-seat, low-wing tourer with fixed undercarriage; O-320-A2B engine	More than 32,700; Arrow, Archer LX, Archer TX and Warrior III in production
PA-32 Cherokee Six and Saratoga	6 December 1963	Stretched six-seat PA-28; Lycoming O-540 piston engine	4409
PA-36 Pawnee Brave	5 December 1969	Improved Pawnee; Continental Tiara 285 piston engine	938
PA-38 Tomahawk		Two-seat trainer; Lycoming O-235-L2C piston engine	2519
PA-46 Matrix	2007	Six-seat tourer/business aircraft; Lycoming TIO-540-AE2A piston engine	In production

Specifications

Crew: 1

Passengers: 5

Powerplant: One 220kW (300hp) Continental
IO-550-B engine

Cruising speed: 326km/hr (203mph)

Range: 409km (254 miles)

Service ceiling: 5443m (17,858ft)

Dimensions: Span 10.21m (33ft 6in);
length 8.38m (27ft 6in);
height 2.62m (8ft 7in)

Weight: 1542kg (3400lb) loaded

▲ Beech V35B Bonanza

1982–present

Introduced in 1970, the V35B Bonanza retained the V-tail of the original Model 35, although Beech always struggled to overcome pilots' suspicion of the arrangement and built several variants with conventional tails. N35YR remained in service in 2012, while today's Beechcraft Bonanza G36 is a direct descendent of the 1946 V-tailed prototype.

Specifications

Crew: 2

Powerplant: One 83.5kW (112hp) Avco
Lycoming O-235-L2C air-cooled flat-four
piston engine

Maximum speed: 202km/hr (126mph)

Range: 8670km (539 miles)

Service ceiling: 4000m (13,000ft)

Dimensions: Span 10.36m (34ft 0in);
length 7.04m (23ft 1¹/₄in);
height 2.76m (9ft ³/₄in)

Weight: 757kg (1670lb) loaded

▲ Piper PA-38 Tomahawk

British Airways Flying Club, 1979

The Tomahawk was Piper's response to Cessna's Model 150/152 line. This Tomahawk was registered to BA's Flying Club in 1979 and sold on in 1991. It remains on the British register as G-BVHM. Piper's 2012 piston offering includes the Mirage, Matrix, Arrow, Archer LX and Archer TX.

gaining FAA certification for its latest aircraft, the M-9-235, a STOL four-seater, capable of carrying its occupants and a useful cargo load out of the shortest, roughest airstrips. Mooney has generally followed a different path with its elegant, fast, low-wing tourers. Al W. Mooney began designing aircraft in 1922, latterly for Culver, before establishing Mooney Aircraft, at Wichita, on 5 July 1946. Mooney's 2012 catalogue includes the Ovation2 GX, Ovation3 and Acclaim Type S, all of them offering luxury travel, and the latter billed as the fastest piston single available.

Piper

W.T. 'Bill' Piper reorganized the Taylor Aircraft Co, responsible for the Taylor Craft Cub, in 1936, when the company fell into financial strife. As Piper Aircraft the new firm began building the J-3 Cub, a machine developed through a bewildering array of variations for civil and, in its thousands, military customers.

Post-war, the Cub provided the early basis for a series of high-wing models before the first Comanche was flown on 24 May 1956 and established the company's future as a manufacturer of low-wing cabin singles and twins.

Cirrus and Diamond

Cirrus was formed in 1984, to make a new series of composite piston singles. Thoroughly modern in design, construction and performance, the resulting Cirrus SR20 and SR22 include Garmin-derived EFIS avionics and the Cirrus Airframe Parachute System, which safely brings the entire aircraft to the ground in the event of a catastrophic problem.

Diamond Aircraft was established in 1991, when the Dries family acquired HOAC AG, producer of the Dimona and Katana motor gliders. It offers the

▲ **Diamond DA20**

The two-seat DA20 is optimized for basic training. It is available with a conventional 'steam gauge' cockpit or a choice of EFIS set-ups and a range of other optional avionics and equipment.

DA20 two-seater and DA40 four-seater, as well as the new five-seat DA50 and a range of DA42 twins. The company has its primary facilities in Wiener Neustadt, Austria, but has a North American branch named Diamond Aircraft Industries Inc and based in London, Ontario, Canada.

▲ **Cirrus SR20**

2000

Cirrus markets the SR20 as the ideal tourer for the new pilot, as well as being comfortable enough for the serious business traveller. It is not uncommon for more ambitious GA pilots to fly themselves to and from meetings, using their aircraft as essential business tools.

Specifications

Crew: 1	Range: 1454km (903 miles)
Passengers: 3	Service ceiling: 0m (0ft)
Powerplant: One 149kW (200hp) Continental	Dimensions: Span 11.68m (38ft 4in); length
IO-360-ES engine	7.92m (26ft); height 2.71m (8ft 11in)
Cruising speed: 288km/hr (179mph)	Weight: 1386kg (3050lb) loaded

Aerobatic specialists
1914–2012

Aerobatics began as little more than a by-product of pilot experimentation, but matured as something rather more defined through air combat.

A S SOON AS AIRCRAFT were able to withstand the structural stresses of more demanding manoeuvres, pilots began flying loops and rolls. The art of air combat, first practised during World War I, was soundly based on primitive aerobatics, but a range of manoeuvres designed to escape or outsmart the enemy was designed and taught.

After the war, barnstorming pilots soon learned that adoring crowds could be enthralled by relatively simple manoeuvres. Before long, series of manoeuvres, or elements, were being put together to form aerobatic displays.

Aerobatics remained a basic requirement in military training and basic trainers like the Avro 504N, Stearman and Tiger Moth found their way onto the civil market as aerobatics became a sport in its own right. Aerobatic variations of production aircraft were developed post-war, typified by the Cessna A150 Aerobat of 1969, but specialist aerobatic machines were developed in earnest following the first Fédération Aéronautique Internationale (FAI) World Aerobatics Championship in 1960.

Curtiss H. Pitts completed his first aerobatic biplane, known as the Pitts Special, in the mid-1940s. Although the aircraft crashed, he persevered, producing a competition-winning aircraft that was primarily available in kit form until 1971, when the tiny S-1S single-seat and S-2A two-seat aerobatic biplanes went into production.

The 1960 FAI event was won by a Czech flying a Zlin 226A monoplane and Zlins dominated the competition for its first three years. The prize was then alternated between Soviet Yak-18 and Zlin machines, before a Pitts S-1S took the title in 1972. Either Yaks or Zlins generally won subsequent competitions, until 1988, when the CAP 230, a machine of French origin, introduced a new order.

Since that first CAP victory, the manufacturer has taken even more titles and in the years when it has missed the title, it has fallen to either Sukhoi-equipped pilots, or those flying Extras. Sukhoi has preferred radial power for its superb Su-26 and Su-31 aircraft, while Germany's Extra uses a rather more elegant inline installation in its phenomenal machines.

Of course, these extreme aerobatic aircraft are also the mounts of choice for air display pilots, but they are quite recognizable even to those who have never attended an air show, since the aircraft competing in the Red Bull Air Races are essentially all modified aerobatic machines.

▲ **Pitts S-1S Special**
Brian Lecomber, 1979

Renowned UK aerobatic pilot Brian Lecomber took delivery of G-BOOK in 1979. The aircraft was delivered in the stock configuration shown here, with 200hp (150kW) AEIO-360-A1A engine and two-bladed propeller, but Lecomber had it modified for 260hp (194kW) and fitted with a three-blader.

Specifications

Crew: 1
Powerplant: One 134kW (180hp) Lycoming IO-360-B4A engine
Cruising speed: 225km/hr (140mph)
Range: 507km (315 miles)
Service ceiling: 6797m (22,300ft)
Dimensions: Span 6.09m (20ft);
 length 5.76m (18ft 9in);
 height 2.04m (6ft 7in)
Weight: 521.6kg (1150lb) loaded

▲ Extra 230

Team Belga, 1984

Using an interesting composite structure of metal-framed fuselage with a mix of metal and fabric covering, plus a wooden wing, the Extra 230 first flew on 14 July 1983. The aircraft was stressed for manoeuvres at up to 10g.

Specifications

Crew: 1

Powerplant: One 149kW (200hp) Lycoming AEIO-360-A1E engine

Maximum speed: 352km/hr (218mph)

Endurance: 2 hours 30 mins

Service ceiling: Unknown

Dimensions: Span 7.40m (24ft 3in);
length 5.82m (19ft 1in); height 1.73m (5ft 9in)

Weight: 560kg (1234lb) loaded

Business jets
1956–2014

Bombardier, Cessna, Dassault and Gulfstream have traditionally dominated the bizjet market, but in recent year's Embraer has also become a force to be reckoned with.

AIRCRAFT HAD BEEN used for business flying to a limited extent from the early years after World War I. Generally, they were little more than multi-seat aircraft allowing an owner or corporation to hire a pilot who conveyed one or more important occupants between business engagements.

As general aviation became more popular in the later 1920s and 1930s, so some business fliers began operating cabin tourers, while the potential of light twin-engined aircraft as high-speed business transports was not ignored, but few manufacturers set out to build aircraft specifically for business use.

After World War II, a surplus of utility twins met the majority of the demands for business travel and a plethora of ambitious conversions of light military transports and, in some cases, bombers, was offered. A handful of visionaries, notably at Lockheed and North American in the United States and de

Specifications

Crew: 2	Range: 4020km (2500 miles)
Passengers: 12	Service ceiling: 12,200m (40,000ft)
Powerplant: Two 15.6kN (3500lbf) Garrett AiResearch TFE731-3R-1D engines	Dimensions: Span 13.56m (44ft 6in); length 13.41m (44ft); height 4.88m (16ft)
Maximum speed: 885km/hr (550mph)	Weight: 7412kg (16,340lb) loaded

▼ Rockwell Sabreliner 65

Acopian Technical Company, 1990s

Acopian took delivery of this Sabre 65 in December 1981, just a year before Sabreliner production closed. The aircraft remained with the company until 2007, when it was sold on and re-registered as N376D.

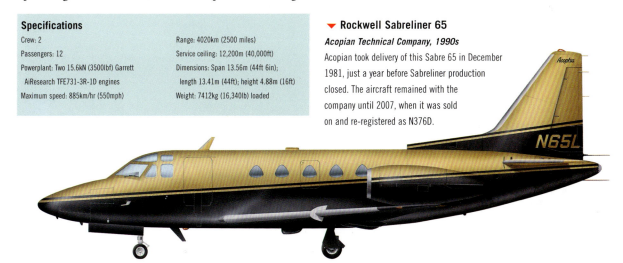

HS.125 and variants

Model	First flown	Description; original powerplant	Number built (all versions)
de Havilland DH.125	13 August 1962	10-seat bizjet; two Bristol Siddeley Viper 502 turbojet engines	2
Hawker Siddeley HS.125 Series 1		Stretched production DH.125; Rolls-Royce Viper 520 engines	86
HS.125 Series 3		Improved Series 2; Viper 522 engines	64
HS.125 Series 400		Improved Series 3	117
HS.125 Series 600		Stretched, 14-seat Series 400; Viper 601 engines	70
HS.125 Series 700		Improved Series 600; Garrett TFE731-3 turbofan engines	215 for civil and military customers
British Aerospace 125 Series 800	26 May 1983	Improved Series 700, designated Hawker 800 from 1993; TFE731-5 engines	Around 650 (including Hawker 850XP) for civil and military customers
Hawker 850XP		Improved Hawker 800 with winglets; TFE731-5BR1H engines	See above
British Aerospace 1000	16 June 1990	Stretched, 15-seat Series 800, designated Hawker 1000 from 1993; Pratt & Whitney PW305 turbofan engines	More than 50
Hawker 750		Short range Hawker 850XP; TFE731-5BR1H engines	47
Hawker 900XP		Hot-and-high Hawker 850XP; TFE731-50R engines	158; in production

Specifications

Crew: 2

Passengers: 4–8

Powerplant: Two 14.65kN (2320lbf) Garrett TFE731-2 turbofan engines

Cruising speed: 912km/hr (566mph)

Range: 3560km (2212 miles)

Service ceiling: unknown

Dimensions: Span 13.08m (42ft 11in); length 13.86m (45ft 5.75in); height 4.61m (15ft 1.5in)

Weight: 8500kg (18740lb) loaded

▼ **Dassault Falcon 10**

VIP-Air, 1980s

Italian bizjet operator VIP-Air used this Falcon 10 during the 1980s. The aircraft remains current in the US in 2012, even the early Falcons offering much better economy in operation than turbojet-powered aircraft like the Sabreliner and pre-fan HS.125s.

Havilland in the UK, nevertheless foresaw a market for jet-powered business aircraft – business jets or, more commonly, bizjets.

Sabreliner and JetStar

Lockheed and North American reacted to a USAF requirement for a high-speed Utility and Combat Readiness aircraft for use as a trainer and light transport. Both companies went for a low-mounted, swept wing, with engines mounted in nacelles alongside the rear fuselage. North American was first into the air with its NA.246 prototype, on 8 May 1956. A pair of General Electric YJ85 turbojets

powered the machine but were replaced by more powerful Pratt & Whitney J60-P-3 engines in the military T-39A aircraft that soon followed.

With the Sabreliner established in production, North American produced the Sabreliner 40 civilian version. Seating as many as nine passengers, but normally taking seven, the model was followed by the stretched Model 60. When North American merged with Rockwell-Standard in 1967, the Sabreliner briefly became the Sabre and development continued so that the Sabre 75 variant was quickly re-engined as the 75A, powered by General Electric CF700-2D-2 turbofans. The last of the production Sabreliners was the Model 65, equipped with a supercritical wing and Garrett TFE731-3R-1D turbofans and though there were certainly bizjets around by this time that made more buying sense, Rockwell was able to sell almost 80 airframes.

Lockheed flew its JetStar for the first time on 4 September 1957. A pair of Bristol Orpheus 1/5 turbojets powered the prototype, but this engine could not be produced under licence in the United States. This major stumbling block was overcome by installing four Pratt & Whitney JT12A-6 turbojets in the second prototype, but although production was begun for civil customers as well as the USAF, production amounted to just 204 aircraft, compared to more than 320 Sabreliners. The first production JetStar I was a striking aircraft seating up to 10 passengers, while the JetStar II introduced TFE731-3 turbofans.

Jet Dragon

The management at de Havilland were perhaps even more prescient than their colleagues at North American and Rockwell. The company may only have announced its DH.125 Jet Dragon in 1961, long after the Sabreliner and JetStar had flown, but unlike the American jets, the DH.125 was aimed at the civilian business user. The prototype flew for the first time on 13 August 1962, but the company was absorbed into Hawker Siddeley soon after and further development fell to the new organization. The Jet Dragon name had been dropped.

Hawker Siddeley remained true to the Viper powerplant of the original DH.125 as it developed the aircraft through several variants. When Hawker Siddeley became part of the nationalized British Aerospace, the designation 125 was retained for its

Dassault's Falcons

Model	First flown	Description; original powerplant	Number built (all versions)
Falcon 10	1 December 1970	Nine-seat bizjet; two Garret TFE731-2 turbofan engines	193
Falcon 100		Improved Falcon 10	36
Falcon 20		12-seat bizjet; two Pratt & Whitney CF700 turbofan engines	449
Falcon 200	24 April 1979	Improved Falcon 20; two Garatt ATF3-6-2C turbofan engines	449
Falcon 50	7 November 1976	12-seat long-range version of Falcon 20; three TFE731-3 engines	355
Falcon 900	21 September 1984	Enlarged, 13-seat Falcon 50; three TFE731-5AR engines	More than 270; Falcon 900LX in production
Falcon 2000	4 March 1993	19-seat bizjet; two General Electric/Allied Signal CFE738 turbofan engines	More than 234; Falcon 2000S in production
Falcon 7X	5 May 2005	14-seat bizjet; three Pratt & Whitney Canada PW307A turbofan engines	More than 131; in production

Specifications

Crew: 2

Passengers: 10

Powerplant: Two 16.24kN (3650lbf) AlliedSignal TFE731-3B-100S turbofan engines

Maximum speed: 885km/hr (350mph)

Range: 4345km (2694 miles)

Service ceiling: 15,545m (51,000ft)

Dimensions: Span 16.31m (53ft 6in); length 16.9m (55ft 5in); height 5.12m (16ft 9in)

Weight: 9979kg (21,954lb) loaded

▼ **Cessna Citation VI**

Vesey Air, 1999

With swept wings and tail surfaces, the Citation VI not only offers high-speed luxury travel to its its 12 passengers, but also assures its owner of considerable 'ramp presence' at the airport.

Cessna's Citations

Model	First flown	Description; original powerplant	Number built (all versions)
Citation and Citation I	15 September 1969	Eight-seat bizjet; two Pratt & Whitney Canada JT15D-1 turbofan engines	691
CitationJet, CJ1, CJ2, CJ3 and CJ4	29 April 1991	Six-seat bizjet; two Williams/Rolls-Royce FJ44 turbofan engines	1531; CJ2+, CJ3 and CJ4 in production
Citation II, Bravo	31 January 1977	Stretched, 12-seat Citation I	842
Citation V, Excel and XLS	18 August 1987	Stretched Citation II; two JT15D-5A engines	1593; XLS+ in production
Citation III, VI and VII	30 May 1979	12-seat long-range bizjet; two Garret TFE731-3b-100S turbofan engines	363
Citation X	21 December 1993	Ten-seat, high-speed bizjet; two Allison GMA3007C turbofan engines	319; in production
Citation Mustang	23 April 2005	Four-seat Very Light Jet; two Pratt & Whitney Canada PW615F turbofan engines	262; in production
Citation Sovereign	27 February 2002	14-seat bizjet; two Pratt & Whitney Canada PW306C turbofan engines	314; in production
Citation Ten	19 January 2012	Improved Citation X; two Rolls-Royce AE3007C2 turbofan engines	Deliveries from 2013

Specifications

Crew: 2

Passengers: 8

Powerplant: Two 13.19kN (2968lbf) Pratt & Whitney JT15D-5 turbofan engines

Maximum speed: 899km/hr (559mph)

Range: 2915km (1811 miles)

Service ceiling: 13,230m (43,400ft)

Dimensions: Span 13.25m (43ft 6in);
length 14.75m (48ft 5in);
height 4.24m (13ft 11in)

Weight: 7303kg (16,100lb) loaded

▼ Beechcraft 400A

1990s

Boasting one of the more complex production histories in the bizjet world, the Beech 400 was last in production as the Hawker 400XP. The aircraft has now been discontinued, Hawker's 2012 bizjet line, including the 200, 900XP and 4000, while Raytheon's entry-level jet is sold as the Beechcraft Premier.

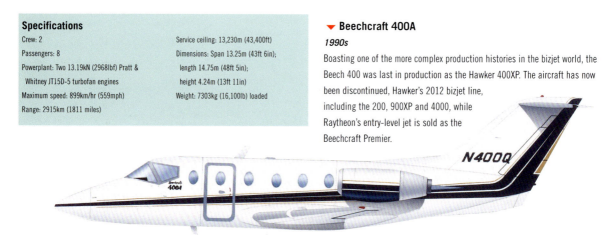

best-selling bizjet and the company soon developed a fan-engined variant as the Series 700. Subsequently, production rights passed to Raytheon, whose Hawker division took on the 125 Series 800 as the Hawker 800. Still development continued and in 2012, the production Hawker 900XP is a direct descendent of the 1962 DH.125.

American Rivals

With the bizjet template established, other manufacturers made their own attempts on the market, which naturally assumed sectors based on the range and capacity of aircraft required. William P. 'Bill' Lear brought the next major bizjet contender to market in 1963. Living in retirement in Switzerland, Lear nevertheless took over the failed design of the P-1604,

a fighter that had been in development for the Swiss air force. Lear used the aircraft's wings and developed a new five/seven-seat fuselage to produce the Learjet 23.

A series of losses marred the aircraft's early service, but with modifications in hand, Lear turned to developing new versions. In 1967, Lear Jet Industries was taken over by the Gates Rubber Company and, like Rockwell and Lockheed before them, the management at Gates realized that the Learjet line would need to be turbofan powered just as soon as such engines became available at the relatively small power ratings required. The eight-seat Learjet 35 was the first such machine in the Lear line, powered by the ubiquitous TFE731.

Gates continued Learjet development as far as the radically wingleted Longhorn 55, but financial

Learjet Variants

Model	First flown	Description; original powerplant	Number built (all versions)
Lear Jet 23 (Learjet 23)	7 October 1963	Eight-seat bizjet; two General Electric CJ610-1 turbojet engines	105
Lear Jet 24 (Learjet 24)		Improved Learjet 23	258
Lear Jet 25 (Learjet 25)	12 August 1966	Stretched, ten-seat Learjet 24; two CJ610-6 engines	368
Gates Learjet 28	21 August 1978	Modified Learjet 25; two CJ610-8A engines	5
Gates Learjet 29		Long-range Learjet 28	2
Gates Learjet 31, 35 and 36	11 May 1987	Learjet 31 is Learjet 35 with Learjet 55 wings and winglets; two Garret TFE731-2 turbofan engines	980
Bombardier Learjet 40, 45, 40 XR and 45 XR		10-seat bizjet; two AlliedSignal TFE731-20 engines	550; 40 XR and 45 XR Gates Learjet 55 in production
Gates Learjet 55		10-seat bizjet with Learjet 28 wing; two Garret TFE731-3A engines	148
Bombardier Learjet 60 and 60 XR	13 June 1991	Stretched, 10-seat Learjet 55; two Pratt & Whitney Canada PW305 turbofan engines	400; 60 XR in production
Bombardier Learjet 85	Scheduled for 2012	All-new, 10-seat bizjet; two Pratt & Whitney Canada PW307B turbofan engines	Deliveries from 2013

Challenger Variants

Model	First flown	Description; original powerplant	Number built (all versions)
Canadair CL-600 Challenger	8 November 1978	19-seat bizjet; two Avco Lycoming ALF502L turbofan engines	890 of all CL-600 variants for civil and military customers; Challenger 605 in production
Canadair CL-601 Challenger	10 April 1982	Improved CL-600 with winglets; two General Electric CF34-1A turbofan engines	See above
Bombardier CL-604 Challenger	18 September 1994	Improved, longer-ranged CL-601; CF34-3B engines	See above
Bombardier Challenger 605		12-seat bizjet; CF34-3B engines	See above
Bombardier Challenger 300	14 August 2001	All-new, 12-seat bizjet; two Honeywell HTF7000 turbofan engines	307; in production
Bombardier Challenger 850		14-seat bizjet based on CRJ200 airliner; two CF34-3B1 engines	54; in production

trouble caused the sale of the Learjet enterprise to Canada's Bombardier in 1990. The Canadians took up the reigns to create a family of new Learjets, which sit comfortably below the larger Challenger series that Bombardier had inherited from Canadair and complement both the Challenger and Global jets to create a complete bizjet range from entry level to the very highest end.

With its successful range of piston singles and executive twins, it was inevitable that Cessna would chase its own share of the bizjet market. The company had extensive jet experience from its T-37/A-37 trainer/light attack aircraft projects and because it was later to the market – its Fanjet 500 first flew on 7 November 1968 – it was able to benefit from turbofan technology from the outset. The Fanjet was renamed as the Citation and development proceeded to allow first deliveries in late 1971. Subsequent development of the Citation line has built on the original Citation, as well as on a series of new airframes, to create several distinct Citation families. Cessna has fought shy of the larger-capacity, high-speed end of the market populated by the big Gulfstreams and the Global Express, instead preferring to offer the very fast, 12-seat Citation X, an aircraft that for many years was the fastest available civil aircraft, at Mach 0.92.

Specifications

Crew: 2

Passengers: 10

Powerplant: Two 16kN (3700lbf) Garrett
TFE731-3A-2B turbofan aero-engines

Maximum speed: 871km/hr (541mph)

Range: 4010km (2492 miles)

Service ceiling: 15.545m (51,000ft)

Dimensions: Span 13.35m (43ft 10in);
length 16.80m (55ft 1in);
height 4.48m (14ft 8in)

Weight: 8845kg (19,500lb) loaded

▼ Gates Learjet Longhorn 55
1980s

Weighing close on twice as much as the original Learjet 23, the Longhorn 55 was, nevertheless, a direct descendent of the earlier machine. The tall winglets of the Learjet 55 were said to resemble the horns of Longhorn cattle, hence the type's name.

Specifications

Crew: 2

Passengers: 19

Powerplant: Two 40.7kN (9140lbf) General
Electric CF34-3A turbofan engines

Maximum speed: 882km/hr (548mph)

Range: 62360km (3875 miles)

Service ceiling: 12,500m (41,000ft)

Dimensions: Span 19.61m (64ft 4in);
length 20.85m (68ft 5in);
height 6.30m (20ft 8in)

Weight: 19,618kg (43,250lb) loaded

▼ Canadair Challenger 601
1980s

Built in 1984, this Challenger was specially modified for navigation aid calibration duties with Nav Canada Ottawa. Calibration work involves specially equipped aircraft – often bizjets – flying precise profiles to calibrate airfield navigation aids.

Specifications

Crew: 2

Passengers: 19

Powerplant: Three 2038kg (4500lb) Garrett
TFE731-5AR-1C turbofan engines

Cruising speed: 922km/hr (572mph)

Range: 7222km (4488 miles)

Service ceiling: 15,544m (51,000ft)

Dimensions: Span 19.35m (63ft 5in);
length 20.2m (66ft 7in);
height 7.5m (24ft 9in)

Weight: 20,639kg (45,500lb) loaded

▼ Dassault Falcon 900
Ford Motor Company, 1987

This Falcon 900 was registered new to the Ford Motor Company in 1987. The third Falcon 900 built, the aircraft was sold to a leasing company in 2001, but remains current on the US register in 2012.

Embraer bizjets

Model	First flown	Description; original powerplant	Number built (all versions)
Legacy 450		Mid-light bizjet; two Honeywell HTF7500E turbofan engines	Deliveries from 2014
Legacy 500		Midsize bizjet; HTF7500E engines	Deliveries from late 2013–2014
Legacy 600	March 2001	16-seat bizjet based on ERJ135 airliner; two Rolls-Royce AE3007A1P turbofan engines	More than 180; in production
Legacy 650		Long-range Legacy 600; two AE3007A2 engines	1; in production
Lineage 1000	26 October 2007	Large bizjet based on E190 airliner; two General Electric CF34-10E7-B turbofan engines	3; in production
Phenom 100	26 July 2007	Four-seat Very Light Jet; two Pratt & Whitney Canada PW617F-E turbofan engines	351 Phenom 100 and 300; in production
Phenom 300	29 April 2008	Stretched, eight-seat Phenom 100 with revised wing; two Pratt & Whitney Canada PW535 turbofan engines	See above; in production

Civilian Gulfstreams

Model	First flown	Description; original powerplant	Number built (all versions)
Grumman Gulfstream I	14 August 1958	21-seat business aircraft; two Rolls-Royce Dart turboprop engines	200 for civil and military customers
Grumman Gulfstream II	2 October 1966	19-seat bizjet; two Rolls-Royce RB163-25 Spey turbofan engines	258
Gulfstream III	2 December 1979	Stretched and improved Gulfstream II	200 for civil and military customers
Gulfstream IV/G300/G350 and IV-SP/G400/G450	19 September 1985	Stretched and improved Gulfstream III; two Rolls-Royce RB183-03 Tay turbofan engines	790 for civil and military customers; G350 and G450 in production
Gulfstream V/G500 and V-SP/G550	28 November 1995	Ultra long-range development of Gulfstream IV; two Rolls-Royce BR710A1-10 turbofan engines	547 for civil and military customers; G500 and G550 in production
Gulfstream G100 and G150	19 March 1984 (Astra)	Gulfstream version of 11-seat IAI Astra; two Garret TFE731-3B-100G turbofan engines	103; G150 in production
Gulfstream G200 and G280	25 December 1997 (Galaxy)	Gulfstream version of eight-seat IAI Galaxy; two Pratt & Whitney Canada PW306A turbofan engines	81; G280 deliveries from 2012
Gulfstream G650	25 November 2009	All-new ultra long-range, high-speed development of Gulfstream V; two Rolls-Royce BR725 turbofan	Deliveries from 2012

Gulfstream developed a series of fast, high-end bizjets, but subsequently added a lower end to its range by acquiring the excellent Westwind and Astra from Israel Aircraft Industries (IAI). It has maintained its relationship with IAI for the subsequent development of new smaller jets.

Other Contenders

In France, Dassault has always been keen to make the most of its jet fighter heritage in marketing its sensational Falcon bizjets. Like Cessna, it was able to use turbofan power from the start, debuting its Falcon 10 in 1970. Later, as it developed its range to offer longer-ranged models, it took the unusual step of adopting a three-engined powerplant, a configuration that it remains faithful to in the current production Falcon 900LX.

An unlikely entrant to the fiercely competitive bizjet market, but one that has, nevertheless, done phenomenally well in a very short space of time, Embraer based its first model, the Legacy 600, on its ERJ135 regional jet. And, just a little over a decade later, it is doing well with its Phenom light jets, even in the face of the continuing global recession, as well as bringing new aircraft into the final phases of their development.

Pistons and props
1930s–2012

The ready market for post-war executive conversions demonstrated just how popular a dedicated business aircraft would be. Grumman was first to respond, with Beech, Cessna and Piper hot on its heels.

DURING THE INTER-WAR YEARS, a handful of aircraft were built specifically for business travel. Lockheed, for example, built a few Vegas for executive use, but because the airliners of the day generally seated so few passengers, there was no real difference in airframe, powerplant, performance or technology between contemporary airliners and aircraft built for business use.

Walter Beech saw the potential for a business-dedicated aircraft and produced his fine-performing

Specifications

Crew: 2
Passengers: 9
Powerplant: Two 429kW (575hp) Garrett
  TPE331 turboprop engines
Cruising speed: 346km/hr (215mph)
Range: 2413km (1500 miles)

Service ceiling: 5943m (19,500ft)
Dimensions: Span 15.17m (49ft 8in);
  length 10.75m (35ft 3in);
  height 2.92m (9ft 7in)
Weight: 4128kg (9100lb) loaded

▼ **Dumod Infinite**

Troy Air

Subsequently known simply as the Dumod I, the Infinite was a nine-seat conversion of the C-45, the military Beech 18. It featured turboprop power in the form of two Garrett TPE331 engines, for improved reliability and the ability to run on more easily available jet fuel rather than Avgas.

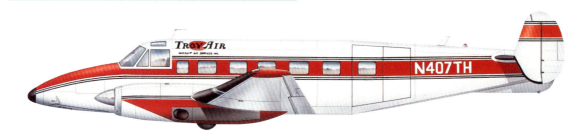

Specifications

Crew: 1
Passengers: 4
Powerplant: One 336kW (450hp) Pratt &
  Whitney R-985-AN-4 Wasp Junior radial
  pistone engine
Maximum speed: 341km/hr (211mph)

Range: 1610km (1000 miles)
Service ceiling: 5805m (19,000ft)
Dimensions: Span 9.75m (32ft);
  length 8.15m (26ft 9in);
  height 2.44m (8ft)
Weight: 1928kg (4240lb) loaded

▼ **Beech Model D17S Staggerwing**

Late 1970s

The Model 17 remains a popular vintage type, thanks to its sleek good looks and fine performance. As well as the pilot, the Staggerwing can accommodate three or four passengers.

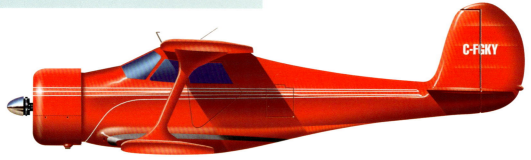

Staggerwing as a result. With an uncanny ability to see what the business operator would want in an aircraft, Beech produced an aircraft that not only performed well, but also looked good, announcing its owner as someone to be reckoned with as soon as it arrived at an airfield.

Beech also produced the Model 18, a twin-engined airliner and utility transport that sold to the military in huge numbers during World War II. Post-war, the Model 18 was particularly sought after as a business transport and many were converted with executive appointments, new engines and other modifications. The Volpar Corporation of

Van Nuys, California specialized in Beech 18 conversions and went as far as producing tricycle undercarriage and turboprop aircraft.

Other machines, including the Douglas A-36 bomber and Lockheed Lodestar, were also popular subjects for conversion, the latter the subject of 'Bill' Lear's Learstar conversion, but it was clear that the manufacturers would need to address the burgeoning market with a range of new types.

New market, new aircraft
Grumman was first off the mark, its twin-turboprop G.159 Gulfstream flying for the first time on 14

Specifications

Crew: 1–2
Passengers: 12
Powerplant: Two 579kW (776hp) Garrett TPE331-6-251M turboprop engines
Maximum speed:547km/hr (340mph)
Range: 2334km (1450 miles)

Service ceiling: 9020m (29,600ft)
Dimensions: Span 11.94m (39ft 2in); length 12.01m (39ft 5in); height 4.17m (13ft 8in)
Weight: 5250kg (11,575lb) loaded

▼ **Mitsubishi MU-2J**
1973
Mitsubishi's UK agent, Express Aviation, used this MU-2J as a demonstrator. The type never found a ready market in the UK, while its popularity in the United States owed much to Mitsubishi's early decision to abandon French Astazou power in favour of the TPE331 turboprop.

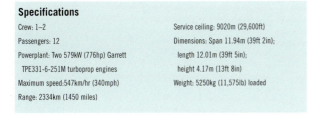

Specifications

Crew: 2
Passengers: 13
Powerplant: Two 634kW (850hp) Pratt & Whitney Canada PT6A-42 turboprop engines
Cruising speed: 523km/hr (325mph)
Range: 3656km (2272 miles)

Service ceiling: 10,668m (35,000ft)
Dimensions: Span 16.64m (54ft 6in); length 13.38m (43ft 9in); height 4.57m (15ft)
Weight: 5670kg (12,500lb) loaded

▼ **Beechcraft Super King Air 200**
1985–1992
This Beechcraft Model 200 stayed only briefly in the UK, before being sold to a new owner in the United States. The King Air/Super King Air line is long and confusing, including the Models 90, 100, 200, 300 and 350.

Specifications

Crew: 2

Passengers: 8

Powerplant: Two 895kW (1200hp) Pratt &
Whitney PT6-67A turboprob pusher engines
driving McCauley five-bladed propellers

Maximum speed: 621km/hr (386mph)

Range: 2657km (1651 miles)

Service ceiling: 10,605m (34,793ft)

Dimensions: Span 16.58m (54ft 5in);
length 14.05m (46ft 1in);
height 3.96m (13ft)

Weight: 6577kg (14,500lb) loaded

▼ Beechcraft 2000 Starship

Raytheon, 1987

The Starship was an ambitious, radical twin-turboprop pusher design with swept wings and moveable canards. It introduced a number of radical structural features and Beech was unable to convince customers that the aircraft was a viable proposition. So few Starships were sold that Beechcraft bought them all back in the 2000s, to avoid having to fund a support network for the type.

Specifications

Crew: 1–2

Passengers: 9

Powerplant: Two 634kW (850hp) Pratt &
Whitney Canada PT6A-66 turboprop engines

Maximum speed: 732km/hr (455mph)

Range: 2592km (1612 miles)

Service ceiling: 12,500m (41,000ft)

Dimensions: Span 14.03m (46ft ¹/₂in);
length 14.41m (47ft 3¹/₂in); height 3.97m
(13ft ¹/₂in)

Weight: 1860kg (4100lb) loaded

▼ Piaggio P.180 Avanti

Piaggio, 1986

I-PJAV was the P.180 first prototype and helped establish the Avanti's unique configuration. Although not unlike the Starship in being a twin-turboprop, canard-equipped pusher, the Avanti employs a straight supercritical wing.

August 1958. The Gulfstream was among the first aircraft designed for business use from the outset, which makes it all the more ironic that the aircraft was later stretched and found popularity as a commuter liner, and is perhaps better remembered today in this capacity.

Beech, Cessna and Piper all built twins for this lucrative market, Piper later taking the unusual step of adding a turboprop single to its range. Beech progressed through the six-seat Twin Bonanza, Baron and Duke piston twins to the various Queen Air twin turboprops. From the latter it developed the King Air, a basic design that has evolved into

today's ultimate King Air, the 350i, considered one of the best turboprop twins available. As well as the King Air 350i, Beechcraft's 2012 catalogue includes 250 and C90GTx version of the aircraft, plus the Baron G58.

Cessna no longer contests the propeller twin market, having built such classics as the Titan, Chancellor and Golden Eagle piston twins in the past. Piper, on the other hand, remains active with the Seneca V and Seminole, both of them piston twins and the latter aimed at multi-engine training. Piper also offers the single-engined Meridian, Mirage and Matrix. Of these various related aircraft, the Meridian is powered by a PT6A-42A turboprop.

The Competition

Competition for the Meridian comes from the DAHER SOCATA TBM850, a machine developed from the original French-designed SOCATA TBM750. Pilatus also has a turboprop business aircraft, although its cabin seats six as opposed to the four of the Meridian. The Pilatus PC-12 is also widely regarded as a versatile utility and special missions aircraft.

Competing twins have included the Mitsubishi MU-2 from Japan. An elegant design, the MU-2 found considerable popularity in the United States, despite its comparatively high price tag. The aircraft also became popular as a light transport and many remain in service.

Undoubtedly the most elegant of the competition, the P.180 Avanti is built by Italy's Piaggio. Offering an unusual configuration and excellent performance, the Avanti overcame its early disappointing sales record to enjoy a revival in the 2000s and continues to sell strongly in 2012.

Specifications

Crew: 1
Passengers: 5
Powerplant: Two 283kW (380hp) Lycoming TIO-541-E1C4 turbocharged six-cylinder, horizontally opposed direct drive engines
Maximum speed: 460km/hr (286mph)
Range: 2274km (1413 miles)
Service ceiling: 9145m (30,000ft)
Dimensions: Span 11.97m (39ft 3?in); length 10.31m (33ft 10in); height 3.76m (12ft 4in)
Weight: 3073kg (6775lb) loaded

▼ **Beech Model 60 Duke**

1990s

This Duke was registered to a private owner in Austria. Duke production ended in 1982 after 593 aircraft had been built. Beechcraft's current production piston twin, the Baron G58, has its origins in the Model 56TC Baron of 1967.

Specifications

Crew: 1–2
Passengers: 9
Powerplant: One 895kW (1200shp) Pratt & Whitney Canada PT6A-67P turboprop engine
Cruising speed: 500km/hr (312.4mph)
Range: 2804km (1753 miles)
Service ceiling: 9150m (30,000ft)
Dimensions: Span 16.23m (53ft 3in); length 14.40m (47ft 3in); height 4.26m (14ft 0in)
Weight: 4700kg (10,450lb) loaded

▼ **Pilatus PC-12NG**

Western Aircraft, 2011

This PC-12 represents the latest NG version of the high-performance Swiss turboprop. The aircraft offers accommodation and performance comparable to that of smaller business jets, a fact not lost on Pilatus in its advertising.

Chapter 8

Rotary Workhorses (1948–2013)

The helicopter became a practical, controllable reality during the 1930s, but limited installed power and tricky handling restricted its utility. Pioneering post-war work by Bell in the United States made regular civilian and military helicopter operations a possibility through the Model 47. Soon helicopters were being used for agricultural and police work, for example, but it was not until the advent of larger, more powerful machines that helicopters became a major part of day-to-day aviation operations. As soon as multi-engined types became available, civilian operators began flying passenger services, as well as performing aerial crane work and a host of other duties unique to the helicopter.

◀ **Bell 222 and 230**

While Sikorsky was busy developing helicopters for the military, Bell had produced the Model 47, a light helicopter eminently suited to civilian and military operations. Later it established its phenomenally successful JetRanger in service, but its attempt to follow the single-engined machine with an executive twin, the Model 222, was met with rather less enthusiasm from potential purchasers.

American rotors
1940–2012

The United States has spawned several of the world's most successful helicopter manufacturers, serving the entire market range, from the basic Robinson R22 to the large Sikorsky S-92.

SIKORSKY HAD BEEN FLYING workable helicopters in the United States during the 1930s, and in 1940 it flew its VS-300 for the first time. The aircraft clearly had potential and from 1943 the company delivered several R-4, R-5 and R-6 helicopters for wartime military use. The military continued to monopolize Sikorsky's output post-war, so that the first American helicopter with real civilian potential was the Bell Model 47, first flown on 8 December 1945.

Available power and airframe size/weight were the limiting factors in early helicopter operations and the first commercial Model 47, the 47B, could accommodate a pilot and passenger, and limited useful load. As more power was added and airframe refinements made, however, the Model 47 soon became established in key helicopter roles, including agricultural and light crane work.

The Model 47 continued in production until 1974, by which time Bell was already doing well with civilian expressions of its seminal UH-1 'Huey' military design. In the meantime, it had produced the first of the Model 206 JetRangers. These five-seat

transports became the mainstay of the Western world's light helicopter fleet, but when Bell came to replace the ageing type in production, it ran into trouble. Faced with intense competition from Eurocopter with its Ecureuil, Bell achieved some success with the Model 407, but poor design decisions led the derived Model 427 into failure. Bell was also competing in the executive twin market with Sikorsky's S-76 and Agusta's A109, and losing badly.

Obliged to replace the Model 427 with the much-improved Model 429, Bell is working hard to re-establish itself, as seen in the Model 525 Relentless, which the company announced early in 2012.

Other Players

Sikorsky flew its first civil helicopter, an optimized S-55 variant, in 1949. The Connecticut manufacturer has continued to sell small volumes of helicopters into the civil market, with its S-61L and N finding favour as the offshore support industry evolved through the 1960s. The most successful of Sikorsky's civil aircraft is undoubtedly the S-76, which will be delivered from

▲ **Bell Model 206B JetRanger III**

Fairfax County Police, Virginia, 1990s

Readily available and supported by an extensive network of maintenance facilities, the JetRanger was an ideal platform for a number of special roles. This police aircraft has an undernose searchlight, with a sensor ball located just aft.

Specifications

Crew: 1	Service ceiling: 4115m (13,500ft)
Passengers: 4	Dimensions: Rotor diameter 10.16m (33ft 4in);
Powerplant: One 310kW (420shp) Allison 250-C20J turboshaft engine	length 12.11m (39ft 8in); height 2.83m (9ft 4in)
Maximum speed: 224km/hr (139mph)	Weight: 1451kg (3200lb) loaded
Range: 693km (430 miles)	

later in 2012 in its latest incarnation as the advanced S-76D. Sikorsky has also developed the S-92, which is gradually building support with offshore operators and government customers.

Several US manufacturers established themselves as the producers of smaller helicopters, including Hiller, Brantly, Hughes, Enstrom and Robinson. Hiller flew its UH-12 for the first time in 1948 and more than 2000 of the two/three-seat helicopters were built for the civil and military markets before production closed in 1965. Brantly, later Brantly-Hynes, flew its B-1 in 1948, but entered production with the B-2 in 1958. Several hundred of the B-2

two-seater and enlarged Model 305 had been built when production came to an end in 1983.

Hughes became deeply entrenched in the helicopter business: along with its licencees, it built more than 2000 of the two-seat Model 269 for civil and military use, before the type was further developed as the Model 300. Schweizer took the Model 300 on in the early 1980s, developing the turboshaft-powered Model 330 and 333, which remain in production by Schweizer as a Sikorsky subsidiary.

Hughes also developed the Model 369/500 series of high-performance light helicopters, roughly in the

Bell production civil helicopters			
Model	First flown	Description; original powerplant	Number built (all versions)
47	8 December 1945	Two-seat light helicopter; Pratt & Whitney R-985 radial piston engine	4991 for civil and military customers
204B		11-seat civil version of military UH-1B; Lycoming T5309A turboshaft engine	199
205A and 205B		15-seat civil version of military UH-1D; T5311A engine	
206A Jet Ranger, 206B Jet Ranger II and 206B-3 Jet Ranger III	10 January 1966	Five-seat civil version of military Model 206; Allison 250-C18A turboshaft engine	More than 7700 for civil and military customers
206L Long Ranger, 206L-1 Long Ranger II, 206L-3 Long Ranger III and 206L-4 Long Ranger IV	11 September 1974	Stretched, seven-seat Model 206; 250-C20B engine	More than 1650 for civil and military customers; 206L-4 in production
212		16-seat transport; Pratt & Whitney PT6T-3 Twin Pac turboshaft engine	1052 for civil and military customers
214B Big Lifter		Improved Model 205; Lycoming LTC4B-8D turboshaft engine	73
214ST Super Transport	21 July 1979	Stretched, 20-seat Model 214; two General Electric CT7-2A turboshaft engines	103
222	13 August 1976	Ten-seat executive transport; two Lycoming LTS101-650C-3 turboshaft engines	230
230	12 August 1991	Improved Model 222; two 250-C30G2 engines	More than 38
407	29 June 1995	Improved Model 206L; Rolls-Royce 250-C47B turboshaft engine	More than 1082; in production
412		Model 212 with four-bladed main rotor; PT6T-3B Twin Pac engine	More than 860 for civil and military customers; in production
427	15 December 1997	Enlarged Model 407 with four-bladed main rotor; Pratt & Whitney Canada PW206D turboshaft engine	
429	27 February 2007	Redesigned eight-seat replacement for Model 427; two Pratt & Whitney Canada PWC207D-1 turboshaft engines	In production
430	25 October 1994	Improved Model 230 with four-bladed main rotor; two 250-C40 engines	136
525 Relentless		Future all-new, 16-seat helicopter; two CT7-2F1 engines	

Specifications

Crew: 2

Passengers: 16

Powerplant: Two 1491kW (2000hp) Pratt & Whitney Canada PT6T-3 turboshaft engines

Maximum speed: 198km/hr (123mph)

Range: 293km (182 miles)

Service ceiling: Unknown

Dimensions: Rotor diameter 17.07m (56ft); length 17.28m (56ft 8.5in); height 4.85m (15ft 11in)

Weight: 6350kg (14.000lb) loaded

▲ Sikorsky S-58T

New York Helicopter, 1980s

Turbine conversion brought a new lease of life to the S-58, allowing the type to hold its own alongside more modern equipment – New York Helicopter flew a pair of S-58Ts alongside eight Dauphins.

Specifications

Crew: 1

Passengers: 14

Powerplant: One 1342kW (1800shp) Pratt & Whitney Canada PT6T-3 or -3B turboshaft engine

Maximum speed: 223km/hr (138mph)

Range: 439km (273 miles)

Service ceiling: 5305m (17,400ft)

Dimensions: Rotor diameter 14.64m (48ft); length 17.43m (57ft 1.68in); height 3.83m (12ft 6.8in)

Weight: 5080kg (11,200lb) loaded

▲ Bell 212

Chinese government, 1980s

The additional power of the PT6T Twin Pac endowed the Model 212 with excellent hot-and-high performance. Around eight Model 212s were delivered to the Chinese Government from 1979.

Specifications

Crew: 1–2

Passengers: 5

Powerplant: One 313kW (420hp) Allison 250-C20B Turboshaft engine

Maximum speed: 282km/hr (175ph)

Range: 429km (267 miles)

Service ceiling: 4877m (16,000ft)

Dimensions: Rotor diameter 8.1m (26ft 5in); length 9.4m (30ft 10in); height 2.6m (8ft 5in)

Weight: 1157kg (2250lb) loaded

▲ Hughes 500D

Slone Aviation, 1976–77

This Model 500D was used by Slone Aviation as a demonstrator for five months in the mid-1970s, before being sold to a private operator. The Model 500 is renowned for its exhilarating performance rather than its slightly cramped accommodation.

Sikorsky production civil helicopters

Model	First flown	Description; original powerplant	Number built (all versions)
S-55	10 November 1949	12-seat transport; Wright R-1300-3 radial piston engine	1281 for civil and military (military version) customers
S-55T		Re-engined S-55; Garret TSE331-3U-303N turboshaft engine	50 conversions
S-58	8 March 1954	Transport; Wright R-989-C9HE-2 radial piston engine	1821 for civil and military (military version) customers
S-58T	26 August 1970	Re-engined S-58; Pratt & Whitney PT6T-3 Twin Pac turboshaft engine	160 conversions
S-61L	6 December 1960	28-seat version of military S-61A Sea King; two General Electric CT58-1-40 turboshaft engines	11
S-61N		Amphibious, improved S-61L; two CT58-110-1 turboshaft engines	126
S-62	14 May 1958	12-passenger amphibious helicopter with S-55 rotor system; General Electric T58-GE-6 turboshaft engine	145
S-64E		Civil version of military S-64A Skycrane; two Pratt & Whitney T73-P-1 turboshaft engines	9
S-64E and F Aircrane		Military CH-54 remanufactured by Erickson Air Crane; two Pratt & Whitney JFTD12A-4A turboshaft engines	In 'production'
S-76 Spirit	13 March 1977	12-seat executive transport; two Allison 250-C30 turboshaft engines	More than 770; S-76C++ in production, S-76D for delivery from 2012
S-92	23 December 1998	22-seat transport; two General Electric CT7-D turboshaft engines	More than 130; in production

JetRanger class. With these helicopters the company achieved huge sales before being taken over by McDonnell Douglas, which was itself then consumed by Boeing. The latter divested itself of all the former Hughes products except for the AH-64 Apache attack helicopter, with a new company, MD Helicopters, then continuing to develop the Model 500 line, including the stretched Model 600 and all-new Explorer.

Enstrom flew its Model F-28 for the first time on 12 November 1960 and the piston-engined, two/three-seat F-28F Falcon and 280FX Shark remain in production in 2012. The company also developed a

Specifications

Crew: 2
Passengers: 12
Powerplant: Two 485kW (650shp) Rolls-Royce (Allison) 250-C30 turboshaft engines
Cruising speed: 287km/hr (178mph)
Range: 761km (473 miles)

Service ceiling: 4200m (13,800ft)
Dimensions: Rotor diameter 13.41m (44ft);
length 16m (52ft 6in);
height 4.415m (14ft 6in)
Weight: 5307kg (11,700lb) loaded

▼ Sikorsky S-76A

1980s

An elegant helicopter seating up to 12 passengers and featuring retractable undercarriage, the S-76 took on Bell's Model 222 and derivatives, consistently outselling them.

▲ Robinson R22 Beta

1980s

Thousands of GA pilots have been trained on the R22, which has been built in variants that include the Alpha and Beta. Robinson recognized, as had the lightplane manufacturers before it, that a newly fledged pilot will often stick with the manufacturer of the aircraft on which he or she trained when making a first aircraft purchase. It built the R44 partly to address this market.

Specifications

Crew: 1 (+1 trainee)	Service ceiling: 4267m (14,000ft)
Powerplant: One 119kW (160hp) Lycoming	Dimensions: Rotor diameter 7.7m (25ft 2in);
0-320-B2C piston engine	length 8.7m (28ft 8in);
Maximum speed: 190km/hr (118mph)	height 2.7m (8ft 11in)
Range: 322km (200 miles)	Weight: 635kg (1370lb) loaded

▲ Bell Model 222UT

University of Tennessee Research Center and Hospital, Knoxville, Tennessee, 1990

The skid-equipped 222UT brought additional utility to the Model 222 and Bell hoped that it would make the aircraft more appealing to operators looking for a more versatile machine.

Specifications

Crew: 2	Service ceiling: 4816m (15,800ft)
Passengers: 8	Dimensions: Rotor diameter 12.8m (42ft);
Powerplant: Two 505kW (677hp) Honeywell	length 15.32m (50ft 3in);
(formerly Lycoming) LTS-101-750C engines	height 3.56m (11ft 8in)
Maximum speed: 250km/hr (155mph)	Weight: 3742kg (8250lb) loaded
Range: 700km (434 miles)	

▲ Enstrom 280FX

1990s

Enstrom's range of light helicopters has proven popular with private and military owners over a period of five decades, both for training and personal transport. The 280FX is a refined version of the F-28 base model.

Specifications

Crew: 1	Range: 446km (277 miles)
Passengers: 2	Service ceiling: 2743m (9000ft)
Powerplant: One 167kW (225shp) Lycoming	Dimensions: Rotor diameter 9.75m (32ft);
HIO-360-F1AD piston engine	length 8.91m (29ft 3in); height 2.74m (9ft)
Maximum speed: 137km/hr (85mph)	Weight: 1170kg (2600lb) loaded

Specifications

Crew: 1

Passengers: 0

Powerplant: One 1342kW (1800shp) Honeywell
T53-17 turboshaft engine

Maximum speed: 185.2km/hr (115mph)

Range: 494.5km (307 miles)

Service ceiling: 7620m (25,000ft)

Dimensions: Rotor diameter 14.7m (48ft 3in);
length 15.8m (51ft 10in);
height 4.14m (13ft 7in)

Weight: 2721kg (6000lb) loaded

▲ Kaman K-MAX

Erickson Air-Crane, 1994–95

Erickson leased a pair of K-MAX in the mid-1990s, but has since focused on its own conversions of ex-military Sikorsky S-64 helicopters. The intermeshing main rotors of the K-MAX allow it to dispense with the traditional tail rotor, for safer operations in tight spaces, such as during logging work, for example.

▲ MD Helicopters MD 520N

Los Angeles County Sheriff, early-2000s

MD Helicopters offers the MD 520N, MD 600N and Explorer with its NOTAR (No Tail Rotor) technology. Using air blown through slots at the end of the tail boom rather than the thrust of a tail rotor, NOTAR results in quieter operation and eliminates the risk of tail rotor strikes in confined areas, but increases fuel consumption.

Specifications

Crew: 1–2

Passengers: 5

Powerplant: One 313kW (420hp) Allison 250-
C20B Turboshaft engine

Maximum speed: 282km/hr (175mph)

Range: 429km (267 miles)

Service ceiling: 4877m (16,000ft)

Dimensions: Rotor diameter 8.1m (26ft 5in);
length 9.4m (30ft 10in); height 2.6m (8ft 5in)

Weight: 1361kg (3000lb) loaded

MD Helicopters civil production helicopters

Model	First flown	Description; original powerplant	Number built (all versions)
MD 500E	28 January 1982 (Hughes 500E)	Five-seat light helicopter, improved Hughes 500D; 250-C20B turboshaft engineAllison	More than 4700 Hughes, McDonnell Douglas and MD Helicopters Model 500s for civil and military customers; in production
MD 530F		Hot-and-high MD 500E; 250-C30 engine	See above; in production
MD 520N	1 May 1990 (as McDonnell Douglas 520N)	Improved McDonnell Douglas 520N; 250-C20R engine	See above; in production
MD 600N	22 November 1994	Stretched, 8-seat MD 520N; 250-C47M engine	More than 70; in production
MD-900, MD-902	18 December 1992	Eight-seat utility helicopter; two Pratt & Whitney Canada PW206B turboshaft and Explorer engines	Explorer in production

Model 480 turbine-engined derivative of the 280FX and this remains in production as the five-seat 480B.

Among the world's most significant helicopter builders in terms of production quantities, Robinson was founded in 1973 to build a small, lightweight, inexpensive GA helicopter. The company began with the two-seat R22, progressing to the R44 four-seater and then the turbine-powered R66, which it delivered for the first time in November 2010. One year later, Robinson delivered its 10,000th helicopter.

Niche Helicopters

Two US manufacturers have built helicopters aimed at niche markets. Boeing Vertol first flew its Model 234 Commercial Chinook in August 1980. It was aimed at the long-range offshore market, but a British Airways Helicopters example was lost in 1984 and the market for the type effectively dried up. The survivors continue to serve as heavylift cranes.

Kaman's niche helicopter, the K-MAX, is also a flying crane. First flown in December 1991, it has been sold in limited numbers, but remains available in 2012.

▲ **Bell Model 407**

Closely resembling the Model 206, the Model 407 features a four-bladed main rotor and FADEC control for its Rolls-Royce 250 turboshaft. The aircraft's fuselage and cabin are based on those of the Model 206.

▼ **Bell Model 47**

With the Model 47D, Bell introduced the type's distinctive 'goldfish bowl' cockpit glazing. Model 47s were produced in considerable numbers under licence, notably in Italy by Agusta, as here, and in Japan, by Kawasaki.

▲ **Schweizer 330**

Schweizer, late 1980s

The 330 was designed to combine safety and mission flexibility with outstanding performance. The usualual fuselage shape, combined with large stabilisers, make the 300 especially stable. The helicopter also includes a crash resistant fuel bladder.

Specifications

Crew: 1–2	Hover ceiling: 4300m (14,100ft)
Passengers: 1–3	Dimensions: Rotor diameter 8.31m (27ft 3in);
Powerplant: One 313kW (420hp) Rolls Royce	length 9.46m (31ft 1in), height 3.35m
250-C10A engine	(11ft 0in)
Cruising speed: 200km/hr (124mph)	Weight: 1012kg (2226lb) loaded
Range: 498km (309 miles)	

European domination
1948–2013

Between them, Eurocopter and AgustaWestland dominate Europe's helicopter manufacturing, as well as controlling much of the market for civil helicopters. Russia's Mil is highly regarded for its tough, capable Mi-8 series.

EUROPE HAS NOT SEEN the proliferation of helicopter manufacturers that the United States has enjoyed, but dominates important sections of the civil helicopter market, especially for light helicopters, where the Ecureuil and its derivatives reign supreme.

Eurocopter, formed by the merger of the helicopter division of the French Aerospatiale concern and Germany's MBB, in January 1992, dominates the European helicopter industry. Aerospatiale had entered the helicopter business with the Alouette II, which first flew as a Sud-Aviation product on 12 March 1955. Subsequent models, all primarily for the military market, included the Alouette III and Super Frelon. In later years the company produced the AS 350/355 Ecureuil and AS 360/365 Dauphin. In co-operation with the UK's Westland, Aerospatiale built three designs: the SA 330 Puma, which achieved limited civil success, but was then developed into the best-selling Super Puma; the Lynx, of which only a handful were sold on the civilian market; and the Gazelle, an ex-military machine that only really appeals to civilians.

Messerschmitt-Bölkow-Blohm's primary type was the BO 105, a high-performance aircraft that was again a primarily military type, but which civilian operators found useful, especially in the air ambulance role. MBB also worked with Japan's Kawasaki on the BK117 development of the BO 105, and with the creation of Eurocopter this formed the basis of the current EC145. Eurocopter also retains the Ecureuil and variants in production, as well as the Dauphin and Super Puma. It has added the EC135 as a BO 105 replacement, the EC120B light helicopter and the EC175 medium twin.

Agusta Westland

Europe's second helicopter dynasty is founded on the businesses of Italy's Agusta and the UK's Westland. Agusta began building the Bell Model 47 under licence in 1954 and has continued this relationship with Bell through the AB204/205/206/212/412 series, to the BA609 tiltrotor. It eventually took a controlling interest in the co-developed AB139, which is now the standard aircraft in the medium twin class, as the AW139.

Westland founded its business on the modification and licence production of Sikorsky designs, working through the S-55, S-58 and S-61, but barely addressed the civil market. Westland first worked with Agusta during the 1960s, when it began building AB47G helicopters for the British Army. The companies later

formed EH Industries to produce the EH101, which became the AW101 when the companies merged in 2001. In 2010, AgustaWestland acquired Poland's PZL-Swidnik, with the remainder of Poland's helicopter industry going to Sikorsky.

AgustaWestland's range of civilian products include the AW119e light single, variations on the classic AW109 light twin, the forthcoming AW169

▲ Kamov Ka-26 'Hoodlum'

Aeroflot, 1970s

The Ka-26 features a detachable rear fuselage pod, allowing great versatility from one airframe. Passenger or cargo-carrying pods were developed, or the pod could be dispensed with and replaced by chemical tanks and spray bars for agricultural work.

Specifications

Crew: 1	Range: 400km (250 miles)
Passengers: 7	Hover ceiling: 800m (2625ft)
Powerplant: Two 242.5kW (325hp) Vedeneyev	Dimensions: Rotor diameter 13m (42ft 7in);
m-14v-26 nine-cylinder air-cooled radial	fuselage length 7.75m (25ft 5in); height
piston engines	4.05m (13ft 4in)
Maximum speed:170km/hr (105mph)	Weight: 3250kg (715lb) loaded

Specifications

Crew: 2	Service ceiling: 4600m (15,100ft)
Passengers: 24	Dimensions: Rotor diameter 15.60m (51ft 2in);
Powerplant: Two 1184kW (1590hp) Turbomeca	length 16.29m (53ft 5in); height 4.92m
Makila 1A1 turboshaft engines	(16ft 2in)
Cruising speed: 266km/hr (165mph)	Weight: 8600kg (18,920lb) loaded
Range: 870km (539 miles)	

▲ Aerospatiale AS 332L Super Puma

A-S Lufttransport, 1983

The Super Puma has become the primary large transport helicopter for offshore support. This aircraft was delivered to Norway's A-S Lufttransport for such operations in 1983 and is shown with both its Norwegian and French delivery registrations.

Specifications

Crew: 1 or 2

Passengers: 11

Powerplant: Two 625kW (838hp) Turboméca
   Arriel 2C turboshaft engines

Maximum speed: 306km/hr (190mph)

Range: 827km (514 miles)

Service ceiling: 5865m (19,242ft)

Dimensions: Rotor diameter 11.94m (39ft 2in);
   length 13.73m (45ft 1in);
   height 4.06m (13ft 4in)

Weight: 4300kg (9480lb) loaded

▲ Aerospatiale AS 365N Dauphin

Tokyo Fire Department, 1982

Aerospatiale developed the Dauphin through the single-engined SA 360, into the twin-engined SA 365C. Subsequently, and with a change of designation from 'SA' (Sud-Aviation) to 'AS' (Aerospatiale), it produced the AS 365N, which Eurocopter offers in 2012 as the AS365N3+ and EC155B1.

▲ Mil Mi-8P 'Hip-C'

Aeroflot, 1980s

The Mi-8P was designed as a civil passenger transport, with rectangular cabin windows and accommodation for 28 passengers, or 32 if the wardrobe for winter coats was removed.

Specifications

Crew: 3

Passengers: 28

Powerplant: Two 1454kW (1950shp) Klimov
   TV3-117Mt turboshaft engines

Maximum speed: 208km/hr (155mph)

Range: 930km (575 miles)

Service ceiling: 4500m (15,000ft)

Dimensions: Rotor diameter 21.29m (69ft
   10in); length 25.24m (82ft 9in); height 5.65m
   (18ft 6in)

Weight: 12,000kg (26,400lb) loaded

▲ Aerospatiale AS 355F1 Twin Squirrel

Independent Television News, 1989

Used in the UK as a news-gathering helicopter, G-OITN represents the twin-engined Ecureuil, known in the UK as the Twin Squirrel and in the United States as the TwinStar (the AS 350 is the Squirrel in the UK and the AStar to a US customer).

Specifications

Crew: 1

Passengers: 5

Powerplant: One 540kW (724hp) Turbomeca
   Arriel 1D1 turboshaft engine

Maximum cruising speed: 246km/hr (153mph)

Range: 690km (428 miles)

Hover ceiling: 3200m (10,500ft)

Dimensions: Rotor diameter 10.69m (35ft);
   length 10.93m (35ft 10in); height 3.14m
   (10ft 4in)

Weight: 2250kg (4950lb) loaded

multi-role helicopter, the AW139 and the AW101, although the latter has struggled on the civilian market even as it sells well to military customers.

Russian Helicopters

Russia's helicopters, especially those of Mil origin, are renowned for their rugged construction and dependability, albeit with lower levels of technology, efficiency and customer support than might be expected from their Western equivalents.

Mil flew its first helicopter, the Mi-1, in September 1948 and since then the majority of its models have been built for both civil and military use, with many licence-built and further developed by PZL. The Mi-8/17 'Hip' series has undoubtedly been Mil's most successful design and the latest variants of the 'Hip' remain in production at two Russian facilities.

Kamov's co-axial helicopters do not need a tail rotor, as the torque of their main rotors is neutralized by their opposite directions of rotation. Kamov's first helicopter for the civil market, the Ka-26, was developed into several versions for a variety of applications from crop spraying to cargo transport. It flew for the first time in 1965 and was later developed into the turboshaft-powered Ka-126.

Specifications

Crew: 5	Service ceiling: 4600m (15,000ft)
Passengers: 90	Dimensions: Rotor diameter 32m (105ft);
Powerplant: Two 8390kW (11,237hp) ZMDB	length 33.72m (110ft 7in); height 8.14m
'Progress' (Lotarev) D-136 turboshaft engines	(26ft 8in)
Maximum speed: 295km/hr (183mph)	Weight: 56,000kg (12,350lb) loaded
Range: 2000km (1243 miles)	

▼ **Mil Mi-26 'Halo'**
Aeroflot, 1984

CCCP-06141 appeared at the 1984 Farnborough Airshow, causing quite a stir as the world's largest helicopter. Capable of carrying more than 100 passengers, the Mi-26 also has a formidable crane capability and has even been built as a tanker for the ground delivery of liquid fuels.

▲ **Eurocopter EC135B-1**
Eurocopter, 1994

D-HECZ was the third pre-production EC135 and flew for the first time in 1994. Successor to the BO 105, the EC135 features the fenestron tail rotor developed by Aerospatiale, in which a multi-blade fan rotates within a shroud to provide anti-torque control.

Specifications

Crew: 1	Service ceiling: 6096m (20,000ft)
Passengers: 7	Dimensions: Rotor diameter 10.20m (33ft 6in);
Powerplant: Two 417kW (560hp) Turbomeca	length 10.16m (33ft 4in);
Arrius 2B turboshaft engines	height 3.62m (11ft 11in)
Maximum cruising speed: 261km/hr (162mph)	Weight: 2500kg (5500lb) loaded
Range: 715km (443 miles)	

Aerospatiale and Eurocopter civil production helicopters

Model	First flown	Description; original powerplant	Number built (all versions)
Aerospatiale SA 319B Alouette III	28 February 1959 (SE 3160 Alouette III)	Seven-seat version of military Sud Aviation SA 319; Turbomeca Astazou XIV turboshaft engine	1392 including SA 316, for civil and military customers
Sud Aviation/ Aerospatiale SA 321F Super Frelon	7 December 1962 (SA 321 Super Frelon)	27-seat version of military SA 321; three Turbomeca Turmo IIIC turboshaft engines	112 for civil and military customers
Aerospatiale SA 330 Puma (military SA 330)	14 April 1965	Civil versions of military SA 330; two Turbomeca Turmo III.C4 turboshaft engines	686 built by Aerospatiale and Westland for civil and military customers
Aerospatiale/ Eurocopter AS 332 Super Puma and Eurocopter EC225	13 September 1978 (military AS 332)	Civil versions of military Aerospatiale AS 332, Eurocopter AS 532 Cougar and EC725; two Turbomeca Makila 1A turboshaft engines	More than 540 for civil and military customers; in production
Aerospatiale/ Eurocopter AS 350 Ecureuil/A-Star and AS 355 Ecureuil II/ Twin Star, and Eurocopter EC130	26 June 1974	Six-seat light helicopter; Turbomeca Arriel turboshaft engine	More than 3000 for civil and military customers; in production
Aerospatiale SA 360 and SA 361 Dauphin, Aerospatiale SA/AS 365/Eurocopter AS 365 Dauphin and Eurocopter EC155	2 June 1972	11-seat helicopter; Astazou XVIIIA engine	More than 670 for civil and military customers; in production
Eurocopter EC120 Colibri	9 June 1995	Four-seat light helicopter; Turbomeca Arrius 2F turboshaft engine	660 by March 2012; in production
Eurocopter EC135	5 June 1991	Seven-seat helicopter; two Arrius 2B2 or Pratt & Whitney Canada PW206B2 turboshaft engines	More than 1000; in production
Eurocopter EC145	13 June 1979 (BK117)	11-seat development of MBB/Kawasaki BK117; two Arriel 1E2 engines	More than 580 for civil and military customers; in production
Eurocopter EC175	4 December 2009	Medium helicopter; two Pratt & Whitney Canada PT6C-67E turboshaft engines	Deliveries from 2012

▲ **Mil Mi-34 'Hermit'**

Mil, 1990s

A lack of funds has hampered Mil's development of the Mi-34 light piston single. The type is roughly equivalent to the Enstrom F-28, but has failed to find a customer base in a marketplace already crowded by excellent products.

Specifications

Crew: 1–2

Passengers: 2

Powerplant: One 239kW (320hp) Vedeneyev M-14V-26V nine-cylinder air-cooled radial engine

Maximum speed: 210km/hr (130mph)

Range: 450km (280 miles)

Hover ceiling: 1500m (4920ft)

Dimensions: Rotor diameter 10m (39ft 7in); length 11.4m (37ft 5in); height 2.8m (9ft 2in)

Weight: 1080kg (2380lb) loaded

Chapter 9

Special Purpose Aircraft (1935–2012)

Aircraft have been converted or built for almost every conceivable role. From the smallest general aviation types flying as crop sprayers, through bushplanes and converted firebombers, to grossly modified jet transports, the world of special purpose aviation is varied, surprising and endlessly fascinating. It has inspired some of the most incredible aircraft ever flown and demands some of the most exacting, dangerous flying undertaken in the civilian world. Apart from the commercial freighters, few special purpose aircraft operate within regular airways or within the general regulations that govern civil aviation, and many perform operations that could not be accomplished by any other means.

◀ **SATIC A300-600ST Beluga**
Built by SATIC to support Airbus's distributed supply chain, the Beluga adds a grossly enlarged upper fuselage and modified tail surfaces to an A300-600R airframe. The entire nose section above the cockpit hinges upwards for straight-in loading. Five aircraft were built, and following changes of ownership and organization, they are now offered for charter under the name Airbus Beluga by Airbus Transport International.

Firebombers
1935–2012

Although many firebombers are conversions of ex-military aircraft, some purpose-built aircraft have also entered service, including the spectacular Canadair CL-215/Bombardier 415 series.

AERIAL FIREFIGHTING, or firebombing, makes exacting requirements upon an airframe. It must be spacious in order to carry a useful load of water or retardant, and it must have power reserves sufficient for safe low-speed manoeuvring at low altitudes, often in confined operating environments where smoke and heat haze are constant hazards. The firebomber's crew must be able to deliver their payload accurately and, if at all possible, have the means to return to base – or a nearby water source – to replenish their tanks quickly after each drop.

Helicopters have obvious utility as firefighters and many types are able to carry a tank of water, generally called a Bambi Bucket, as an underslung load, for release over the fire scene. Indeed, Erickson Air-Crane has developed a Sea Snorkel system that allows its S-64 Aircrane conversions to refill an onboard tank from any suitable water source from the hover, but helicopters are generally limited in payload and must be flown alongside larger, fixed-wing assets.

Fixed-Wing Firebombers

Many types of aircraft have been converted for firebombing, ex-military aircraft with weapons bays proving particularly suitable. The Grumman Avenger, Douglas Invader and Lockheed Orion have all been modified, while Grumman's Tracker and the upgraded Turbo Tracker have been so successful that Conair Aviation produced a series of converted aircraft under the names Firecat and Turbo Firecat.

Flying boats have shown great utility as firebombers. In Canada, Coulson Flying Tankers keeps the last airworthy examples of the Martin JRM-3 Mars in service as high-capacity firebombers. The aircraft are able to scoop from any suitably large body of water, refilling their tanks without the need to return to base. Coulson has invested heavily in upgrading the 1945-vintage aircraft and one of the two machines now features an EFIS cockpit and datalink for the inflight transmission of key aircraft and environmental data to a ground station.

Canadair created a purpose-designed amphibian firebomber as the CL-215. Later redesigned for turboprop power, the aircraft remains available as the Bombardier 415 and is also able to scoop water as it flies at low level along a river, lake or across the sea – for the North American market it is known as the Super Scooper.

Some agricultural aircraft have also been modified for firefighting, including the vintage Grumman AgCat, while Air Tractor produces two variants of its AT-802F turboprop firebomber, including the Fire Boss amphibian.

▼ Douglas A-26 Invader

Airspray, 1980s

Canada's Airspray operated as many as 18 converted Invaders at one time, using the type over three decades. The company also used three CL-215s, but sold them in 2009 to concentrate its operations on the L-188 Electra and Aero Commander Turbo Commander 690.

Specifications

Crew: 3

Powerplant: Two Pratt & Whitney R-2800-27 "Double Wasp" radials, 1500kW (2000hp) each

Range: 570km/h (355 miles)

Service ceiling: 6700m (22,000ft)

Dimensions: Span 70m (21.34);
    length 50m (15.24m); height 5.64m (18.3ft)

Weight: 10,365kg (22,850lb) loaded

Specifications

Crew: 2

Powerplant: Two Pratt & Whitney R-2800-83AM
18-cylinder radial engines, 1566kW (2100hp)
each

Maximum speed: 290km/hr (180mph)

Range: 2260km (1405 miles)

Dimensions: Span 28.6m (1080ft);
length 19.82m (65ft); height 8.98m (26ft 6in)

Weight: 19,730 kg (43,500 lb) loaded

▼ Canadair CL-215

Sécurité Civile, 1970s

Among other duties, Sécurité Civile flies firebombing missions for the French
Ministry of the Interior. It took 10 CL-215s in 1970 and the aircraft have since
been replaced by the Bombardier 415. Sécurité
Civile also operates Turbo Firecats,
converted Dash 8s and a large fleet
of helicopters.

Specifications

Crew: 2

Powerplant: Two Pratt & Whitney Canada PT6A-
67AF, 761kW (1220hp) each

Maximum speed: 407km/h (253mph)

Endurance: 5 hours 6 min

Dimensions: Span 22.12m (72ft 7in);
length 13.26m (43ft 6in); height 5.05m
(16ft 7in)

Weight: 12,473kg (27,500lb) loaded

▼ Conair Firecat

Conair, 2000s

As part of the Firecat conversion, Conair moves the Tracker's cabin floor upwards
by 20.30cm (8in) to make extra space for retardant tanks. The company also flies
its own operations, using a fleet of
firebombers that includes AT-802s,
CL-215s, CV-580s, a DC-6, an
Electra and Firecats.

Specifications

Crew: 4

Powerplant: Four Wright R-3350-24WA Duplex
Cyclone 18-cylinder radial engines, 1900kW
(2500hp) each

Maximum speed: 356km/h (221mph)

Range: 8000km (5000 miles)

Service ceiling: 4450m (14,600ft)

Dimensions: Span 60.96m (200ft);
length 35.74m (117ft 3in); height 11.71m
(38ft 6in)

Weight: 40,820kg (90,000lb) loaded

▼ Martin JRM-3 Mars

Forest Industries Flying Tankers, 1990s

Both operational Mars flying boats are now
operated by Coulson Flying Tankers, but for
many years they were flown by Forest
Industries, from the same Port Alberni,
Vancouver Island base.

Freighters
1971–2012

A large fleet of dedicated freighters, some of them created by passenger to freight conversion, serves the world's air cargo needs. Many airliners are retired from regular service into air cargo, where they continue to fly for many years.

ALTHOUGH A HUGE amount of air freight is moved in the holds of regular airliners, so much cargo is moved by air that many airlines have freight divisions, while other operators exists solely for the movement of cargo and often play a large part in the logistics and onwards movement of that cargo.

While airline freight operations tend to be quite general in nature, more specialist cargo operators might target themselves at the movement of mail or packages; livestock, such as racehorses; luxury or racing cars; or even fresh flowers and produce. A variety of aircraft are used as freighters and the conversion market for the modification of passenger aircraft to freighters – so called P2F conversions – is so important that for many operators the potential resale value of an airliner for P2F is considered during purchase negotiations.

Widebody and single-aisle conversions include those for the 747, 767, A300, A310, DC-10 and MD-11, and 737 and 757, for example, while Airbus

Specifications

Crew: 3	Service ceiling: 13,716m (45,000ft)
Passengers: 366	Dimensions: Span 59.64m (195ft 7in);
Powerplant: Two Pratt & Whitney JT9D-7J	length 70,51m (2313ft); height 19.33m
2166kN (0hp)	(63ft 4in)
Maximum speed: 969km/hr (602mph)	Weight: 267,570kg (589,900lb) loaded
Range: 13,149km (8170 miles)	

▼ **Boeing 747-200F**

Nippon Cargo Airlines, 1984

JA8167 was delivered to the freight arm of All Nippon Airlines in 1984. As well as the visor nose door, the 747F also has a large upwards-hinging cargo door in its rear left fuselage. For ease of ground handling and continuity, side doors are always cut into the port, or left side of an aircraft.

▼ **McDonnell Douglas DC-10-30CF**

Federal Express, 1984

This aircraft was delivered to Trans International Airlines as a standard DC-10-10 in 1973 and passed to Air Florida in 1981. It was then bought by FedEx and converted as a freighter in 1984, and later upgraded to MD-10 standard under FedEx's programme to bring its DC-10 and MD-11 freighters to a common cockpit standard.

Specifications

Crew: 3	Service ceiling: 12,802m (42,000ft)
Passenger: 255 (two class, typical)	Dimensions: Span 47.34m (155ft 4in);
Powerplant: GE CF6-50C 226.9kN (51,000lbf)	length 51.97m (170ft 6in); height 17.7m
Maximum speed: 982km/hr (610mph)	(58ft 1in)
Range: 10,620km (6600 miles)	Weight: 259,459kg (572,000lb) loaded

Specifications

Crew: 2

Powerplant: Two 249kN (56,000lb thrust) Pratt
  & Whitney PW4156 engines

Maximum speed: 876km/hr (544mph)

Range: 4850km (3014 miles)

Service ceiling: 12,200m (40,026ft)

Dimensions: Span 44.85m (147.1ft);
  length 54.08m (177.4ft);
  height 16.62m (54.5ft)

Weight: 170,500kg (376,000lb) loaded

▼ Airbus A300F4-200

Korean Air Cargo, 1984

The A300F4-200 version of the standard A300B4 was built to the
extent of two examples, the first going to Korean Airlines in
August 1986. Many more A300s were converted as
freighters, while Airbus had great success with the
long-range A300-600F.

Specifications

Crew: 2

Powerplant: Two 490kN (110,100lbf)
  GE90-110B1 engines

Maximum speed: 950km/hr (590mph)

Range: 9070km (5636 miles)

Service ceiling: 13,140m (43,100ft)

Dimensions: Span 64.8m (212ft 7in);
  length 63.7m (209ft 1in);
  height 18.6m (61ft 1in)

Weight: 347,800kg (766,800lb) loaded

▼ Boeing 777F

FedEx Express, 2011

FedEx Express took its first 777F in 2009, but N861FD was delivered
in 2011 and deliveries were continuing in 2012. FedEx ordered
777Fs when Airbus could no longer provide guaranteed
delivery dates for the A380F, an aircraft that has fallen
into abeyance.

has recently postponed its A320 P2F programme. Ironically, among the older airliners, the DC-8 proved to be a far more practical option for P2F than the Boeing 707 – and the Douglas jet, said by some to have been built to a far higher standard in the first place, is now the more common in service, largely thanks to freight operations.

Purpose-Built Freighters

Boeing revolutionized air freight when it flew its 747-200F, or simply 747F, for the first time on 30 November 1971. There had been freighter versions of the 707 and DC-8, but with the 747F, the airlines got not only widebody capacity, but also the possibility for straight-in loading of longer cargoes via the aircraft's upwards hinging 'visor' nose. Later, Boeing created the 747-400F and the Extended Range 747-400ERF, while the first of the new 747-8s into service was the 747-8F.

All the other mainline freighters oblige their operators to load cargo through large side doors, using special ground-handling equipment to turn larger loads as they enter the fuselage. In the wake of the 2008 global financial crisis, the freight market has fallen into decline and is recovering far more slowly than the passenger market. However, airfreight remains vitally important, especially in the Far East, and two new freighters have come to market in recent years.

Boeing launched the 777F into a booming freight market in 2005, but delivered the first aircraft to launch customer Air France in the depths of recession, on 19 February 2009. The 777F is based on the 777-200LR and uses that aircrafts 489.18kN (110,000lb) thrust GE90 engines. A typical load might be 27 standard pallets on the main cargo deck, with 17m³ (600 cu ft) of bulk cargo, or 10 pallets, on

Specifications

Crew: 2	Service ceiling: 12,527m (41,000ft)
Powerplant: 320kN (71,930lbs)	Dimensions: Span 60.30m (197ft 8in); length
Maximum speed: 871km/hr (537mph)	58.82m (193ft); height 16.88m (55ft 4in)
Range: 7400km (5950 miles)	Weight: 65.000kg (143,300lb) loaded

▼ Airbus A330-200F

Turkish Cargo, 29 September 2010

TC-JDO was delivered direct to Turkey from Airbus' Toulouse facility on 29 September 2010. Turkish Airlines was the third customer to receive A330-200Fs, after Etihad Airways and Hong Kong Airlines.

the lower deck; such a payload can be carried over as much as 9045km (5620 miles).

With the Airbus A300-600F selling strongly into the 2000s, Airbus saw no reason to make an early commitment to an A330F, especially while engineers and resources were focused on A380 development, and launched the project only on 17 January 2007, with six months of A300 production left to run. At roughly the same time, orders for the standard A330 models began to flood in as airlines sought to cover capacity shortfall caused by delays to Boeing's Dreamliner. Struggling to meet demand, Airbus decided to slow A330F development, a decision given additional weight by the 2008 economic crisis, delaying first flight to 5 November 2009 and first delivery, to Etihad, to 2010.

Airbus was forced to work rather harder at the A330F than Boeing had needed to on the 777F, since the A330's natural nose-down stance on the ground would have forced freight loading to be conducted 'up hill'. The problem could have been solved by a lengthened nose gear leg, but this complex solution was rejected in favour of mounting the leg lower down in the wheel well, providing a level cabin floor for loading, but forcing Airbus to add a fairing to cover the retracted undercarriage assembly.

▼ Boeing 747-8F

The freighter version of the 747-8 was first into service, bringing much of the Dreamliners 'all-electric' technology to the cargo market. All 747 freighters built as such have the small upper fuselage 'hump' of the -100/200 Classics.

Outsize specialists
1961–2012

Aero Spacelines really began the outsize cargo business with its Guppy conversions, a theme continued by SATIC and Boeing. Military freighters have also found commercial use, satisfying the needs of customers with bulky or especially heavy cargoes.

EARLY IN THE 1960s, NASA found itself in urgent need of a means to carry large sections of Saturn rockets and other equipment for the Apollo programme quickly, safely and securely. Ex-USAF bomber and transport pilot John 'Jack' Conroy came up with a solution. BOAC, Northwest and Pan Am had recently retired their Stratocruiser fleets and, with aircraft broker Lee Mansdorf, Conroy formed Aero Spacelines to create an outsize freighter from

Stratocruiser parts. He took an ex-Pan Am machine and inserted a fuselage section from an ex-BOAC aircraft behind its wing. He then took the roof off this stretched machine and added a grossly swollen upper fuselage 'bubble', creating what became known as the B377PG Pregnant Guppy.

The modified aircraft flew for the first time on 19 September 1962 and by summer 1963 it was working on contract to NASA. But the space agency

Specifications

Crew: 3	Service ceiling: 9100m (30,000ft)
Passengers: 160	Dimensions: Span 43.37 m (142ft 4in);
Powerplant: Four Rolls-Royce Tyne 515/50	length 41.73m (136ft 11in); height 11.18m
turboprops 4270kW (5730hp) each	(36ft 8in)
Maximum speed: 646km/hr (402mph)	Weight: 29,959kg (66,048lb) loaded
Range: 8990km (5588 miles)	

▼ Canadair CL-44D4-2
Flying Tiger Line, 1961

The CL-44D4-2 was a specialized freighter based on Canadair's CL-44 development of the Bristol Britannia. The aircraft's entire tail section could be swung to starboard, allowing straight-in loading of even the longest items of cargo.

Specifications

Crew: 3–4	Service ceiling: 7620m (25,000ft)
Powerplant: Four 5145kW (6900shp) Pratt &	Dimensions: Span 47.63m (156ft 4in);
Whitney T34-PI-WA turboprop engines	length 43.8m (143ft 8in);
Maximum speed: 565km/hr (351mph)	height 14.78m (48ft 6in)
Range: 3211km (1995 miles)	Weight: 77,111kg (170,000lb) loaded

▼ Aero Spacelines B377SG Super Guppy
Aero Spacelines, late 1960s

The Super Guppy was so modified that very little of the KC-97 could be discerned from the finished product. The aircraft served NASA until 1991, before going into storage. Its place at NASA was later taken by one of the retired Airbus Guppy 201s.

Specifications

Crew: 6

Powerplant: Four 229.5kN (51,600lbf) Ivchenko
Progress D-18T turbofans engines

Maximum speed: 865km/hr (537mph)

Range: 5410km (3360 miles)

Service ceiling: 12,000m (39,370ft)

Dimensions: Span 73.3m (240ft 5in);
length 68.96m (226ft 3in); height 20.78m
(68ft 2in)

Weight: 405,000kg (893,000lb) loaded

▼ Antonov An-124 Ruslan 'Condor'

Aeroflot, 1980s

Wearing Aeroflot titles and military red stars, this An-124 is typical of the type in Soviet service. In terms of its load-carrying capability the An-124 is unmatched and attempts to reinstate it in production are ongoing.

Specifications

Crew: 6

Powerplant: Six 229.47kN (51,355lb thrust)
ZMKB Progress (Lotarev) D-18T turbofan
engines

Maximum speed: 850km/hr (530mph)

Range: 15,400km (9570 miles)

Service ceiling: 11,000m (36,100ft)

Dimensions: Span 88.4m (290ft 2in);
length 84m (275.6ft); height 18.1m (59.3ft)

Weight: 640,000kg (1,410,000lb) loaded

▼ Antonov An-225 Myria 'Cossack'

1989

The An-225 flew with Buran in place during 1989, but had already made history with a number of world records, including the fact that it was the first aircraft to be able to fly at a gross weight in excess of 453,600kg (1,000,000lb).

Interestingly, the A380 became the first aircraft to complete its maiden flight at a take-off weight of more than 453,600kg.

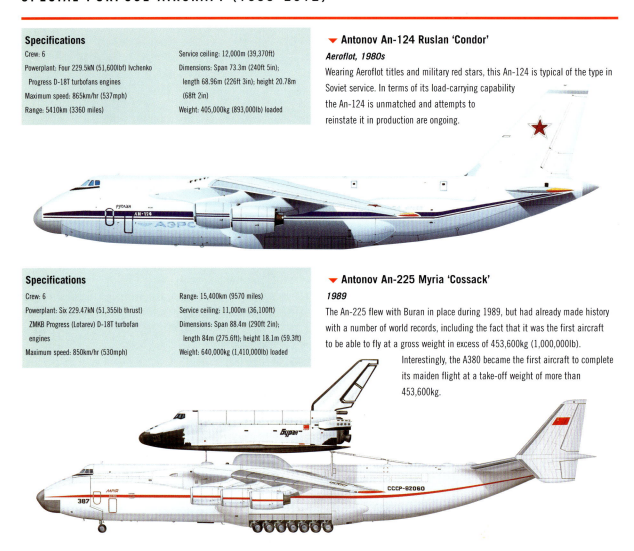

required an even larger machine. In response, Aero Spacelines produced a second Guppy, increasing its wingspan and stretching its fuselage even more radically. A taller fin was installed, along with a swinging nose for ease of loading and a T34 turboprop powerplant. This B377SG Super Guppy was soon also serving NASA, while Conroy designed Guppies for other markets, including the Mini Guppy and productionized Guppy 101.

Conroy also created a Guppy from a Canadair CL-44 propliner, but his definitive aircraft was the turboprop Guppy 201. The aircraft was designed under subcontract from Sud-Aviation, specifically to move Airbus components between its multinational factories. Based on a KC-97, with the engines and nacelles of a Lockheed P-3 Orion, the Guppy 201

flew for the first time on 24 August 1970. Two aircraft were delivered, but then Airbus bought the type's production rights and had two more built. The Guppy 201s served into the mid-1990s, when a new outsize specialist replaced them.

Beluga and Dreamlifter

Airbus realized during the 1980s that the Guppy 201s would soon need replacing and proposed a not dissimilar modification of the A300B4 to replace them. It put the work out to tender and an Aerospatiale/DASA consortium was successful, being contracted to build four aircraft as the Super Airbus Transport International Company (SATIC). In the event, the new aircraft were based on the A300-600R and named A300-600ST Beluga.

The Beluga completed its first flight on 13 September 1994 and the fleet of five, after an additional aircraft was ordered, has worked hard for Airbus ever since.

When Boeing decided to build its 787 along similar lines to the Airbus production model, it too required an outsize freighter. Clearly, it would never do to buy the SATIC product and the manufacturer contracted Evergreen to convert three 747-400 airframes. Performed in Taipei, the modification work produced the 747 Large Cargo Freighter (LCF), or Dreamlifter, the first of which arrived in Seattle on 16 September 2006.

Airlifters

With the exception of Flying Tiger Line's swing-tail CL-44D, most of the aircraft flying outsize cargoes have been, and continue to be, either ex-military airlifters or similar aircraft built for the commercial market. During the build-up to the 1982 Falklands War, the British Government found itself in the ignominious position of having to charter Heavylift to fly supplies to Ascension Island in the Shorts Belfast outsize freighters that the Royal Air Force had been forced to retire in budget cuts just a few years earlier.

A similar aircraft to the Belfast, though slightly smaller, the Lockheed C-130 Hercules was built for commercial operators as the L-100 and achieved a degree of success, particularly in support of oil drilling and other prospecting work.

The regular outsize market belongs to Russia, however. Back in Soviet times, the divide between military airlifter and civilian freighter was often blurred as Aeroflot aircraft wore military markings for exercises and immediate mobilization should war break out, while air force machines often wore Aeroflot titles. During the 1990s, the Antonov An-124 Ruslan 'Condor', the world's largest production aircraft, became increasingly available for charter and the more it was used by Western organizations, the more they appreciated its load-hauling capabilities.

Generators, fleets of cars, drilling equipment and even trains – all have been swallowed by the cavernous maw of the An-124, with loading eased by its kneeling undercarriage, integral ramps, visor nose and wide-opening rear doors. Even with a full cargo hold, the aircraft has space for 88 passengers on its pressurized upper deck, and it has become a vital component of Coalition operations in Afghanistan and Iraq, as well as serving the outsize freight market globally.

Antonov's other giant jet airlifter, the An-225 Mriya (Dream) is little more than an enlarged, six-engined An-124. It was designed primarily to carry the Buran space shuttle piggyback fashion, but also features a massive cargo hold. First flown on 21 December 1988, the sole example fell out of use during the 1990s, but was made airworthy again in 2001. A second aircraft was never completed.

Specifications

Crew: 2	Service ceiling: 10,700m (35,105ft)
Powerplant: Two 262kW (59,000lb thrust) GE	Dimensions: Span 44.84m (147ft 1in);
CF-6-80C2A8 turbofan engines	length 56.15m (184ft 3in); height 17.24m
Maximum speed: 778km/hr (483mph)	(56ft 7in)
Range: 4632km (2878 miles)	Weight: 45,000kg (100,310lb) max take-off

▼ **SATIC A300-600ST Beluga**

Airbus, 2000s

Although the Beluga fleet is dedicated to the Airbus network, it is available for charter should spare capacity become available, and has been used to support the European Space Agency. The 'ST' of its designation refers to 'Special Transporter'.

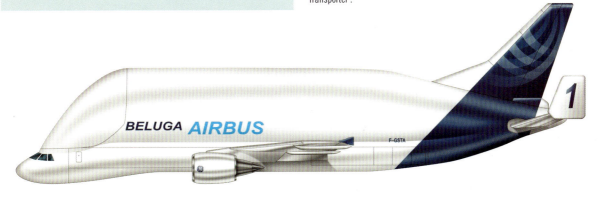

Specifications

Crew: 3–4

Powerplant: Four 3360kW (4510shp) Allison
501-D22A turboprop engines

Maximum speed: 570km/hr (354mph)

Range: 2470km (1535 miles)

Service ceiling: 7000m (23,000ft)

Dimensions: Span 40.4m (132ft 7in);
length 34.37m (112ft 9in);
height 11.6m (38ft 3in)

Weight: 70,300kg (155,000lb) loaded

▼ Lockheed L-100-30 Hercules

Pacific Western Airlines, December 1978

Pacific Western took delivery of C-GHPW in December 1978, having become the first operator of the L-100 during the 1960s. The aircraft were used in support of energy and mineral exploration, as well as on general freight work. The -30 models had a stretched fuselage compared to the 'vanilla' L-100.

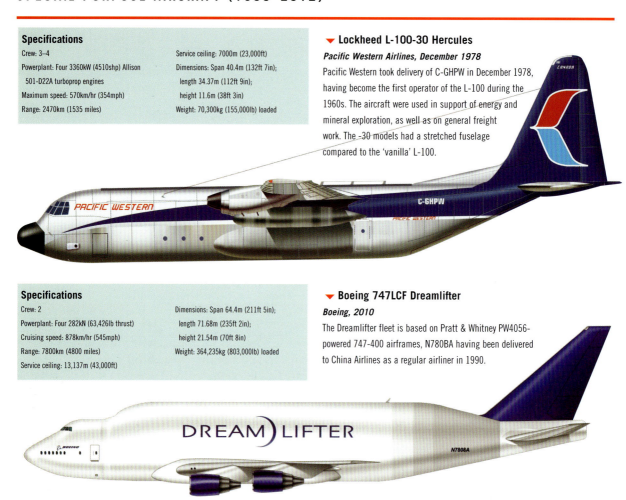

Specifications

Crew: 2

Powerplant: Four 282kN (63,426lb thrust)

Cruising speed: 878km/hr (545mph)

Range: 7800km (4800 miles)

Service ceiling: 13,137m (43,000ft)

Dimensions: Span 64.4m (211ft 5in);
length 71.68m (235ft 2in);
height 21.54m (70ft 8in)

Weight: 364,235kg (803,000lb) loaded

▼ Boeing 747LCF Dreamlifter

Boeing, 2010

The Dreamlifter fleet is based on Pratt & Whitney PW4056-powered 747-400 airframes, N780BA having been delivered to China Airlines as a regular airliner in 1990.

Agricultural aircraft
1960s–2012

Agricultural aircraft have an obvious role in the application of chemicals to crops, but are also important in the wider control of pests, such as locusts. Several countries have thriving agplane manufacturing facilities.

THE DEMANDS OF agricultural flying are in many ways similar to those of firebombing and some agricultural machines, notably the AT-802F, have made the transition to the more dangerous role. There have also been some quite extreme agricultural aircraft, such as DC-6 propliners converted as sprayers and the PZL M-15 Belphegor, a huge jet biplane. First flown in the early 1970s, the Belphegor

was nominally optimized for the delivery of large quantities of chemicals over Soviet collective farms, but is just as likely to have been used to deny NATO's armies cover, by the defoliation of Western Europe should conflict have broken out.

In general terms, agricultural aircraft (commonly known as agplanes) are usually single-engined machines and fairly large – they must hold a hopper

▲ Ayres S2R-T65 Turbo Thrush

US Department of State Narcotics Eradication Delivery System (NEDS), 1980s

Nine S2R-T65 aircraft were ordered for the NEDS programme, as armoured sprayers for the delivery of herbicide against narcotics plants in South and Central America during the 1980s. Like all modern agplanes, the Turbo Thrush cockpit is sealed against penetration by chemicals, but the S2R-T65 had more power to allow the installation of armour and the carriage of an observer to spot groundfire.

Specifications

Crew: 1–2	Service ceiling: 7620m (25,000ft)
Powerplant: One 559kW (750hp) Pratt &	Dimensions: Span 13.55m (44ft 5in);
Whitney Canada PT6A-34AG turboprop	length 10.06m (3ft);
Maximum speed: 256km/hr (159mph)	height 2.8m (9ft 3in)
Range: 1239km (770 miles)	Weight: 2721kg (6000lb) loaded

for their chemical payload. They have excellent manoeuvrability, allowing them to work around a field at very low altitudes. Finally, ease of maintenance is desirable, since many agplanes are flown by owner pilots, or in small fleets by dedicated operators. An agplane might be 'on the road' away from base for weeks at a time during a spraying season, moving from job to job as crops, jobs and the weather demand. In terms of piloting, most importantly from the client's point of view, agplanes must be flown accurately. Farmers want to avoid too much chemical being applied to one swathe of crop, but equally need to avoid overspray, which can be harmful to plants other than the target crop and is liable to pollute water courses and waste expensive chemicals.

Several manufacturers have produced agplanes over the years, including Air Tractor, Ayres, Cessna, Grumman and Piper in the United States; Embraer in Brazil; PZL in Poland; and Antonov in the Soviet Union. With the advent of broad-swathe, wheeled sprayers, aerial application is now very uncommon over the UK's relatively small fields, but over the vast fields of the Americas and Russia, it still has an important role to play.

▲ Ayres Turbo Commander

1980s

Ayres, in common with other agplane manufacturers, has had piston and turboprop-powered aircraft in its range. The Thrush Commander used a Pratt & Whitney Wasp, but in 2012 all of Ayres range – the 510P, 510G, 550P and 710P – were turboprop powered.

Specifications

Crew: 1	Range: 648km (403 miles)
Powerplant: One 448kW (600hp) Pratt &	Service ceiling: 4575m (15,000ft)
Whitney R-1340 Wasp 9-cylinder air-cooled	Dimensions: Span 13.51m (44ft 4in); length
radial engine	8.89m (29ft 2in); height 2.79m (9ft 2in)
Maximum speed: 225km/hr (140mph)	Weight: 3130kg (6900lb) loaded

Bushplanes/utility
1935–2012

The demands of bushplane operations have produced a handful of dedicated designs, optimized for operations from austere strips in the worst conditions all year round.

BUSHPLANE OPERATIONS, flights servicing remote locations with limited or no facilities, began between the wars, but became a major facet of general aviation after World War II. Early bush operations were flown using whatever aircraft were available, typically into Canadian or Alaskan forests, but also into the Australian bush and other remote areas of the world.

Some manufacturers considered building aircraft specifically for bush operations, however, and among the first was Canada's Noorduyn, which flew its first Norseman on 14 November 1935. The aircraft exhibited all the characteristics of the classic bushplane: it was simple and easy to maintain; it offered accommodation for eight passengers, freight, or a mix of both; and, perhaps most importantly, could be operated off wheel, ski or float landing gear, so that operations could continue all year round and were not restricted to locations with a suitable stretch of clear ground. In the Canadian bush, a stretch of water suitable for landing a floatplane is seldom far away.

More than 900 Norsemen were sold and the aircraft was then joined on the market by de Havilland Canada's DHC-2 Beaver in 1947. Reacting to the requirements of the Ontario Department of Lands and Forests, de Havilland Canada produced an aircraft that was generally similar to the Norseman, but offering STOL performance and built to modern standards. The aircraft was very successful and de Havilland followed it with the larger DHC-3 Otter in 1951. Both designs remained so popular that turboprop conversions were developed many years later.

Cessna entered the bushplane market with the smaller Model 185 in July 1960 and the larger 206 in 1964, and finally addressed the modern bushplane market with the turboprop Caravan in 1982. Australia's piston-powered Gippsland GA8 and the United States' turboprop Quest Kodiak, both of them high-wing bushplanes currently in production, have now joined the Cessna on the bushplane market.

▲ **de Havilland DHC-2 Beaver**

Royal Canadian Mounted Police, 1963–83

The capabilities of the Beaver appealed to more than regular passenger/freight operators, its versatility being especially appreciated by the Royal Canadian Mounted Police. Configured as a floatplane, the Beaver gained an auxiliary ventral fin beneath its tail, to ensure directional stability.

Specifications

Crew: 1
Passengers: 7
Powerplant: One 936kW (1255hp) Pratt & Whitney R-985 Wasp Junior radial piston engine
Maximum speed: 262km/hr (163mph)

Range: 1180km (733 miles)
Service ceiling: 5485m (18,000ft)
Dimensions: Span 14.63m (48ft);
length 9.22m (30ft 3in); height 2.74m (9ft)
Weight: 2313kg (5100lb) loaded

▲ Antonov (PZL-Mielec) An-2 'Colt'
Arctic Directorate

First flown in 1947, the Soviet An-2 was roughly equivalent to the Beaver, albeit in biplane form. It offered the same versatility in terms of undercarriage arrangement and this Polish-built example is painted and equipped for Aeroflot's Arctic Directorate, although it lacks the airline's titles.

Specifications

Crew: 1–2	Range: 845km (525 miles)
Passengers: 12	Service ceiling: 4500m (14,750ft)
Powerplant: One 750kW (1000hp) Shvetsov	Dimensions: Span 18.2m (59ft 8in);
ASh-62IR 9-cylinder radial engine	length 12.4m (40ft 8in); height 4.1m (13ft)
Maximum speed: 258km/hr (160mph)	Weight: 5500kg (12,000lb) loaded

▲ de Havilland Canada DHC-3 Otter
Wardair, 1970s

Wardair was unusual, as a mainline carrier that also flew bush operations. It used as many as five Otters, with this example on skis for winter use. Undercarriage options included standard wheeled gear, low-pressure balloon tyres for rough-field operations, skis and floats.

Specifications

Crew: 1	Range: 1520km (945 miles)
Passengers: 9–10	Service ceiling: 5730m (18,800ft)
Powerplant: One 448kW (600hp) Pratt &	Dimensions: Span 17.69m (58ft); length
Whitney 9-cylinder air-cooled radial engine	12.80m (41ft 10in); height 3.83m (12ft 7in)
Maximum speed: 257km/hr (160mph)	Weight: 3629kg (8000lb) loaded

Specifications

Crew: 1	Range: 2000km (1243 miles)
Passengers: 12	Service ceiling: 8410m (27,600ft)
Powerplant: One 505kW (677hp) Pratt &	Dimensions: Span 15.88m (52ft 1in); length
Whitney PT6A-114A engine	12.67m (41ft 7in); height 4.32m (14ft 2in)
Maximum speed: 317km/hr (197mph)	Weight: 3970kg (8752lb) loaded

▲ Cessna Model 208 Grand Caravan
Cessna, 2012

Cessna's Grand Caravan can be equipped with seats for up to 12 passengers, for fewer passengers in a luxurious executive configuration, or cargo carrying. As well as the Grand Caravan, the Caravan is available in baseline Caravan 675, Caravan Amphibian and Super Cargomaster versions.

Index

Page numbers in *italics* refer to illustrations and tables.

Aerial Steam Carriage *6, 12*
Aero O/Y, Finland *50*, 54, *93*
Aero Spacelines
    B377PG Pregnant Guppy 179
    B377SG Super Guppy *179*, 180
    B377SGT Guppy 201 180
aerobatics 146, *147*
Aeroflot, USSR
    helicopters *168, 169, 170*
    interwar period *50*
    latest developments 132, *133*
    modern period *82*, 83, 85, 95, *99*
    post-war period *78*
    regional routes *117*
    special purpose aircraft *180*
    widebodied aircraft *105, 107*
Aerospatiale
    Aerospatiale/BAC Concorde 109,
        110, *111*
    Alouette II 167
    Alouette III 167, *171*
    AS332 Super Puma 167, *168, 171*
    AS350/355 Ecureuil 160, 167,
        169, 171
    AS360/365 Dauphin 167, *169, 171*
    Lynx 167
    SA 321 Super Frelon 167, *171*
    SA 330 Puma 167, *171*
    SA 341/342 Gazelle 167
    see also Eurocopter
agricultural aircraft 182–3
Agusta
    A109 160
    Agusta/Bell AB47 168
    Agusta/Bell AB139 168
    Bell/Agusta BA609 168
AgustaWestland
    AW101 168
    AW139 168
Air France
    Concorde 109, *111*
    interwar period *50*, 52, *55*, 59
    modern period 83, 87, *96*
    post-war period 69, 76–7, 77
    regional routes 124

widebodied aircraft *107*
air mail, interwar years 34–5, 42–3,
    44, 52, 56
Air Tahiti 115, 116
Air Tractor AT-802 174, 182
Airbus Industrie
    A300 101, *104*, 105, 122, 173,
        176, *177*, 178, 180
    A310 105, *106*, 176
    A318 124–5
    A319 124, 131
    A320 123–5, 129, 131, *177*
    A320neo 129, 131
    A321 123–4, 131
    A330 *107*, 108, 178
    A340 *107*, 108
    A350 *126*, 131
    A350 XWB 130
    A380 128, 129, 130, 178, 180
    Guppy 201 179
Aircraft Manufacturing Co Ltd (Airco)
    DH.4A 22, 29
    DH.4B 34
    DH.9 22, *32*, 54
    DH.9A 23
    DH.9C 26
    DH.16 22–3
Aircraft Transport & Travel Ltd, UK
    16–17, 22, *50*
Airspeed Ambassador 75
Alcock, Captain John *13, 20*, 21, 32–3
Alitalia *65*, 78, *124*
American Airlines
    interwar period 56, 57, *58*
    modern period 87, 93
    post-war period 70, 71
    widebodied aircraft 105
American Airways 43, *44*
American Export Airlines 67, 69
Antonov
    An-2 'Colt' *185*
    An-124 Ruslan 'Condor' *180*, 181
    AN-225 Mriya 'Cossack' *180*, 181
Archdeacon, Ernest *12*, 13
Armstrong Whitworth
    Argosy *26*, 27, *33*, 36, *48*
    A.W.XV Atalanta *26*, 38–9
    A.W.27 Ensign *26*
Atlantic Aircraft 26

Australia
    earliest flying machines 8
    interwar period 25, 31, *32, 33*,
        38–9, 46, 60
    post-war period 75, 76
Austria *51*, 54, 145
autopilots, earliest 30, *32*
Aveline, Georges 30, *32*
Aviation Traders ATL.98 Carvair *76*
Avions de Transport Régional (ATR)
    ATR 42 119
    ATR 72 115, 119
Avro
    504K *136*, 146
    618 Ten *36*
    Avian 137
    Lancaster 75
    Lancastrian 75–6
    RJ 120
    Tudor 75
    York 75
Ayres
    S2R-T65 Turbo Thrush *183*
    S2R Thrush *183*

BAC
    Aerospatiale/BAC Concorde 109,
        110, *111*
    One-Eleven 85, 89, 91, 94
Batten, Jean 46
Beech, Walter and Olive 139, 143, 154
Beechcraft
    Hawker Beechcraft 800 series *148*,
        150
    Model 17 Staggerwing 143, 154
    Model 18 154, 155
    Model 35 Bonanza 143, *144*
    Model 50 Twin Bonanza 156
    Model 55 Baron 156
    Model 58 Baron 156
    Model 60 Duke 156, *157*
    Model 80 Queen Air 117, 156
    Model 99 Airliner 117
    Model 200 Super King Air *155*
    Model 350i King Air 156
    Model 400 *134, 150*
    Model 1900 Airliner 117–18, *119*
    Model 2000 Starship 156
Belgium 22, 26, *51, 52, 56, 70*, 137

Bell Helicopter
  Agusta/Bell AB139 168
  Bell/Agusta BA609 168
  civil helicopter range *161*
  Model 47 159, 160, *161, 166,*
    167, 168
  Model 206 JetRanger 160, *161,*
    166, 167
  Model 212 *161, 162,* 167
  Model 222 *158, 161, 164*
  Model 230 *158, 161*
  Model 407 160, *161, 166*
  Model 427 160, *161*
  Model 429 160, *161*
  Model 525 Relentless 160, *161*
  Model UH-1 160, *161*
Bellanca Skyrocket *48*
Bennet, Floyd 32, *33*
Berlin Airlift 64, *66*
Bernard 191GR *31*
Blériot, Louis *11,* 15, 29
Blériot Aéronautique
  Blériot-SPAD S.33 29, *49*
  XI *11–12,* 15
Bloch
  MB.160/161 77
  MB.220 59
Blohm und Voss
  BV 142 *60*
  BV 222 *60*
  Ha 139 *48, 55*
Boeing
  707 82–3, 84, 87, 89, 90–1, 93,
    102–3, 177
  717 90, *93*
  727 *80, 88,* 89, 98, 122
  737 *88,* 89, 91, 94–5, 123, 124,
    125, 129, 176
  737 MAX 129
  747 102–4, 108, 128, *176,* 177,181
  747-8 128–9, 177, *178*
  747LCF Dreamlifter 181, *182*
  757 *100,* 122–3, 124, 176
  767 101, 105, *106,* 122–3, 176
  777 108, 125, 177–8
  787 Dreamliner 108, 128, 131,
    178, 181
  2707 110
  B-1 *13*
  B-17 73
  B-29 73
  B-47 86
  B-50 73
  B-52 86

C-97 73
  KC-97 87, 180
  Model 1 *14*
  Model 40A 42
  Model 80 42
  Model 200 Monomail 48
  Model 234 Chinook 166
  Model 247 *18,* 48, 56, *57*
  Model 247D *57*
  Model 307 Stratoliner 48, 58, *59,*
    67, 73
  Model 314 Clipper *48, 59,* 67, 73
  Model 367-80 86–7, 90
  Model 377 Stratocruiser 69, *72,* 73,
    75, 86, 179
  Sonic Cruiser 128
Boeing Air Transport, US 42, 43, *48*
Bombardier
  415 174, 175
  Challenger series 151
  CRJ 121, 133
  CSeries 127, *132,* 133
  Gates Learjet 151
  Q400 116, 118
Boulton & Paul P.64 Mail Carrier *39*
Braniff International Airways, US 87
Brantly Helicopter 161
Brazil 41, 47, *114,* 118, 121, *122*
Breguet
  763 Provence 76, *77*
  Bre.14 29
  Bre.14T2 Salon 29
  Bre.19 Super Bidon *31*
  Bre.19GR 33
  Bre.280T 29
  Bre.393T *52*
Bristol
  Brabazon 74
  Britannia 96, 179
  Tourer 25, 29
  Type 62 *23,* 25
British Aerospace (BAe)
  Advanced Turboprop (ATP) 96
  BAe 125 *148,* 150
  BAe 146 120
  Jetstream 31 *112,* 118
  Jetstream 41 118
British Air Ferries *76*
British Airways (1935) *50,* 53, 54
British Airways (1974) *89, 104,* 109,
  110, 122, 123
British Caledonian (BCal) *85,* 123
British European Airways (BEA)
  modern period 84–5, 94, 96

post-war period 74, 75, 76
  regional routes 112
British Overseas Airways Corporation
  Concorde 109
  interwar period 39, *50,* 53
  modern period 82, 84, 85, 90, 96
  post-war period *65,* 73, 74–6
  World War II 59, *61*
Britten-Norman
  BN-2A-21 Islander *111,* 115
  BN-2A Mk III Trislander 115
Brown, Lieutenant Arthur Whitten *13,*
  20, 21, 32–3
Brymon Airways, UK 122
Buran space shuttle *180,* 181
bushplanes 184, *185*
business jets 147–53
Byrd, Lieutenant Commander Richard
  E. 32, *33,* 47

Canada
  general aviation 151, *152*
  interwar period 35, 184
  latest developments 127, *132,* 133
  modern period 82
  regional routes *112, 113, 114, 117,*
    121
  special purpose aircraft 174, *175,*
    184, *185*
Canadair
  C-4 *71,* 75
  Challenger series 121, 151, *152*
  CL-44 *179,* 180, 181
  CL-215 174, *175*
  Regional Jet 121
CAP Aviation CAP 230 146
CASA-Nurtanio CN235 118, 119
Caudron C.640 Typhon *55*
Cayley, Sir George 8–9
Cessna, Clyde V. 138–9, 143
Cessna Aircraft Company
  120 139, 141, 142
  140 141
  150 *140, 141,* 142
  152 *141,* 142
  162 Skycatcher *141,* 142
  170 140, 141, *141*
  172 *139,* 141, 142
  180 140, *141*
  182 140, *141*
  185 Skywagon *140, 141,* 184
  190 141
  208 Caravan 142, 184, *185*
  210 Centurion *140, 141*

404 Titan 156
414 Chancellor 156
421 Golden Eagle 156
A150 Aerobat 146
Citation series *149–50, 151*, 153
CW-6 139
Model A 139
Model C 139
post-war singles *141*
T-37/A-37 151
T-50 139
Chanute, Octave 9, 10
China 8, 67, *97, 113,* 127
Cirrus SR20/22 145
Civil Aviation Administration of China
(CAAC) *97*
Cobham, Sir Alan 25, *32, 33*
Commercial Aircraft Corporation of
China (COMAC)
ARJ21 127, 132–3
C919 133
Compagnie de Messageries Aériennes,
France 29, *50*
Compagnie Franco-Roumaine de
Navigation Aérienne, France 52
Compagnie Générale d'Enterprises
Aéronautiques, France 49, 52
Compagnie Internationale de Navigation
Aérienne, France 29, *49, 50,* 52
Conair Firecat 174, *175*
Conroy, John 'Jack' 179, 180
Consolidated Commodore *43*
Construzioni Meccaniche Aeronautiche
SA (CAMSA) 29
Continental Express, US *114, 120*
Convair
CV-240 Convair-Liner 73, 78, 93
CV-340 *72, 73*
CV-440 *73*
CV-880 93
CV-990 Coronado *92*
Cornu twin-rotor *10*
Costes, Dieudonné 33
Coulson Flying Tankers 174, 175
Curtiss
AT-32B Condor 42, *44*
BT-32 Condor II *47,* 57
C-46 Commando *66*
C-55 *61*
JN-4 Jenny 34
Model 40 Carrier Pigeon *35,* 42
Curtiss Swallow 42
Czechoslovakia *50,* 54, *78, 79,* 146

DAHER-SOCATA TBM850 156
Daily Mail 13, 15, 21, 46, 136
Daimler Air Hire, UK 23, 25, *50*
Daimler Airways, UK 30, 31, *32,* 36,
50
Dassault
Falcon 10 *148,* 153
Falcon 900 *152,* 153
Mercure 94–5
de Havilland
Comet I 75, 82, 86–7, 90, 94
Comet 4 82, *83,* 90
DH.16 23
DH.18 23, 25, 30
DH.34 *24,* 25, *32,* 36
DH.50 *32, 33*
DH.50J *25*
DH.60 Moth 136
DH.60G Gipsy Moth 46, 136
DH.60M Moth 31, *32,* 46
DH.66 Hercules *24, 27, 33,* 38
DH.75 Hawk Moth 136
DH.80A Puss Moth 46
DH.82 Tiger Moth 146
DH.83 Fox Moth 136
DH.85 Leopard Moth 136, *138*
DH.86 38, 39
DH.87 Hornet Moth 137, *138*
DH.88 Comet 48
DH.89 Dragon Rapide 74, 75, 112
DH.91 Albatross 59
DH.121 Trident 84
DH.125 Jet Dragon 149
Dove 75
Heron *75,* 112
interwar aircraft *24*
Mosquito FB.Mk.IV *61*
see also Aircraft Manufacturing Co
Ltd; Hawker Siddeley
de Havilland, Geoffrey 22–3, 82, 136
de Havilland Canada
DHC-2 Beaver *113,* 142, 184
DHC-3 Otter *113,* 142, 184, *185*
DHC-6 Twin Otter *113, 114,* 115,
116, 117, 118
DHC-7 Dash 7 *113,* 118, 120
DHC-8 Dash 8 *113,* 116, *117*
Denmark *50,* 54
Deutsche Aero Lloyd, Germany 26, 40,
51
Deutsche Luft-Reederi, Germany 17,
26, 40, *51*
Dewoitine D.338 52, *55,* 59
Diamond Aircraft 145

Dobrolet, USSR 25, 31, *32, 51*
Dornier
Delphin 28–9
Do X 29, *54*
Do 17 *60*
Do 18 41
Do 228 *112,* 118
Do 328 118
Do J Wal 29, 41
Do P *60*
Do R2 Super Wal 41
Komet 28, 40
Merkur 28, *40*
Douglas
A-26 Invader 154, 174
C-47 *62,* 64, 73, 75
C-54 58, 63, 67, 68, 71
DC-1 48
DC-2 39, 48, 53, 54, 56–7
DC-3 48, 54, 57, *58,* 61, *62,* 67,
73, 74, 76
DC-4 58, 67, *70,* 75, 76
DC-6 69, 70, 71–2, 73, 182
DC-6A 70, *71,* 72
DC-6B 70–1, 72
DC-7 71, 72, 73
DC-7C *71,* 72
DC-8 84, 90–1, 93, 102, 177
DC-9 89, 91, *92,* 93, 94–5, 124
Douglas Sleeper Transport 57
DWC *30, 32*
M-2 42
post-war aircraft *71*
Dumod Infinite 155

Earhart, Amelia 46
earliest flying machines *6,* 7–17
Eastern Air Lines, US
interwar period 43, 56
post-war period *68,* 69, 70
widebodied aircraft 105
easyJet, UK *124*
EH Industries EH101 168
Elliot, A.B. *32, 33*
Embraer
commercial aircraft range *115*
E195 *115,* 116
EJet series *115,* 121, 133
EMB-110 Bandeirante *114, 115,*
118
EMB-120 Brasilia *115,* 118, 121
ERJ-145 *115,* 121, *122*
Legacy series 153
Phenom series 153

Enstrom
    280FX Shark 163, *164*
    480 163
    F-28 163, *164*
Eurocopter
    AS365 Dauphin 167, *171*
    EC120 167, *171*
    EC135 167, *170, 171*
    EC145 167, *171*
    EC175 167, *171*
    see also Aerospatiale
Extra Aircraft EA-230 146, *147*

Fairchild
    F-27 Friendship *97,* 98
    FC-2 *33*
    Saab-Fairchild SF340 118
Fairey
    IIIC/D *32*
    Long Range Monoplane *33*
Farman, Henry 9
Farman F.60 Goliath *17,* 29, 30
FedEx Express, US *176, 177*
Fiat G.12 78
Finland *50,* 54, *93*
firebombers 174–5
Florida Airways, US 42, 43
flybe, UK 116, *122*
Flying Doctor Service, Australia 25, *33*
Flying Tiger Line, US *179,* 181
Focke-Wulf
    A 43 Falke 137
    Fw 200 Condor *58,* 60
Fokker
    50 *119*
    100 120, *121*
    C-2 32, *33*
    decline of 60, 78, 120–1
    Dr.I 20
    D.VII 20
    E-series 20
    F.I 25
    F.II *22,* 25–6
    F.III *22,* 26, *27*
    F.V 26
    F.VII *22,* 26
    F.VII-3m *22,* 26
    F.VIIa *49*
    F.VIIa-3m *22,* 31, 32, *33*
    F.VIIb-3m *29,* 32, *33, 34, 36*
    F.XII 53
    F.XVIII 53
    F.27 Friendship 94, 96, 98, 115, 118
    F.28 Fellowship 94, 120

interwar aircraft *22*
    T-2 32
Fokker, Anthony 20, 25–6
Fokker-Grulich F.II 26
Ford
    2-AT 42
    4-AT Tri-Motor 31, *33,* 42
    5-AT Tri-Motor *45*
France
    earliest flying machines *9,* 10,
        11–12, 15, 16
    general aviation *139, 142,* 146
    helicopters 167, *168–9, 171*
    interwar period 17, 29, *31,* 49, *50,*
        52, 58–9
    modern period 83, 94–5, *96,* 105
    nationalized aircraft industry 76, *77*
    post-war period 69, 76–7
    regional routes 115–16, 124
    special purpose aircraft *175*
    supersonic transports 109–10, *111*
    widebodied aircraft *107*
freighters 176–81
French Polynesia 115–16

Gates Learjet 150–1
    Learjet 55 Longhorn *151, 152*
general aviation *134,* 135–57
Germany
    earliest flying machines 9
    general aviation 146
    interwar period 17, *20,* 26, 28–9,
        40–1, *48,* 49, *51, 52,* 53, 58–9,
        60
    modern period 89, *94, 104,* 108
    post-war period 64, *72*
    regional routes *112,* 118, *125*
Gippsland GA8 184
Grumman
    AgCat 174
    Avenger 174
    Gulfstream *98, 153,* 154
    Tracker 174, *175*
Gulfstream Aerospace 153

Handley Page
    Halifax 64, 65, 76
    Halton 64, *65,* 76
    Herald 96, *99*
    H.P.42 36, 38
    H.P.42W *37,* 38
    O/10 *17,* 22, 30, *32*
    O/400 *13, 16,* 17, 21, 22, 30, *32*
    Type 75 25

V/1500 22
    W.8b 22, *23, 32,* 36
    W.9 22
    W.10 22
Handley Page Transport Ltd *16, 17,* 22,
    23, 25, 30, 36, *51*
Hapag-Lloyd, Germany *104, 125*
Harbin Y-12 *113*
Hargrave, Lawrence 8
Hawker Beechcraft 800 series *148,* 150
    see also Beechcraft
Hawker Siddeley
    HS.125 *148*
    HS.146 120
    HS.748 96
    Trident 81, 84–5, *86*
    see also Airbus Industrie; British
        Aerospace; de Havilland
Heinkel
    He 70 53, 54
    He 111 53, *60*
helicopters 10, *158,* 159–71
Henson, William Samuel *6, 12*
Herndon, Hugh, Jr. 47, *48*
Hiller UH-12 161
Hughes, Howard 70, 93
Hughes Helicopters
    AH-64 Apache 163
    Model 269/300 161
    Model 369/500 161, *162,* 163
Hungary *51, 95*

Iberia, Spain *51,* 54
Ilyushin
    Il-12 'Coach' *78*
    Il-14 'Crate' *79*
    Il-18 'Coot' *97,* 98
    Il-62 'Classic' 95
    Il-86 'Camber' *105,* 107, 108
    Il-96 *107,* 108
Imperial Airways 22, *27,* 31, *32,* 36–9,
    48, 49, *51,* 53, *57,* 59, 60
Instone Air Line, UK 23, 25, 36, *51*
interwar period 17, *18,* 19–61, 67,
    136–9, 184
Irkut MS-21 132
Italy
    general aviation *148, 156,* 157
    helicopters 167–8
    interwar period 29, 58–9, 60
    modern period *124*
    post-war period 64, *65,* 78

Japan
    general aviation *155,* 157
    interwar period 46, 47
    latest developments 127, 133
    modern period 98, *99*
    World War II 67
Johnson, Amy 46, 47, 136
Junkers
    F13 *13, 20,* 28, 40
    G24 40
    G38ce *54*
    interwar aircraft *28*
    Ju 46 28, *52*
    Ju 52 28
    Ju 52/3m 28, 41, *60, 65*
    Ju 86 *60*
    W33 28, *33*
    W34 28, *35*
Junkers Luftverkehr 40, *51*

Kaman K-MAX *165*
Kamov
    Ka-26 'Hoodlum' *168,* 170
    Ka-126 170
Kingsford Smith, Sir Charles *33, 34,*
    38, 47, *48*
KLM 39
    interwar period 26, *27, 49, 51,*
    52–3
    modern period *97, 102*
    post-war period 69

Latécoère
    17 29
    25 29
    26 29
    631 77
latest developments *126,* 127–33
Lear, William P. 'Bill' 148, 154
Lear Jet Industries Learjet 23 150, *151*
LET L-410UVP-E *117*
Lignes Aériennes Latécoère, France 49,
    51
Lilienthal, Otto 9, 10
Lindbergh, Charles 32–3
Lisunov Li-2 *78,* 79, 83
Lockheed
    14 53, 58
    Altair 47, *48*
    C-5 Galaxy 102, 105
    C-69 63, *67,* 68, 69
    JetStar 149
    L-049 Constellation 67, 68–9, 70,
    73, 76, 77

L-100 Hercules 181, *182*
L-188 Electra *97,* 98, 174
L-649 Constellation *68,* 70
L-749 Constellation *69,* 70
L-1011 TriStar *104,* 105
L-1049G Super Constellation *69,*
    70–1, *72*
L-1649A Starliner *69,* 71, 72
Lodestar 154
Model 9 Orion *43,* 54, 174, 180
Model 10 Electra *44,* 53, 57–8
Model 18 Lodestar *61*
Vega 46, 47, 154
Loganair, UK 112, 115, 116
LOT Polish Airlines *29, 51,* 54, 77, *79*
Luft Hansa, Germany
    interwar period *20,* 26, 40–1, *48,*
    49, *51, 52,* 53, 54, *55, 58,* 60
    latest developments *128,* 129
    modern period 89, 108
    post-war period *72*

McDonnell Douglas
    DC-10 *102,* 105, 108, *176*
    MD-11 *106,* 108, 176
    MD-80 series 89, *92–3,* 123, 124,
    132–3
    see also Douglas; MD Helicopters
MacRobertson Air Race 46, 48, 53
Martin
    2-0-2 73, 78
    4-0-4 73
    JRM-3 Mars 174, *175*
    M-130 *45*
Maule M-9-235 143–4
MD Helicopters
    Explorer 163, *165*
    MD 500 series 163, *165*
    MD 600 163, *165*
Messerschmitt-Bölkow-Blohm
    BO 105 167, 170
    MBB/Kawasaki BK117 167
Mil
    Mi-1 170
    Mi-8/17 'Hip' series *169*
    Mi-26 'Halo' 170
    Mi-34 'Hermit' *171*
Miles Marathon 75
Mitsubishi
    Diamond 135
    MRJ 127, 133
    MU-2 *155,* 157
modern period *80,* 81–125
Mollison, Jim 46, 47–8

Mooney Aircraft
    Acclaim Type S 144
    Ovation2 and 3 144
Moore-Brabazon, John T.C. 15, 74

National Air Transport (NAT), US *35,*
    42, 43
Netherlands
    interwar period 25–6, 39, *49, 51,*
    52–3, 59, 60
    modern period 94, *97, 102*
    post-war period 78
New Zealand 76
Nihon Aircraft Manufacturing
Corporation (NAMC) YS-11 98, *99*
Noorduyn Norseman 184
North American Sabreliner 148–9
Northrop
    Alpha *42*
    Gamma 2D *44*
Northwest Airlines, US *44,* 73
Norway *50,* 54

Österreichische Luftverkehrs *51,* 54
Ovington, Earl L. *12,* 16

Pacific Air Transport (PAT), US 42, 43
Pan American Airways
    interwar period 32, *33,* 43, *45,* 48,
    58, *59*
    modern period 87, 90, 91
    post-war period *66,* 67, *68,* 69, *71,*
    72, 73
    widebodied aircraft 102–4
Pangborn, Clyde E. 47, *48*
Percival Gull series 46, 137
Piaggio P.180 Avanti *156,* 157
Pilatus PC-12 156–7
Pilcher, Percy S. 9
Piper Aircraft
    J-3 Cub *143,* 144
    PA-24 Comanche *143,* 144
    PA-34 Seneca 156
    PA-44 Seminole 156
    PA-46 series 156
    piston singles *143*
Pitcairn Aviation, US 42, 43
Pitts
    S-1S Special 146
    S-2A Special 146
Poland *29, 50, 51,* 54, 77, *79,* 137,
    168
Portugal *88*
post-war period *62,* 63–79, *141,* 184

Progress in Flying Machines (Chanute) 9
PZL M-15 Belphegor 182
PZL-Swidnik 168, 170

QANTAS (Queensland and Northern Territory Aerial Service) 25, 31, *32*, 38–9, 75
Quest Kodiak 184

regional routes *100*, 101, 111–25
Reims Cessna
    F172F Skyhawk *139*
    FA152 *142*
Rickenbacker, Eddie 56
Riley Turbo Skyliner *75*
Robinson
    R22 *164*, 166
    R44 166
    R66 166
Rockwell Sabreliner 65 *147*, 148–9
Roe, Alliot Verdun 10
Roe I *10*
Rohrbach Roland 40
Rolls, Honourable Charles Stewart *12*, 16
Russia 16, 127, 132, *133*
    see also Soviet Union
Ryan NYP 32–3

Saab
    340 *114*, 118
    2000 118
    Scandia 78, 79
SABENA, Belgium 22, 26, *51*, 52, *56*, *70*, 87
Santos-Dumont, Alberto 10, *12*
Santos-Dumont 14bis 10, *12*
SATIC A300-600ST Beluga *172*, 180–1
Savoia-Marchetti
    S.73 54, 56, 60
    SM.83 *56*, 60
    SM.95 64, *65*, 78
Scandinavian Airlines System (SAS) 70, *79*, 83
Schneider Trophy 14
Short
    330 118
    360 *116*, 118
    Belfast 181
    interwar aircraft *37*
    L.17 Scylla 38
    Mayo Composite *57*
    No. 2 15
    S.8 Calcutta *33*, *37*, 38, *48*

S.17 Kent *37*, 38
S.20 Mercury *37*, *57*, 60
S.21 Maia *37*, *57*, 60
S.23 C-class Empire 39, 48, 60
Sandringham 76
Skyliner 112, 118
Solent 76
Sunderland 76
Siebel Si 204 *60*
Sikorsky
    civil helicopters *163*
    R-4/5/6 160
    S-42 *45*
    S-55 160, *163*
    S-58T *162*, *163*
    S-61L/N 160, 163
    S-76 160, 161, *163*
    S-92 161, *163*
    VS-44 67
    VS-300 160
Sikorsky, Igor *13*, 16
Smith, Captain Ross and Lieutenant Keith *13*
SOCATA TBM750 156
Sopwith Tabloid *14*
South Africa 38, 60, 75
Soviet Union
    general aviation 148
    helicopters *168*, *169*, 170, *171*
    interwar period 25, 28, 30–1, *32*, *50*, *51*
    modern period *82*, 83, 85, 95, 98, *99*
    post-war period 64, *78*, 79
    regional routes *117*
    special purpose aircraft *180*, 181
    supersonic transports 109–10
    widebodied aircraft *105*, *107*, 108
    see also Russia
Spain 28, *51*, 54
special purpose aircraft *172*, 173–85
Standard JR-1B 34
Stearman, Lloyd 139
Sud-Aviation
    Caravelle 83, 89, 91
    see also Airbus Industrie
Sud-Est Languedoc 77
Sukhoi
    Su-26 146
    Su-31 146
    Superjet 127, 132, *133*
Supermarine Sea Eagle *32*, 36
supersonic transports 101, 109–10, *111*
Sweden 28, *50*, 54, 79, *114*, 118

Swissair *51*, 54, *92*, *106*
Switzerland
    general aviation 156–7
    interwar period 29, *50*, *51*, 54
    modern period *92*, *106*
    post-war period *65*
Syndicat National d'Etude du Transport Aérienne (SNETA), Belgium *51*, 52

Taylor, Captain P.G. 47, *48*
Taylor Aircraft Co 144
Trans World Airlines (TWA), US 93, 105
    see also Transcontinental and Western Air
Transcontinental Air Transport (TAT), US 42, 43
Transcontinental and Western Air (TWA)
    interwar period *42*, 43, *44*, 48, 56–7, 58, *59*
    post-war period 69, 70
    World War II 67
Travel Air Manufacturing Company 139, 143
Tupolev
    ANT-1 30, *32*
    Tu-104 'Camel' *82*, 83
    Tu-114 95, 98, 99
    Tu-116 *99*
    Tu-124 85
    Tu-134 'Crusty' 85, 95
    Tu-144 'Charger' 109–10
    Tu-154 'Careless' 95, 132
Tupolev, Andrei Nikolayevich 30–1, *32*

Ulm, Charles T.P. *33*, 34
United Airlines, US
    interwar period *18*, 31–2, 43, 48, 56, *57*
    modern period 89, 90, 91
    post-war period 73
    widebodied aircraft 105, 108
United Kingdom
    earliest flying machines *6*, 8–9, *10*, 11, *12*, *14*, 15–16, 16–17
    general aviation 136–7, *138*
    helicopters 167–8
    interwar period 21–3, *24*, 25, *27*, 30, *32*–3, 36–9, 46, 47–8, 49, *50*–1, 53, 58–60, *61*, 136–7
    modern period 82–3, 84–5, 88–9, 90, 94, 96
    post-war period 64, *65*, 73, 74–6
    regional routes 112, *113*, 115, 116, 120, *122*

supersonic transports 109–10, *111*
widebodied aircraft *104,* 105
World War II 59, *61*
United States
earliest flying machines *8,* 9–10,
11, *12,* 13, *14,* 15, 16
general aviation *134,* 137–49,
150–1
helicopters *158,* 159–63, *164–5,*
166
interwar period *18,* 19, 21, 26,
31–2, 34–5, 41, 42–3, *44–5,*
46–7, 48, 56–8, *59,* 67
latest developments 128–9
modern period *80,* 81, 84, 86–93,
97, 98, 110
post-war period *66,* 67–73

regional routes *114,* 116–17, *119,*
122–3, 125
special purpose aircraft 179–80,
181
widebodied aircraft 102–5
World War II 67–8, 73

Varney Air Lines, US 31, *33,* 42, 43
Vickers
Super VC10 *84*
Vanguard 96
VC10 84, *85,* 94, 95
Viking *74,* 76
Vimy *13,* 21, *32*
Vimy Commercial *15,* 36
Viscount 75, 96
Wellington 76
Voisin-Farman 1bis *9*

Wakefield, Sir Charles 25
Western Air Express (WAE), US 42, 43
Westland Lynx 167
see also AgustaWestland
widebodied aircraft 101–8
World War I 16–17, 20–1, 26, 29, 64,
139
World War II 58, 59, *61,* 63–4, 67–8,
73
Wright, Orville and Wilbur *8,* 10, *12,*
13, 15
Wright Flyer 8, 9, 10, *12*
Wright Flyer III 11, 13

Yakovlev Yak-18 146

Zlin 226A 146